To

Thanks
intellectual c

Bill Menlow
27 March 2013

How To Be An Excellent Human

How To Be An Excellent Human

Mysticism, Evolutionary Psychology and the Good Life

Bill Meacham, Ph.D.

Earth Harmony
Austin, Texas

Contact the author at *http://www.bmeacham.com*.

Published in the United States of America by Earth Harmony
Inc., 603 Kingfisher Creek Drive, Austin TX 78748-2424.

ISBN-13: 978-0615727004

ISBN-10: 061572700X

Dedication

I dedicate this work in memoriam to Laszlo Versenyi and Nathaniel Lawrence, two exceptional teachers of philosophy, the love of wisdom, at Williams College. From these men I gained a lifetime of inspiration.

Contents

Acknowledgements

This book is for Casey Bledsoe. I asked Casey for editorial help with the collection of papers that I had originally thought would be a book and gave her an outline of what I thought the book should be. She came back with insightful comments and a different outline, and I now see that it is a better one. I figure she gave me a writing assignment, and I hope this work lives up to her expectations.

I am also grateful to Dr. Edwin Allaire at the University of Texas, who advised me that my original collection was not a book but could be made into one, and to members of the Austin Philosophy Discussion Group, who have provided many enjoyable occasions for kicking ideas around and inspiring me to write.

Deep thanks to my teacher, Shahabuddin David Less, who told me seven or eight years ago just to start writing and not wait till I retire.

And, of course, my deepest gratitude goes to my wife, friend, teacher and colleague, Patricia Michael. Without her encouragement I never would have started this journey. Sometimes it is not easy to live with a fussy writer who is, at times, too focused on his work to be warm and loving, but she has done it with aplomb.

Bill Meacham
Austin, Texas
December 2012

Part I: Setting the Stage

Chapter 1, Introduction

The theme of this book can be summed up in a simple proposition: *To be an excellent human being, you have work for the good in all things.*

By "excellent human being" I mean one who does well what humans do, who exemplifies the best in what makes humans unique and different from other beings. In a nutshell, that is the exercise of second-order thinking, the ability to pay attention to and think about ourselves as well as the many objects, events and concerns that surround us. We have lots of talents, but the one that distinguishes us most sharply from other living beings is just this: that we can take ourselves as objects of concern. In so doing we can, within limits, actually change who we are and develop ourselves to be able to function better and more efficiently.

And to what end? To survive and thrive, to live a life that is fulfilling and happy. In order to do that, we have to function well. And in order to function well, the environment in which we live, which nourishes and supports us, has to function well also.

We do not live apart from the world. Each of us is deeply and intimately embedded in the physical world, the animate world of living beings, the social world of others like us, and the world of what mystics call the unseen, that which unifies all of reality into a single coherence. That we are uniquely able to appraise ourselves as entities in the world does not make us separate from it. We are not so special that we can afford to ignore our essential connection with all of reality.

By working for the good—that is, the healthy functioning—of the world around us, we nourish that which nourishes us, and we thrive. By working for our own good—that is, our own healthy

functioning, our own thriving—we become better able to intervene and give helpful guidance to the world. We create an upward spiral of health and well-being.

That's the thesis. The rest of the book unpacks and explains
it, clarifying (I hope) the concepts that I use and giving evidence
for my assertions.

Chapter 2, Posing the Question

The goal is to find out how to live a fulfilling life. To do that we need to determine what human nature is. That's because the nature of a thing (here "thing" means anything, animate or inanimate, human or not)—what a thing is, essentially—determines or at least gives us very good clues to two things: what it is good for or good at, and what is good for it. When a thing is doing what it is good at and getting what is good for it, then it is functioning well. The internal experience of functioning well is—in human terms—fulfillment, a fulfilling life.

By "fulfilling life" I mean what the Classical Greeks called *eudaimonia*. Often translated as "happiness," or "human flourishing," the word is composed of *'eu'* meaning "well" and *'daimon'* which refers to a spirit being. A *daimon*, the Greeks thought, is a disembodied being somewhere between mortals and gods. It is not necessarily malevolent, as the English term "demon" denotes. There were *eudaimons,* beneficial spirits, and *kakodaimons,* malicious spirits. If one were accompanied by a *eudaimon,* a sort of guardian angel, then one's life would go well; hence, the translation "happiness."[1]

Whether or not you believe that people can be accompanied by beneficial or malicious spirits, there is one spirit that always accompanies each one of us, our own spirit, our own soul, in the sense of coherence of interiority. By extension of the Greek idea, then, we can say that *eudaimonia* means wellness of soul. If our own interiority is healthy and functioning well, then we experience a feeling of well-being. Our interiority, of course, is not separate from our exteriority, so if we are healthy and functioning well, then we are happy.

Consider physical exercise. If your body is functioning well—meaning, purely mechanically, all the bones and muscles and sinews operate together smoothly, and each element has sufficient strength and endurance—then it feels good to move. The pleasure of exercising a healthy body is not something separate from the exercise, not something that comes about as a result of the exercise. It is simply the exercise itself, experienced from the inside.

Similarly, the feeling of well-being that we experience when our life is going well is not separate from the healthy functioning of the various aspects of who we are; it is simply our own healthy functioning observed from the inside, from the first-person point of view. Functioning well means doing what we are good at and doing it in a good way, a way that promotes and enhances our ability to do it. When we function well, we experience happiness, fulfillment, *eudaimonia*.[i]

Happiness in this sense is not the same as pleasure. It is possible to feel pleasure but not be functioning well, as anybody who has experienced an addiction such as alcoholism can attest. The goal is not pleasure, although certainly the feeling of well-being that accompanies healthy functioning is pleasurable.

Nor, interestingly, is the goal the feeling of well-being. The goal is healthy functioning, and a feeling of well-being typically accompanies such functioning. If you focus on the feeling rather than the functioning, however, it is easy get sidetracked and end up with temporary pleasure but long-term misery, or at least less-than-optimal functioning and, hence, less fulfillment than otherwise possible.

There are things that some of us are good at and others are not. Some have special talents for sports, for instance, or mathematics or music, but not everyone does. On an individual level,

---

[i] This is my restatement of a remark by Aristotle: "[A clearer account of happiness] might perhaps be given, if we could first ascertain the function of man. For just as for a flute-player, a sculptor, or an artist, and, in general, for all things that have a function or activity, the good and the 'well' is thought to reside in the function, so would it seem to be for man, if he has a function." (Aristotle, *Nichomachean Ethics*, I.7 1097b 22–29.)

each of us needs to find out what he or she is good at personally, or idiosyncratically, and pursue and develop those talents.

There are also things that everybody is good at, by virtue of being a human being. That's what this book is about: what humans are essentially and how we can function in an excellent way. The Greek word for "excellence" was *areté*. Sometimes translated as "virtue," it really means effectiveness in the world.[2] For instance, the excellence of a ship-builder is to build ships that are themselves excellent, that is, that stay afloat, handle easily, travel quickly and haul people and goods safely. An excellent horse trainer produces excellent horses; and the excellence of a horse is that it runs fast, is easily trained, does not flinch in battle, and so forth. An excellent teacher imparts knowledge skillfully and accurately, and an excellent student learns quickly. These are all examples—and there are many more—of people and things fulfilling their functions and doing so well. To be an excellent human being, then, means to do well what humans do.

* * *

And what is that? Before we get to a detailed answer, we need to take a philosophical detour to clarify the concept underlying that of excellence, the good.

Chapter 3, The Good

To be excellent means to be really, really good. But what does it mean to be good? Or to do what is good? I want to explain this concept because too often people use the same word to mean different things, and that does not help at all.

What is good has to do with benefits. Something that benefits something or someone is called good for that thing or person. We can think of this instrumentally or biologically. Instrumentally, a hammer is good for pounding nails, and what is good for the hammer is what enables it to do so well. Biologically, air, water, and food are good for living beings.

Instrumentally, what is good for a thing enables that thing to serve its purpose. To make sense, an instrumental usage of the term "good" requires reference to somebody's purpose or intention. Thus, a hammer is good for pounding nails, and nails are good for building things such as furniture or housing, and we build furniture and housing because we want the comfort and utility they afford us. The instrumental usage is expressed in terms of usefulness, of utility for achieving a purpose or intention. Some hammers are better than others in that they have better heft or weight or balance and thus can be used to pound nails more effectively.

The instrumental usage leads to the biological usage. Why is it good for human beings to have comfort and utility? Because comfort and utility nourish us and keep us alive. Unlike the instrumental usage, the biological usage does not require reference to conscious purpose or intention.

The biological usage is expressed in terms of health and well-being. Biologically, what is good for an organism is what helps it survive and thrive, what nourishes it. Some things are better for us than others in this respect. For instance, a diet of whole grains and vegetables is better, in the sense of providing better health for humans, than a diet of simple carbohydrates and fats. Another example: some plants need full sunlight to thrive, and others need shade; thus, full sunlight is good for the former, and shade is good for the latter. The good, in this sense, is that which enables a thing to function well.

The instrumental usage intersects the biological when we consider what is good for something that is itself good for a purpose or intention. For instance, keeping a hammer clean and sheltered from the elements is good for the hammer; if it gets too dirty to handle easily or too rusty to provide a good impact on a nail, it is not useful as a hammer. So we can talk about what is good for the hammer in a way that is analogous to what is good for a living being. The good, in this sense also, is that which enables a thing to function well.

Just as good is defined in relation to an end, the value of the end is defined in relation to another end. As mentioned above, a hammer is good for driving nails. Driving nails is good for building houses. We build houses to have shelter and warmth. And we desire shelter and warmth because they sustain our life.

This chain of goods and ends stretches in both directions from wherever we arbitrarily start looking. A hammer is good for driving nails. So what is good for the hammer? Whatever enables it to perform its function. It is not good to leave it out in the rain; it is good to handle it carefully, swing it accurately with grace and force, and put it away safely.

Both the instrumental and the biological usage give meaning to the term "good" by referring to the consequences or effects of an action or event. That whole grains are good for humans means that the effect of eating them is healthful. That a hammer is good for pounding nails means that using it for that purpose is likely to have the effect you want, namely that the nails go in easily and straight. Some synonyms for "good" are "helpful," "nourishing," "beneficial," "useful" and "effective." Some synonyms for "bad" are the opposites of those terms: "unhelpful," "unhealthy," "damaging," "useless" and "ineffective."

There are degrees of goodness and its opposite, badness. That some plants need full sunlight to thrive and others need shade means that full sunlight is good for the former and not so good for the latter.

There is no end to the chains of goods and ends, no *summum bonum* (highest good) in which all chains culminate or from which all goods are derived. The world is a web, not a hierarchy. The only ultimate good would be the good of the entire universe and all that is within it, not an abstract entity or concept apart from it.

An ethic—a set of moral principles or values—can focus on specific actions or on qualities of character and motives for action. Focusing on specifics, we can ask what we should do in a particular situation or evaluate what someone else has done. Focusing on character, we can ask what sort of virtues we should cultivate. In either case, the goodness approach looks at benefits and consequences. If we are concerned about choices between courses of action, we will ask questions about the anticipated or hoped-for benefits of one choice or another. If we are concerned about character, we will ask questions about the anticipated or hoped-for effects on our habitual way of approaching life.[ii]

* * *

All this leads up to the point of my whole argument, which I call the Goodness Ethic.

[ii] Goodness is not the only approach to ethics, of course. The other one is Rightness, which I discuss in *Chapter 22, Ways to Say "Should"*. I contrast the two approaches in *Appendix A, The Good and The Right*.

Chapter 4, The Goodness Ethic

In order to know what is good for something or somebody, we need to know some facts, and one of the basic facts about all things and persons is that *everything is connected to everything else.*

Nothing exists in isolation. A change in an organism affects its surroundings, or environment, and a change in the environment affects the organism. This is easy to see in the case of living beings. It is also true of non-living things, but the timescale is longer. Consider: we all breathe the same air, drink the same water and get our nutrients from and recycle our wastes into the same environment. Thus, all of us—humans, animals, plants and minerals—on the planet earth are connected. We are connected to the rest of universe as well in that we are subject to the gravitational attraction of the planets and can see the light of distant stars.

Certainly we humans are all connected to other humans; if we were not, we would not be able to survive. As babies we are born helpless except for our powers—and very strong powers they are—to influence other humans, powers such as our ability to cry to summon aid and to smile and respond with love and cuteness to the attention of others. The few stories we have of people raised by animals rather than by other humans reveal beings that are more animal-like than human, without language or the ability to relate in a sociable and mutually respectful way to others. We learn to express ourselves in language, and there is no such thing as a private language; language is essentially communal. We have the capability or capacity to imagine another's point of view, to experience things as they do, and it is fulfilling to do so. If we were not connected, we would not have this capability.

I will return to this point, that we are all connected, in different ways throughout the rest of the book. For now, take it as a premise of my argument.

Given that everything is related to everything else, it makes sense to try to maximize the good in all situations, that is to maximize what is good for all concerned. Another way of saying this is that it is good to be of service, to help everybody, as best you can. As you maximize the good of everybody and everything in the environment, you thereby promote your own health as well. (By "you" I mean everyone, each of us individually; and by "environment" I mean everything that surrounds us: people, animals, plants, non-living things, the earth, the atmosphere, the water, etc. Everything.)

Acting this way is enlightened self-interest, as opposed to unenlightened self-interest, which seeks to maximize your own welfare without regard to the effects on your actions on others. Commonly called "selfishness," such an unenlightened approach is actually self-defeating.

(This view is not the Utilitarian argument that one should act to maximize pleasure and minimize pain. For one thing, it is not clear that pleasure is always good and pain is always bad. For another, Utilitarianism, even though expressed in terms of consequences, is actually a form of rules-based ethics. For the Utilitarian, the moral rightness of action is a function of the amount of pleasure or pain that it produces. One is supposed to calculate the net long-term outcomes of all of the available options—the "hedonic calculus"—and then choose the option that will yield the greatest pleasure. Such calculation, of course, is impractical; at what point does "long-term" end?)

The goal of the Goodness Ethic is to maximize the good for all so far as you can determine at the time, without excessive conscious calculation.

The Goodness Ethic may be stated in a number of ways. The simplest is this:

Work for the good in all things.

Here are other ways of saying it:

- Live with an intention to maximize what is good for all concerned.
- Align yourself with what is good all around, for everyone.
- Act for the benefit of yourself and your environment.
- Do the best you can to maximize goodness for all.
- Act for the benefit of the whole.
- We are all in it together, so let's make it good for everybody.

This is not altruism, if by that term we mean acting for the benefit of others without regard to your own benefit. Nor is it selfishness, acting for your own good alone. It is a false dichotomy to think of self-interest being opposed to the interest of a larger whole. For example, you are happy when your spouse is happy. It is a win-win situation. The motivation is both your own happiness and your spouse's happiness. Another example: you profit when your company benefits all the stakeholders: customers, owners, workers, suppliers and neighbors.[3] Again, a win-win. The motivation is both your own profit and the other stakeholders' benefits.

The goal is for *both* you and your environment to survive and thrive. To benefit yourself at the expense of others or to the detriment of your environment is self-defeating. If you act selfishly in the usual sense of that term, for your own good alone as if you were separate from your environment, you will not thrive as much as if you worked for the larger good. On the other hand, if you act altruistically, in the sense of working for others' benefit or the benefit of your environment without regard to your own benefit, you will likely become stressed and exhausted and be unable to contribute. Instead, you should act so as to flourish mutually with your environment. If you do good for what is around you, it will nourish you

If you adopt these principles, then you find yourself in an environment in which things work out well for everyone. If they work out well for the benefit of all elements of the environment and you are one of those elements, then they work out well for you. And you get to be thankful to have had a good effect.

Method

The method for putting the Goodness Ethic into practice is this:

1. Pay attention.
2. Intend to benefit.
3. Think about the situation. Figure out how to benefit what is around you and yourself as best you can determine at the time.
4. Act. Do what you think will benefit you and your surroundings.
5. Do this cycle repeatedly.

Pay attention. This is the fundamental precursor to any form of effective action in the world. You need accurate knowledge about what you are acting on, so you must pay attention to it.

Intend to benefit. This step is unique to the goodness approach to ethics. You could act effectively while intending to harm, and some people, whom we call evil, do just that. Many act effectively while intending to be morally obedient to the rules of right and wrong regardless of the consequences. The Goodness Ethic asks us to intend to benefit all elements of whatever situation or predicament we find ourselves in.

Think about it. One of the things human beings do well is to plan, to envision states of affairs not currently present and think about how to bring them about. Exercising this function is essential to achieving our goals, including the goal of benefiting all concerned. The Goodness Ethic asks us to think about what will benefit us and our surroundings as best we can determine at the time.

Act. In order to be effective, it is not enough merely to have an intention. You must act as well. Only by acting will you achieve any effect, and only by acting will you find out what works and what does not.

Repeat the cycle. Having acted, pay attention to the results, compare them to what you intended to accomplish, adjust your tactics if needed, and act again. This cycle is essential to any form of process improvement, including the process of being of benefit to yourself and your world.

* * *

Having clarified what goodness is, we are ready to proceed. The Goodness Ethic is premised on the idea that everything— including us human beings—is connected to everything else. The chapters in Part II explore that idea in more detail.

Part II: The Broadest Vision

Chapter 5, Our Place in the Grand Scheme

One of the premises of the Goodness Ethic is that everything is connected to everything else. This chapter gives a metaphysical explanation of how that is.

Metaphysics is the investigation of the underlying nature and structure of reality as a whole. It places our understanding of our capabilities as humans in a larger context. It is different from particular scientific inquiries, such as physics, biology and the like. Physics tells us about how the material world works. Biology tells us how the living world works. Anthropology, psychology, sociology, history, economics and other such fields of study tell us how the human world works. Some disciplines, such as neuroscience, span the boundaries, explaining human behavior in terms of another aspect of reality. But what are the fundamental categories that would enable us to understand all the specialized disciplines? That question is the subject of metaphysics.

Metaphysics is important because the fundamental conceptual categories within which we frame how we think about the world determine how we feel about it, evaluate it and react to it. In other words, how we conceive of the world as a whole and our place in it determines—or at least strongly influences—how we act. If we are to act wisely, we had better have a good metaphysical understanding, one that is thought out well, that makes sense and that we can rely on.

There are two basic paradigms for understanding the world as a whole: that the world is dead and that the world is alive. We'll take a look at both.

The Mechanistic World View

What is the most fundamental characteristic of all that is? Throughout European history from the Greeks onwards, the answer has most often been framed in terms of substance, inert stuff that occupies space and persists through time. Space and time are conceived of as mere containers. The ancient Greek philosopher Democritus held everything to be composed of atoms, which are physically indivisible, separated in space and always in motion. Aristotle gave a privileged position to substance among his ontological categories; for him the primary sense of the word "being" is substance. In this view the properties of substances are never touched by change, which affects only the relations between substances.

In the 18th century, with the rise of modern science, Sir Isaac Newton asserted that reality consists of solid, impenetrable particles; and ever since then we have thought ourselves to live in a world that is, when all is said and done, physical and causally determined, a Newtonian mechanistic universe in which inert matter is all there is and every change is determined, much like the movement of billiard balls. The success of the technological accomplishments we have enjoyed since then lends credence to such a view. But such a cold universe leaves no room for human freedom and creativity.

René Descartes conceived both physical and mental reality as substance. The former he called *res extensa*, Latin for "extended thing," after its primary attribute, extension in space. The latter he called *res cogitans*, or "thing that thinks," after its primary attribute, the ability to be conscious. The problem with such a dualistic metaphysics is that it is incoherent. Ever since Descartes, philosophers have grappled with the so-called "mind-body problem," how to explain how two such ontologically disparate substances can influence each other. I say "so-called" because it is a problem only given the metaphysical assumptions within which it is framed. Descartes himself had to resort to yet a third category, a benevolent, all-powerful and supernatural God, to reconcile the two.

Scientific discovery no longer supports a wholly deterministic view of the universe. The Newtonian mechanistic view of universe has now been superseded by quantum physics, which reveals that at the tiniest, most fundamental level of physical reality things and events are indeterminate: the outcomes of events cannot be predicted in advance, except in statistical terms. Matter acts sometimes like particles and sometimes like waves of probability. The philosophical impetus toward dualism has been blunted.

Dualism has a certain appeal. It is not surprising that we find the idea that things endure through space and time comfortable and familiar, because in our ordinary experience they do. Our minds have evolved to have an intuitive grasp of the physics of objects. It is also not surprising that we do not like the idea that our experience, feeling and cognition—in short, our mentality—is a mere byproduct of material causes. We know our own subjectivity, experience and volition first-hand and we have an intuitive grasp of the psychology of others like us, which has likewise proven to work out correctly over and over again in the long history of our race. The two realms—body and mind—have different qualities and seem quite distinct. But dualism is unsatisfactory, because it lacks a coherent explanation of how body and mind can influence each other. Other attempts to solve the problem—asserting that the mind is just an effect of physical causes or that mind is primary and the physical is an illusion or that mind somehow emerges from the physical as the latter becomes more complex—are all unsatisfactory as well. There must be something better.

Process Metaphysics

Fortunately, there is another explanation of reality that does not suffer from such defects: process metaphysics, also called process philosophy. This is the view that reality is best understood as processes rather than things, that the fundamental character of all that exists is change and that enduring objects are persisting patterns amid change, much like the flame of a candle. The process view too has been present in European thought from the time of the Greeks. Heraclitus used the metaphor of a river, which remains what it is by changing what it contains. Change is a necessary condition for constancy; without it we would have only lifeless uniformity and would not even know it, because knowing itself is a temporal process.

In the 20th century the most elaborate and thoroughly developed version of this ontology is that of Alfred North Whitehead. Whitehead was a mathematician who finished his career teaching philosophy at Harvard, where he formulated a metaphysical system based on the idea that reality is made up of atomic or momentary events, not inert particles. This is not an intuitive idea, and his major work, *Process and Reality*, is dense and highly technical, over 500 pages long. I'll try to summarize it briefly.

These events, which Whitehead calls "actual occasions" are a bit like subatomic particles, with some important differences:

- Each is momentary, coming into being, going through various phases and then passing away.
- The final phase of an actual occasion is not fully determined by the beginning. There is room for novelty, for the possibility of something new coming into being.
- Each actual occasion has awareness. In a primordial way it experiences its past and its present surroundings. Whitehead calls it an "occasion of experience."
- What we think of as a particle is actually a series of these actual occasions. A single electron is a series of momentary electron-occasions that form an enduring object much as the momentary frames of a movie form a continuous moving picture.
- Nonliving things are composed of streams of actual occasions whose primordial experiences randomly cancel each other out.
- The primordial experiences of the actual occasions comprising living things, such as plants, animals and human beings, bind together and reinforce each other, giving birth to a higher-level experience. The richest and most intricate example we know of is our own conscious experience.

According to Whitehead, the smallest quantum event is a moment of experience; the event comes into being by incorporating aspects of its surroundings and its past into itself by means of processes akin to the full-blown conscious experience that we know as perception. Such elementary events cohere into temporal strands that appear to us (through the medium of scientific instruments) as elementary particles. Particles cohere into molecules, then into objects and living cells. Mere objects are different from living cells. Nonliving objects lack the unified coherence of interiority, built up of the interiority of their constituents, that living cells have. Objects cohere into substances. Cells cohere into organs and living beings. All of reality has interiority, a private experiential aspect, as well as exteriority, a publicly observable aspect.

Panpsychism

The doctrine that everything has at least some rudimentary awareness is known as *panpsychism*.[4] The term comes from the Greek *pan*, meaning "all," and *psyche*, meaning "soul." The root meaning of *psyche* is "breath," or "that which breathes," or by extension, "life." Panpsychism says that everything, from the smallest quantum event to the most complex living being, is mental as well as physical.

Panpsychism does not assert that rocks have psyches in the same way that humans do. That would be ridiculous, as rocks exhibit none of the complex behavior of humans. But if we take a broader view of mentality, the view that mentality consists of sensory and emotional experience, then the theory becomes more plausible. Whitehead says that the fundamental building blocks of reality are events that have two aspects, interiority and exteriority. Everything has an inside and an outside. By "interiority," I mean that events take into account their surroundings in a manner analogous to human experience, albeit in a much more primitive fashion. (Whitehead calls this taking into account "prehension.") By "exteriority," I mean that each event is present for the proto-experience of other events. Sequences of events form what we know as quantum objects, which behave as both waves and particles. From there we can in theory construct the variegated world of things and living beings that we know in our everyday experience. Perhaps a better, although clumsier, term would be *pan-proto-experientialism*.

The point is, rather than assuming that life mysteriously emerges when brute matter becomes organized in sufficient complexity and that consciousness emerges when it becomes even more complex, we can assume that a primitive form of experience is present at every level of reality. Then we need make no unverifiable suppositions about which animals are conscious and which are not, nor do we have to puzzle over how mere complexity of matter gives rise to consciousness. Reality is a continuum, all aspects of which have some degree of mentality as well as physicality.

Panpsychism solves the mind-body problem, the question of how the mind, immaterial and without physical extension, can have any influence on the body or on physical reality generally. The usual answers are to say that reality is fundamentally physical and the mind is an epiphenomenon of the body or that reality is fundamentally mental and the physical is in some way an outgrowth or extension or construct of the mental. A more balanced approach is to say that the mental is an emergent property of the physical, that mentality arises when physical reality reaches a certain complexity. But the well-known problem with emergentism is how to specify the conditions under which consciousness emerges. Just what is the threshold above which there is consciousness and below which there is none?

The mind-body problem is only a problem, however, if we assume that the mind is distinct and separate from the body, that mental events are in some fundamental way different from physical events. If we assume that everything is both mental and physical, that everything has an inside and an outside, then the problem disappears. Of course the mental can influence the physical, because it is the same as the physical viewed from a different vantage point. From the outside, everything is physical. From the inside, each of us is clearly mental as well. If we assume that everything has an inside, then from the inside of each thing, or each event, reality is mental as well as physical.

Another way of saying this is that to be real is to have an effect. If you think of something that has no effect, then what you are thinking of cannot be real. The minimal effect something has is to be detected by something else. We never find something being real without something else being real as well. Relatedness, as well as process, interiority and creativity, is fundamental to the way things are.

Inside And Outside

I want to explore in a bit more detail the idea that everything has a mental, or subjective, aspect and a physical, or objective, aspect. I like to say that everything has an inside and an outside. By "mental," "subjective" and "inside" I mean that everything has experience, is in some way aware, and, like all experience, that experience is private. By "physical," "objective" and "outside" I mean that everything can be perceived, or at least detected, by something else. In that sense, everything is public.

You can easily understand the difference between private and public from your ordinary experience. Take a look around you. You see things that others can see, such as tables and chairs, trees, other people, etc. You hear sounds that others can hear, smell odors that others can smell. These are public things. You can describe what you see, hear or smell and listen to others' descriptions of what they see, hear or smell, and conclude that you both perceive the same thing. In this sense, much of what you experience is public. However, some of what you experience is private. For instance, think of something—a color or a word or a card, etc. As you think of it, there is no way another person can know what you are thinking of. Your thought is entirely private, subjective. Your thoughts are private, and so are other aspects of your experience, such as your emotions and your physical feelings, your perception of your own body. In addition, the particular appearance of each public thing, the particular way it is presented to you, is private. We each see a slightly different aspect of every public thing.

In fact, all experience is private. We learn to interpret much of what is contained in our experience as public. But the public world is presented to us in our experience; and each of us, individually, has direct acquaintance only with our own experience.

It is easy to understand the idea that everything has an outside. Less obvious is the tenet of panpsychism, that everything, down to the smallest quark or muon, is in some way aware of its surroundings. This is not so much a claim, as it is unverifiable, as a way of thinking about reality.[iii]

It is unverifiable because there is no way to experience the inside, the subjectivity, of anyone or anything else, so there is no way to know for sure that it exists. Certainly some things exhibit external, public behavior that suggests they have an inside. There is a range of such behavior, from purposive, like humans, to inert, like a rock. Animals and plants are in between. We infer that other people have intentions, desires, aversions and feelings as we do because we observe them acting in ways similar to the way we act, and we know how it feels to be us. So we conclude that others have an interior life as we do, even though we cannot directly experience it. We extend this inference to animals. Dogs and cats appear to have desires and aversions; they respond to verbal communication from humans (cats less so than dogs, but we interpret that behavior as being aloof rather than as being less conscious); they seem to be happy at times, bored or unhappy at others, and so forth. Some people extend the inference to plants. My wife, a gardener, says plants are happy when they get watered.

Most people in advanced civilizations conclude that nonliving things, which exhibit no external sign of having any subjectivity, in fact have none. But there is no way to know that for sure. It's just a convenient way to divide up the world conceptually, into living and nonliving things. People commonly assume that nonliving things have no awareness of their surroundings, but we can imagine that they do. We cannot directly experience their internality, the world from their point of view, as we cannot directly experience any entity's internality but our own, so it might be true that even a rock has some experience of the world. Try

---

[iii] See *Appendix C, In Defense of Panpsychism,* for the logic of the argument in favor of it.

imagining being a rock. Your world would be very, very slow, but you can imagine feelings of pressure, of heat and cold, of heaviness.

Even a glass table top has interiority, although probably without enough cognition to distinguish itself from anything else. It has feelings, but they are not directed toward anything. The table top is very simple, lacking the coherency of pattern—of sensation, perception, emotional feelings, thoughts, physical feelings, etc.—that makes a fully developed self. So there is no sense of self that perceives anything else; there is only feeling. We can imagine the feelings. Fundamentally there would be a sense of attraction downward. There would be feelings of heat and cold, perhaps pressure from above. There would be a kind of orderliness, solidity, but there would not be a sense of being lined up like a crystal.

Physicists call the sense of attraction downward gravity. Sufis call it *Ishq*, love. That gravity is love is described well by Daniel Dennett, although he scoffs at the idea:

> Imagine that we visited another planet and found that the scientists there had a rather charming theory: Every physical thing has a soul inside it, and every soul loves every other soul. This being so, things tend to move toward each other, impelled by the love of their internal souls for each other. We can suppose, moreover that these scientists had worked out quite accurate systems of soul-placement, so that, having determined the precise location in physical space of an item's soul, they could answer questions about its stability ("It will fall over because its soul is so high"), about vibration ("If you put a counterbalancing object on the side of the drive wheel, with a rather large soul, it will smooth out the wobble"), and about many much more technical topics.
>
> What we could tell them, of course, is that they have hit upon the concept of a center of gravity ... [and] ... all they have to give up is a bit of unnecessary metaphysical baggage.[5]

Dennett thinks to say that things are attracted by love has no value, that it is an unnecessary hypothesis. But I say that the theory that things are attracted by love does have value. If you live as if it is true, if you live as if everything has an inside as well as an outside, you'll be happier and function better than if you live as if some things don't. (See *Implications*, below.)

As physical things combine into more organized wholes, their interiority combines as well into more coherency and richness. A plant has more organization than a rock, and its interiority is richer. Animals are more complex than plants and humans more complex yet, viewed physically from the outside. And the experience of the more complex organisms is more coherent: each has more memory, more ability to anticipate the future and more conceptual understanding than the next order down (humans as compared to animals, animals as compared to plants, and plants as compared to nonliving things). Each has more self-consciousness as well, in the sense of having an idea of oneself as separate from other things or beings and, through the lens of that idea, paying attention to one's internal states as well as one's knowledge of how one acts and appears to others.

If we assume that everything has an inside and an outside, then what appears to be dead is just living at a very slow pace. A dead animal's interiority has decomposed into its constituent elements, the interiority of the elements, but the larger coherent interiority of the whole organism is gone.

If everything has an inside as well as an outside, then everything has will, the drive to actualize intention. The fundamental drive in everything, every occasion or event—every actual occasion, to use Whitehead's terminology—is to actualize intentions. One imagines and desires, however dimly, some state of affairs, and one does something to bring about that state of affairs. Plants, for instance, turn toward the sun. They are aware of the current state of affairs, that sunlight is coming from a certain direction to which their leaves are not optimally oriented, and they imagine and desire that their leaves be oriented better, so they act on that desire and turn their leaves. That humans and animals act on intentions is obvious. Even inanimate matter, in this view, actualizes intention, the intention to cohere and persist.

The drive to actualize intention is will and passion. Will can exist without much passion, for instance when you are just gritting your teeth through an unpleasant situation because you have to for some reason or you need to do your duty. Passion can exist without much will. In that case what you have is unfocused energy and desire, and nothing gets done. Just as every mental event has both a cognitive and an affective aspect, every intention has both an imagination of a state of affairs, and a desire for that state of affairs to come about. (Desire, I am suggesting, is a form of emotion.)

Implications

Panpsychism is a metaphysical theory, neither verifiable nor falsifiable by scientific experiment. But it is not thereby meaningless. It ties together quite coherently everything we know about the world from our own personal experience and from objective scientific knowledge.

And it makes a difference. It determines whether we feel as if we are strangers in a dead universe or at home in a world of life. It determines where we look for wisdom and inspiration. And it determines how we treat ourselves and our environment.

If we think of ourselves as an anomaly, as a mere byproduct of mindless matter, then we have to find a way to cope. We might lose ourselves in religious faith, huddling fearfully against the fall of night, praying for something to save us. Or we might rebel, heroically but foolishly, against the absurdity of it all in order to stave off anomie and despair. Or we might just party harder. In any case, we treat the world as a thing, extracting its resources unsustainably and risking collapse, attempting to dominate it because we feel apart from it. But we're not, so it will bite back.

If we think of ourselves as living in a world full of life, we feel connected and nurtured. We live in confidence, not fear, recognizing ourselves as an integral part of a larger whole. We pay attention to ecosystems and natural processes and adapt our technology to work as nature does, increasing abundance for all. We cooperate with our living environment and each other to increase the welfare of all.

I am exaggerating these two extremes, of course, to make the point starkly. No doubt many materialists are compassionate and wise, and many who believe that the world is alive fall prey to pettiness and fear. And I am not suggesting that we should adopt a biocentric view just because it feels better. I am suggesting that panpsychism makes the most sense as a metaphysical system, a conceptual scheme that encompasses everything, and that thinking in those terms will lead us to adopt better strategies for being in the world, strategies that will help us all survive and thrive and be joyful.

* * *

That the world is alive, is animated, is one thing. The mystical traditions of the world go further. They suggest that not only is the world animated, it is animated by a single center of consciousness, that it is a single organism. In the next chapter we find some hints of this in the biological world.

Chapter 6, A World Alive

Off the western coast of the Big Island of Hawai'i in Keala-kekua Bay lives a remarkable fish, known as Akule or, less color-fully, Big-Eye Scad.[6] It is remarkable, not because of the individual fish (which is said to be quite tasty), but because of its behavior. The fish clump together in very tight schools, which form arresting three-dimensional shapes in the water. They move in unison in the form of quivering clouds. When a predator comes near, the Akule formation shape-shifts, confusing the assailant. It makes a hole through which the predator passes harmlessly. Or it becomes a tornado-like column, twisting and writhing to evade the enemy. Or perhaps sometimes it writhes just for fun. It is impossible to escape the intuition that the school as a whole is acting as one organism.

We think so because of the way our minds work. Cognitive psychologists have found that we have two ways of thinking, two distinct mental modules—sets of cognitive apparatus similar to software modules—for thinking about and dealing with the world: thinking in terms of objects and thinking in terms of agents. Both have been engrained in us over hundreds of thousands of years of evolution. We might call these Folk Physics and Folk Psychology. They are "folk" because we don't have to study physics or psychology to figure out how to think in these ways. They are built in.

Research with very young infants reveals that people have innate ideas—ideas formed in advance of experience and through which experience is interpreted—about how the world of objects works.[iv] We know intuitively that an object cannot pass through another object, that objects move along continuous trajectories, that objects are cohesive (their parts move together), that they move each other by contact only, and so forth.

We also have innate ideas about agents: "Agents are recognized by their ability to violate intuitive physics by starting, stopping, swerving, or speeding up without an external nudge, especially when they persistently approach or avoid some other object. The agents are thought to have an internal and renewable source of energy ... which they use to propel themselves, usually in service of a goal."[7] This cognitive domain is adapted to understanding and dealing with animals, including humans. Agents have minds, and we interpret their behavior in terms of beliefs and desires.

Both forms of thinking are built into the machinery of our minds, presumably for very good evolutionary reasons: our ancestors who thought in these ways had more offspring than their contemporaries who didn't. And the reason these ways of thinking work is that they reflect how the world actually is. But what if we have, at times, misapplied them, thinking in one category when the other would be more appropriate?

For centuries Western thought has tried to reduce life and consciousness to the nonliving, interpreting the world as a mechanism, as nothing but matter, inert and lifeless. We have gotten very, very good at understanding the world of physical objects and manipulating it to produce unparalleled wealth and physical

---

[iv] The methodology is fascinating. Babies can't talk, but they exhibit interest and boredom by looking at something intently or by looking away. Researchers set up a screen that hides part of the baby's visual field and allows the baby to see things on either side, such as something sticking out from the left and something sticking out from the right. "It's especially informative when a screen first blocks part of the infant's view and then falls away, for we can try to tell what the babies were thinking about the invisible part of their world. If the baby's eyes are only momentarily attracted and then wander off, we can infer that the scene was in the baby's mind's eye all along. If the baby stares longer, we can infer that the scene came as a surprise." (Pinker, *How the Mind Works*, p. 317.)

well-being for millions of people. Nobody would want to lose the advantages of objective, reality-based science and engineering.

But we have lost the other way of approaching the world, the way that interprets confluences of things and events as agential, as the result of beings who take note of what is happening around them and respond to further their own goals. We have no trouble with interpreting individuals, animal and human, as agents. But we tend to dismiss the idea that larger patterns, involving more than one individual, may also reasonably be taken as agential.

Schools of fish, such as the Akule, belie that attitude, as do flocks of birds and herds of animals. They seem, at times, to act as if they have one mind. Take ants traveling back and forth along a trail between food and the colony. Purely physically, we know that they communicate chemically via pheromones with a sort of enhanced sense of smell.[8] But functionally the ant colony appears to act with a collective intelligence, as if each ant is more like a ganglion with legs in an extended nervous system than an individual organism itself.[9] The colony sends out tendrils, which both sense what is out there and carry it back.

So we find in nature instances where disparate physical elements act as one, embodying one mind, one locus of consciousness, one coherence of internality.

And if flocks and herds and colonies act as one, why not other types of beings as well? All human cultures have ideas of gods (with a lower-case "g"), spirits, angels, demons and other such disembodied entities. Some say that these ideas are just cognitive mistakes, a sort of misfiring of our folk psychology, applying agential concepts where they don't fit. But perhaps there really are such beings, only they are not truly disembodied. Instead, their bodies consist of many discrete physical elements, like the individual Akule, only not so obviously choreographed. Think of a sacred place in nature or a shrine, a place where people go to find inspiration and renewal. At such a place you find a certain mood of peacefulness and acceptance, and a sense that somebody or something is watching benevolently, listening to your prayers. Or, if that is too anthropomorphic, you have a sense at least that a being is somehow aware of you and is open and receptive to your needs. Sometimes you receive answers or guidance, a sense of knowing what to do, or a vision of what needs to take place, or even words in your mind, as if the spirit of the place is speaking to you. If disparate physical elements can embody a single mind, then there really is a spirit there, and its body is all the physical stuff, the plants, rocks, trees, animals, insects, water, sky and human structures that make up the place.

This idea might even explain the mystical intuition that all is one. There is a Sanskrit term, *Paramatman*, which means Supreme Self. Ralph Waldo Emerson called it the Over-soul.[10] If it is possible for physical elements that are separated in space to act as if animated by a single intelligence, a single locus of consciousness or interiority, then perhaps the entire world can be viewed as such. If so, we are all part of a vast organism, and what we call "God" is the interiority of the whole thing. Native American traditions speak of the Spirit-that-moves-in-all-things. The world is that spirit's body. Panpsychism is pantheism.

* * *

I admit that is a bit of stretch, from the behavior of herd animals to mystical speculation about the ultimate nature of reality. It might seem more plausible if there were other examples of physically separate objects that seem to act as one. There are, and they are found at the most fundamental level of physical reality.

Chapter 7, The Quantum World: Oneness

This chapter and the next are a bit of a digression, but we'll end up with some useful insights. I want to discuss some findings of modern science about the physical world in its tiniest dimensions, the subatomic world of quantum reality.[11] That world is strange, not like the everyday world we are accustomed to at all. But it underlies our perceived world and has profound (but disputed) implications for metaphysics, so please bear with me for a little while as I try to explain some of it.

By "quantum reality" I mean things and events that are quite tiny, less than about 100 nanometers long. They are called "quantum," from a Latin word meaning "how much," because the magnitudes of certain properties at this level can take on only discrete, not continuous, values. For example electrons orbit their nuclei only at certain discrete distances, not in between, so the electron is said to be quantized. So is light. You may have heard that light behaves sometimes as a wave and sometimes as a particle. The particle aspect of light is the photon, a quantum unit of light.

We can't see electrons or photons, of course, but we can detect them through instrumentation, and their properties and behavior can be described mathematically by a formula called the "wave function." Under certain circumstances the wave function divides into two or more pairs or branches, each with its own consequences. Each of these branches represents a potential future or a potential version of reality. When observed, only one of these branches is perceived; that is, only one of the potential futures becomes the actual perceived present. And you can't tell in advance which one it will be. Things and events at this level are *indeterminate*, meaning that the outcomes of events cannot be predicted in advance, except in statistical terms. An initial configuration of things and forces does not determine a subsequent configuration. Mathematics can describe the probability of a range of outcomes, but cannot predict a single outcome.

Here is an example. The Stern-Gerlach experiment, named after the scientists who first performed it, consists of sending a series of electrons through a magnetic field, which deflects them. The magnetic field is stronger at one end than at the other, a condition that causes the electron to swerve a bit, toward one pole of the field or the other, as it passes through. On the other side of the field from the emitter is a recording medium, which registers where the electron hits the medium. Each electron is detected at one of two places on the medium, depending on a property of the electron called "spin." One finding of this experiment is that electrons are detected in only two places rather than in a range between them. Thus, an electron's spin can take only two values; it is quantized. This finding corroborates the quantum nature of reality at this level.

Another finding is *quantum indeterminacy*: you cannot predict in advance where the electron will be detected. Given a great number of electrons and the known characteristics of the magnetic field, you can predict the relative number of impressions at each detection point. But there is only a probability, not an absolute certainty, that any single electron will end up in one place or another. When you send an electron there are two possible futures, but there is no way of deducing from the mathematics which possibility will become reality.

An electron is not like a billiard ball. If you know the mass of two billiard balls, the amount of force and its direction applied to one, and the angle at which it hits the second, you can predict in what direction and how fast the second ball will travel. Not so with quanta.

This is weird, but it gets even weirder.

A subatomic particle called a pion decays and emits two photons, which travel in opposite directions. Each photon, like an electron, has spin, and you can measure spin in different directions. Think of a globe with a horizontal axis. As you look at the globe, it can spin so the surface you see goes up or so the surface you see goes down. So the globe can be in one of two states, spin-up or spin-down.[v] Now imagine that it has two more axes, each at right angles to the others. We can call the axes X, Y and Z. The photon, unlike a globe, can spin along any of these axes, but along only one at a time. So we have three things to detect, X-spin, Y-spin and Z-spin, each of which can have one of two states, up or down. Thus there are six possible states: X-up, X-down, Y-up, Y-down, Z-up and Z-down.

The photon is a quantum object; before you measure it, its state is indeterminate. There is no way of telling, before you take a measurement, which kind of spin it has along any given axis. If lots and lots of pions decay and emit photons, we know statistically that half of the photons in each direction will be in state up when measured on the X axis and half will be in state down. But there is no way to tell in advance for a given photon which one it will be.

And you can measure only one axis at a time. Once you measure one axis, the others are indeterminate. Imagine several detectors in a line so that the photon goes through one and then another and then another, and so forth. If the first detector measures X-spin and the second one does also, the second one will always agree with the first. So you know that, once measured, the X-spin stays the same. If the first one measures X-spin and the second one measures Y-spin, the Y-spin is indeterminate until you measure it. Half the time it will be up and half the time down, but you can't know in advance which it will be for any particular photon. If a third detector again measures X-spin, that X-spin might or might not agree with the first measurement. (Yes, this is weird. As I said, Nature works differently at the quantum level from how it works at the classical level.)

When you measure one of the pair of photons—call it A—and then measure the other one—call it B—they are always opposite. If photon A is X-up, you know for certain that photon B is X-

---

[v] Having no spin is not an option. The pion was at rest, having no angular momentum. When it splits, the child photons go in opposite directions and have opposite spin. The sum of their spin equals zero, the same as the initial pion.

down. If photon A is X-down, you know for certain that photon B is X-up. This is true no matter how far apart they are, a millimeter or thousands of kilometers. This is true even if the measurements are made simultaneously, so that there would be no chance of a signal traveling from A to B. This is true even if they are so far apart that light would not have time to travel from A to B between the time you measure A and the time someone (not you, because you are too far away) measures B, so that there is absolutely no way a signal could travel from one to the other.

Imagine two observers, typically called Alice and Bob. Alice observes the A photons and Bob observes the B photons. They are too far apart to communicate with each other, and they have not decided their observational strategy in advance, so neither knows exactly what aspect of each photon, X, Y or Z, the other will measure. After the experiment is over, they get together to compare notes. They find that when Alice observed X-up, maybe Bob observed Z-down, and when Alice observed Y-down, maybe Bob observed X-up, and so forth. But whenever they happened to observe the same aspect, the observations were correlated. Every time Alice observed X-up, if Bob observed X, it was X-down. Every time Alice observed X-down, if Bob observed X, it was X-up, without fail. And this is true whether Alice observed before Bob did, or Bob observed first or they both observed at the same time.

So here is the question: How does photon B "know" that Alice is observing X-up so that when Bob observes X, it must be X-down?

You might object that it is not mysterious. Suppose you take a coin and carefully slice it in half along the circumference so that one piece has the heads side and the other has the tails side. If you put each half in an envelope and shuffle the envelopes and then open one and it contains heads, you would know without looking that the other one contains tails. But quantum objects are not like that. They don't exist as heads or tails (up or down) until they are detected. They have only a probability of being one or the other. To use the lingo, they are in a "superposition" of states. Only when a quantum object is detected does it unambiguously take on one property or another.

Albert Einstein and two colleagues, Podolsky and Rosen, developed a thought experiment that, they believed, proved that quantum theory was incomplete. Quantum theory says that you can't know with certainty two different properties of the same quantum object, for instance its position and its momentum, or its X-spin and its Y-spin. The more closely you pin down one, the less precisely you know the other. But in this case you could theoretically know both X-spin and Y-spin. If Alice observes X-up and Bob observes Y-up, then we know that Alice's photon is both X-up and Y-down, and we know that Bob's photon is both X-down and Y-up. This is known as the EPR Paradox, the paradox being that even though theory says you can't know two properties with certainty, here is a way you can. Einstein thought this proved that something, a hidden variable of some kind, one that we do not yet know about, determines the outcome, and that quantum indeterminacy was bogus.

Since then researchers have proved mathematically and experimentally that quantum theory is correct and that Einstein was wrong. Unfortunately, the math quickly gets very complex, and I am not competent to understand it, much less explain it. The gist of it is that classical (determinate) statistics says one thing about how often you would find combinations of properties, such as X-up, Y-up and Z-up, but actual experiment finds a different distribution. The results of the experiment do not agree with classical assumptions, but they do agree with quantum assumptions, so something about the classical assumptions must be wrong.

The primary assumption violated is called "locality," meaning that what happens at one place can't instantaneously affect what happens someplace else. Locality says there has to be some connection between them, some impetus traveling from one to the other. But in this case measuring photon A does in fact instantaneously affect the measurement of photon B. We appear to have what Einstein called "spooky action at a distance."

Except it's not action. No signal, impulse, stimulus or data of any sort is transmitted between the two. Instead the two photons appear to be aspects of the same thing. Each member of the pair is described by the same quantum mechanical wave function, and when it "collapses" into something determinate, both aspects become determinate at the same time. They don't communicate; they are not transmitting information. They are connected, even though physically separate. In the lingo, they are "entangled."

In the previous chapter we saw instances in the biological world where disparate physical elements act as one. Here is an instance at the very foundation of physical reality.

We have to be careful when interpreting quantum physics. The observed facts are unequivocal and repeatable, but what it all means is something else entirely. That quantum objects are sometimes entangled does not prove the mystical intuition that all is one, no matter how many new-age aficionados would like to believe so. But it does open the possibility.

*   *   *

The quantum world contains more than one clue about the ultimate nature of reality. In the next chapter we'll look at another: what happens in our brains.

Chapter 8, The Quantum World: Agency

Quantum indeterminacy operates inside your brain. What does that say about how best to describe what is real?[12]

Indeterminacy

We've seen a couple of examples of quantum indeterminacy in the previous chapter. Here is another. A famous experiment, widely replicated, called the Double-Slit experiment, reveals the strangeness of the quantum level of reality. The experiment consists of sending light through two side-by-side vertical slits to a recording medium, such as film; and it shows, among other things, that light can behave both as a stream of particles and as a wave. When light is sent through one slit at a time, a vertical band appears. In this case light acts like a series of particles that go through the slit, hit the recording medium and make an impression. If you open the slit on the right, the band appears on the right, and if you open the slit on the left, the band appears on the left. You would expect that if both slits were opened, the result would be two side-by-side bands. In fact, however, the result is a strong band in the middle, the expected bands on the left and right, and then dimmer bands extending outward in each direction. Light in this case acts like waves that cause interference patterns. That is, when a crest meets a crest, a more intense crest results; and when a crest meets a trough, they cancel each other out. The bands of light are from the crests reinforcing each other, and the darkness in between is from crests and troughs canceling each other out.

Even more interesting, when light is emitted one photon at a time and aimed at the two slits, it shows the same interference pattern. You would expect that a photon would go through one slit or the other. In fact it appears to act like a wave that goes through both slits, interferes with itself, and results in an impression in one and only one of the bands.

And you cannot predict in advance where the photon will make an impression.

You can predict that given a great number of photons, they will result in bands. That is, they won't all end up in the same place, but rather in various places according to their probability distribution. But there is only a probability, not an absolute certainty, that any single photon will end up in one place or another.

We might well ask what causes the wave, which is mathematically described as a collection of probabilities of being detected in various places, to be in fact detected at only one place. I'll return to this question shortly. For now, note once again the quantum indeterminacy, our inability to predict the final location of any single photon. The sequence in which the singly emitted photons will arrive is completely unpredictable. We have a radical discontinuity of causality.

Causality

In ordinary life and in classical (non-quantum) physics, we have a clear concept of causality: a cause is something that reliably produces an effect. Given the same or a similar set of circumstances, we expect the same or similar results to appear. Hitting a billiard ball at a certain angle and with a certain force will always result in its moving in a certain direction and at a certain speed. This conception of causality has three parts:

- Regularity: A cause always produces its effect according to physical laws that can be discovered by observation and experiment.
- Temporal sequence: The cause always precedes its effect in time. The cause never follows the effect.

- Spatial contiguity: There is always some physical connection or spatial contact between the cause and its effect, or there is a chain of such connections.

At the quantum level, the regularity is missing. (And, as we have seen in the previous chapter, sometimes spatial contiguity is missing as well.) There is no set of circumstances that causes the photon always to be detected in a specific place.

Once the photon has been detected, then the ordinary chain of causality takes over. The beginning of a macroscopic event can certainly be dependent on a microscopic event. In that case, each microscopic possibility at the beginning can lead to a different chain of macroscopic events at the end.

This state of affairs becomes important when we consider that some events in the brain happen at the quantum level.

The Brain

The human brain is a mass of electrochemical activity. It contains approximately 100 billion nerve cells, or neurons, and up to five quadrillion connection points between them. Neurons are the fundamental elements of the brain; they transmit electrochemical impulses to and from other neurons, sense organs or muscles. Some impulses are triggered by sense organs and some by the excitation of neighboring neurons. Some impulses excite or inhibit neighboring neurons, and some cause muscle contractions that move the body.

A neuron consists of several parts: numerous dendrites, which look vaguely like trees with many branches; a cell body; and a single axon, a tube that divides at the end into many terminals. Dendrites are the incoming channels; they receive electrochemical impulses from other cells, which then pass through the body and out the axon terminals. Between the axon terminals and the dendrites of the neighboring neurons are gaps, called synapses, only twenty nanometers wide. On the other side of the synaptic gap from the axon is a receptor area on a dendrite of a neighboring cell. An axon can have many terminals, and each dendrite can have many receptor areas. Thus each neuron transmits impulses to and receives impulses from a great many neighboring neurons. Some neurons receive impulses from up to

10,000 neighbors. Some in the cerebellum receive from up to 100,000. Clearly the brain is an organ of almost unimaginable complexity.

The impulse traveling through the neuron is an electrical charge. A neuron either transmits the impulse (we say it fires) or it does not; it is a binary element, either on (firing) or off (not firing). When the electrical charge reaches the synaptic gap, it triggers the release of chemicals, neurotransmitters, which is why we call brain activity electrochemical. A single release of a neurotransmitter might be too weak to trigger the receiving neuron; but since each neuron forms outgoing synapses with many others and likewise receives synaptic inputs from many others, the combination of several inputs at once can be enough to trigger it. Or the receipt of an inhibitory neurotransmitter can prevent an impulse that otherwise would have fired. The output of a neuron thus depends on the inputs from many others, each of which may have a different degree of influence depending on the strength of its synapse with that neuron.

What is interesting for the present discussion is what happens to cause the neurotransmitters to travel across the synapse. The chemistry is a bit complex, but basically neurotransmitter chemicals sit docked in little pockets, called vesicles, waiting for something to release them. When the electrical impulse arrives at the terminal, it opens up channels that let calcium ions in. The calcium makes the vesicle fuse with the cell wall and open up so the neurotransmitters go out into the synaptic gap and then hit the receiving neuron.

The channels through which calcium ions enter the nerve terminal from outside the neuron are tiny, only about a nanometer at their narrowest, not much bigger than a calcium ion itself. The calcium ions migrate from their entry channels to sites within the nerve terminal where they trigger the release of the contents of a vesicle. At this submicroscopic level of reality, quantum indeterminacy is in play. A given calcium ion might or might not hit a given triggering site; hence, a given neurotransmitter might or might not be released; hence, the receiving neuron might or might not get excited (or inhibited).[vi]

In other words, at the most fundamental level, brain functioning is not causally determined.

And since the ordinary chain of causality takes over after the quantum event happens, quantum uncertainty at the synaptic level can lead to causal uncertainty at the level of the whole brain. And that means—since the state of the brain at least heavily influences, if not causally determines, our perceptions, thoughts, feelings and actions—that human conduct is not fully causally determined in the physical world.

Beyond the Causal Veil

What causes a quantum event—in this case the impact of a calcium ion on a triggering site—to cease being merely a probability and start being something that happens at a certain place? Not anything in the physical world. There is a causal discontinuity in nature. Events at the quantum level of reality have no physical cause but are themselves causes of subsequent events. What is on the other side of the causal discontinuity?

At this point we move beyond what physics can tell us, but clearly these findings leave open the possibility that human will is free and even that something that transcends our ordinary notion of the physical—a soul, perhaps, or a god or a plethora of deities—intervenes in the physical world.

[vi] This account of neural functioning assumes that what is observable in carefully-controlled scientific experiments also pertains to parts of reality that are not directly observable. We cannot actually observe the impact of a calcium ion on a triggering site because the act of setting up the observation would kill the organism containing the nerve being observed. I assume that the behavior of reality is consistent at the quantum level whether we can observe a particular instance of it or not. In order to make that assumption I also assume that the description of the quantum level of reality is not only epistemological, pertaining to our experience of nature, but ontological as well, pertaining to what actually happens in nature whether or not a human being observes it. See the discussions titled "Quantum Theory and Biology" and "The Heisenberg Ontology" in Stapp, *Mind, Matter and Quantum Mechanics*, pp. 123–128.

Some protest that the causal uncertainty at the quantum level of reality is merely statistical. Events happen randomly; hence, we can draw no conclusions about nonphysical causality, free will, the existence of a soul or of God or any such thing. In particular, they say, a decision that is initiated by a random occurrence is no more free than one initiated by physical causality. But random as they may be individually, quantum events considered as a group certainly do exhibit regularities. Light passed through double slits exhibits distinct patterns, not random noise.

Consider a pointillist painting, which consists of distinct dots of pigment. If you look at it up close, all you see is random dots. When you view it from afar, you see identifiable forms and shapes, recognizable objects, patterns. So what are the patterns that we find in the behavior that issues from the firing of our brain cells? Does what is outside the bounds of physical causality have any regularity or structure of its own that we can use to understand and predict what it will do? Are there any categories of causal explanation that might be applicable?

The answer is, yes, of course there are: the concepts that pertain to agents. We explain the behavior of agents not in terms of physics and chemistry but in terms of their perceptions, beliefs, desires and goals.

By "agent" I mean the usual: something with will and intention, something that initiates movement without an external nudge, something that acts or has the power to act on its own rather than merely reacting to events. Agency is a different category of causation from physical causation. What agents do is not uncaused, but what causes agents to act is their beliefs and desires, not mechanical or chemical forces. And what agents do is not completely predictable. We try to influence people by persuasion, but we can only influence them, we cannot completely control them. A person is rather like a single photon: we can never be sure what somebody will do until they have done it. Nor can we be sure what we ourselves will do until we have done it. And afterwards we recognize that we could have acted differently.

What I am suggesting is that, considered *en masse*, the quantum events that take place in our brains exhibit regularities that are best described as agential. The agential is a category of reality that is just as fundamental as—and indeed perhaps more fundamental than—the physical.

* * *

Quantum physics has given us some fascinating clues about the ultimate nature of reality. A further clue is to be found in something that is intimately close to us, but which, paradoxically, we often overlook: the structure of our own experience.

Chapter 9, The First-Person Point of View

Sciences such as biology and quantum physics examine the world from an objective, third-person point of view. Their findings are accepted only if they can be replicated and verified by other investigators. The first-person point of view—how it feels to be you, how the world looks to you, what your experience is like—is most often relegated to the arts: literature, drama, poetry, music, painting, sculpture and so forth. The arts can show us uniquely beautiful things about how the world appears to the artist, an appearance that comes from the artist's singular experience. But what if we approached our experience with the same sort of rigor and objectivity as we use in the sciences? That might tell us tell us something awfully important as well.

The uniqueness of the first-person point of view is that each of us has his or her own, and nobody else has that same point of view. For example, when I see a certain object from my own perspective and you see it from your perspective, we can agree that we are seeing the same object, but I do not see it as it appears to you, and you do not see it as it appears to me. We each have our own experience of it, not anybody else's. To put it another way, the experience each one of us has is private, not public. Our experience is *of* public, objective things, but the experience itself is private, subjective.

Why is this important? After all, the triumphs of the scientific method are triumphs of third-person objectivity, the result of observations that have been publicly replicated and justified by evidence that any competent observer can verify. If you see a rope but everyone else says it is a snake, you would be better off taking another look. If a chemical process requires something to be heated to a certain temperature, you get better results using a thermometer, which anyone can see, rather than relying on your subjective sense of how hot it is. There is no question that the third-person point of view has given us valuable knowledge of what it is to be human, so much so that some philosophers rely on it alone. But to ignore the first-person point of view is to fail to take into account an additional source of information, which turns out to be equally valuable. When we pay attention to first-person experience, we can learn things that are not obvious from the third-person point of view.

The importance of the first-person point of view is this: in a very real sense, it is the only point of view we have! The only contact we have with anything, subjective or objective, is through our experience. The point of all knowledge, whether rigorous science or practical know-how, is to make sense of what we experience. When several researchers independently verify the reading on an instrument or the results of an experiment, each of them sees the reading or the results and communicates their observation to the others. Seeing is a modality of experience. If there weren't any experience, there would be no possibility of any sort of knowledge. The whole of science is the successful attempt to make sense of regularities in our experience of the world, experience that each of us has, individually and privately, and that we communicate to others.

(This is not to judge whether or not there is a real world independent of our experience, by the way, although the assumption that there is seems to work pretty well. It is true whether or not we assume that an objective, real world exists.)

There is a whole field of philosophy, called Phenomenology, devoted to studying the first-person point of view. Phenomenology is the exercise of examining one's own experience without bias. The investigator inspects his or her own experience directly instead of using intermediary channels such as oscilloscopes to measure brain waves or psychological experiments to measure attitudes and responses. The phenomenologist examines, not the objects of experience (bridges, trees, people, art, quarks, and so forth), but the experience itself, how those objects appear to him or her. The phenomenologist attempts to do this examination without bias, without letting what he or she already knows or believes get in the way of just noting what is present in the experience.[vii] Buddhist monks and phenomenological investigators share some similarity in this regard: both just pay attention to what is present in experience, without interpreting it as anything else. Phenomenology is a radically first-person point of view.

And what does this inspection tell us? Lots of things, but I want to focus on two of them, both pertaining to human nature. The first is that what we commonly take ourselves to be is actually a conglomeration of many elements: perceptions, feelings, thoughts, bodily sensations, habitual actions, deliberate actions, beliefs, desires, and more, all organized in an ongoing pattern but none of which are constant. If we examine our experience carefully, we find no specific unchanging thing which is our self. We are not a substance; instead, we are process, an unfolding pattern of change. The pattern has some constancy, like the flame of a candle, but everything within the pattern is continually altering, moving and transforming.

But it is not just any pattern that we experience as our self. It is a pattern of elements that is organized around a center, around a point of view. It is *our* experience that we are directly acquainted with, not somebody else's. And we know it from the "inside," so to speak, not externally as we know everything else. We see the outside of trees, people, animals, etc., but we know directly our own experience, and only our own experience. Who or what is the knower?

That is the big mystery. There is nothing in our experience that is the experiencer. Anything that we can identify is an object of experience, not that which experiences the object. You might think of yourself as your body, but who experiences the body? You might think of yourself as your most intimate, deep-seated beliefs and desires. But even those are things you are conscious of. Who are you, the one who is conscious?

[vii] This lack of bias is how Phenomenology differs from mere introspection.

Who Experiences?

This is so important that I want to spend a little more time on it. What I am saying is that the experiencing subject, the one to whom or to which all the elements of experience are present, is not itself an element in experience. It is certainly not an objective thing or process, there for any third-person observer. Such an observer can see people walking around and doing and saying things, but has no direct access to the private thoughts and feelings of any of them, much less to that which experiences or has those private thoughts and feelings. Nor is the experiencing subject an object of experience in a private sense. We can be conscious of a number of private elements in or aspects of experience: clear and distinct thoughts; less-clear perceptual judgments through which we recognize, for instance, that a squiggly shape is either a stick or a snake; bodily feelings; emotions; and impulsions to action. But none of these private aspects of experience are that which is conscious of them, that which has the experience, the experiencing subject. I call that experiencing subject the Transcendental Self, where "transcendental" means "lying at the root of experience;" but none of us can be conscious of it in any way.

We are barred from becoming conscious of the I, the Self, that is itself aware, for to do so would require that the I be no longer the conscious subject, but an object. The I that is aware cannot be seen or heard, it cannot be intuited through thought (for then we are aware, not of the I, but of an image or concept of the I). The I which is aware, I-the-experiencer, is ungraspable, a void, a nothingness; it is no thing. We can characterize the Self as that to which the world is present, that for which there is the world, but what it is in itself we cannot grasp. We cannot be directly conscious of it in any way. It is a mystery.

This state of affairs is so peculiar and unique that there is no adequate language for it. If by the term "I" or "Self" we mean I-who-experience, then none of us is there in our experience at all! There is no experienceable object which is I-the-experiencer. It seems misleading to use a noun or noun phrase, for there is nothing to which such a noun or noun phrase refers. This conundrum,

I take it, is the point behind Sartre's talk of Nothingness and the Buddhists' talk of the Void and the doctrine of *anatta*, or no-self.

And yet we each take it for granted that we exist, that we experience the world; nothing could be more obvious than that experience is going on and that it is our own experience, if only because it is our own and not someone else's. In the visual field that those of us who are sighted enjoy, everything appears to converge on a central point of view, which each of us takes to be himself or herself. Thus, the Upanishads and the later Hindu tradition speak of the Atman, that innermost Self which experiences the world; and Edmund Husserl, the father of Phenomenology, speaks of the "pure Ego," "the phenomenological Ego which finds things presented to it ... ."[13]

If, following Husserl, we choose to put a name to that-which-experiences, such as the "Transcendental Ego" or the "Transcendental Self," we must always keep in mind that it is not in any sense an object. Husserl says "We shall never stumble across the pure Ego as an experience among others within the flux of manifold experiences ... nor shall we meet it as a constitutive bit of experience appearing with the experience of which it is an integral part and again disappearing ... . It can *in no sense* be reckoned *as a real part or phase* of the experiences themselves,"[14] where "real" means experienceable, present in experience, or present to pure consciousness. Husserl says

> The experiencing Ego is still nothing that might be taken *for itself* and made into an object of inquiry on its *own* account. Apart from its "ways of being related" or "ways of behaving," it is completely empty of essential components, it has no content that could be unraveled, it is in and for itself indescribable: pure Ego and nothing further.[15]

There is a very good reason why it is "in and for itself indescribable." To be able to describe something, you must be able in some way to perceive it; and the pure Ego is that which perceives but which cannot itself be perceived.

The pure Ego or Transcendental Self is not only an observer but an actor as well. Husserl speaks of the ego's "ways of behaving" and of the pure Ego as "free spontaneity and activity," the "primary source of generation," the "subject of the spontaneity."[16] The Transcendental Self is not, in fact, solely passive and receptive; it is also the source of all our action. And the Self as transcendental agent is also unintuitable, unperceivable.

As long as this point is kept clearly in mind, it need not be misleading to use a noun phrase, "Transcendental Self," to refer to the basic state of affairs that is always and everywhere evident regarding oneself, that one experiences and acts. Strictly speaking, we can say that experiencing and acting are functions of the self to which no particular experienceable object corresponds. The important point remains: No one can become aware of himself or herself in the mode, "I myself," for each of us is that which is aware, pure transcendental consciousness. We can characterize the Transcendental Self as that to which the world is present, but what it is in itself—what each of us himself or herself is—we cannot directly experience in any way. At our deepest core we are each a mystery.

*　*　*

This conclusion is as far as the phenomenological evidence will take us. We have reached, in a sense, the ultimate, that beyond which it is impossible to go. Pure transcendental consciousness is of necessity a mystery, unperceivable. But that mystery suggests another way to understand the mystical intuition that all is one: that the Transcendental Self of each of us is the same as the Transcendental Self of all of reality.

Chapter 10, Speaking of the Self

Time out to clarify some concepts. I am about to get grandiose, but I also want to be philosophically rigorous; and the cardinal sin of philosophy, committed all too often, is to use terms that are ambiguous. You start out talking about one thing and end up talking about something else even though you are using the same word. That's called *equivocation*, and equivocation is very bad indeed because it promotes confusion rather than clarity.

I am talking about the self. What is that? By "self," uncapitalized, I mean the human being, emphasizing the view from the inside, from our own subjectivity. When I talk about the human being as perceived from the outside, I use the term "person." The term "self" refers to the constellation of thoughts, emotions, physical perceptions, memories and anticipations that we each commonly think of as "me" or "myself." (By extension, we can think of every being, human or not, as having at least the rudiments of a self. See *Panpsychism* above.)

By "Self," capitalized, I mean the Transcendental Self, that which is conscious of and acts upon the world. That's what I discussed in the previous chapter.

The Transcendental Self is *the unobservable center around which experience is organized and from which action emanates.* By "experience" I mean not just sensation but all the structural elements we find in our experience: thoughts, feelings, emotions, perceptual judgments, etc. (This list is similar to what the Buddhists call the *skandhas*, or "aggregates," which categorize or constitute all individual experience, but it is not identical to the Buddhist list.)

If the Self is unobservable, perhaps Occam's Razor should lead us to drop it entirely from rational discussion, which is what the Buddhists do. However, despite its being unobservable, we can observe its effects and thereby infer something about it.

The term "self," with a lower-case "s," refers to the interiority of a being, recognizing that there are degrees of interior complexity that correspond to degrees of physical, or exterior, complexity. The self in this sense is *coherence of interiority*. The more coherent and the more complex, integrative and harmonious a being's experience, the higher degree of selfness that being has. The higher the degree of selfness, the richer is The God's experience of the All. (Don't worry. I will explain that part in the next chapter.)

Diseases such as Alzheimer's and dementia can be viewed as degenerative diseases of the self in this second sense; and the less coherent the self gets, the less one could say that it survives. People in a persistent vegetative state, such as Terri Schiavo, might be said to lack a self. Or to have only a vegetable self, not a human self.

People with multiple personalities could be said to have more than one self. Not only that, I suspect that one self might animate more than one physical body. Sometimes a flock of birds or a herd of animals will seem to move as one being. Perhaps the selves of the individuals mingle in some way such that a higher-level coherence comes into being, at least for a time. And, of course, the mystical absorption into the One can be understood as an individual self (coherence of interiority) participating in a higher-level coherence.

The Self in the World

We speak as if the Self were an entity, a thing, that endures through time. But when we examine our experience we find no such thing. We could call the Self a locus of consciousness with continuity over time. What is continuous is the pattern and content of the stuff perceived by that locus of consciousness, not the locus itself, because the locus itself is not there.

If the Self, the Transcendental Self, the locus of consciousness, is not there, then what leads us to believe that there is one?
The answer is that we see things from a perspective, that we
have learned that we are "over here" and other people and things
are "over there." We have a visual point of view. We can't see the
seer, but we can see that the visual field extends from a point,
which we occupy.

(We call it a "field" of vision or a "field" of consciousness because it is like an actual field of, for instance, grass or corn. An
actual field is spread out and so is the field of vision. Many of our
metaphors for conscious experience are visual.)

We (each of us, individually) who are "over here" find ourselves thrust into the world of over-there-ness. This is why
Heidegger calls the human being *Dasein*, Being-There.[17] Each of
us is located. Each of us is in context. We are thrust into the
world of the over-there because we have to interact with it.
("Thrust," of course, is a metaphor. I do not propose at this point
to identify who or what has done the thrusting.)

The Self and Others

In the world of the over-there we find other people. People do
not live in isolation, and we humans require other humans for
our survival and well-being. That fact is an important point for
ethical consideration, and there is a huge amount of evidence for
it, but I'll restrict myself for now to the phenomenological evidence.

From a phenomenological point of view, our experience contains interpretations, or perceptual judgments, that tell us that
this over here is different from that over there. Some of our experience can be seen (or heard, or felt, etc.) only from this viewpoint
over here. We call this private experience. Some of the objects of
our experience can be seen by others as well. We call these objects publicly observable things. And some of them are other people.

To put it another way, phenomenologically we find present in
our experience the sense that some objects are private, available
only to the person experiencing them; and others are public,
available to everyone. And we find present in our experience the

sense that some of those publicly available objects are in fact sub-jects as well, conscious of the world as we ourselves are.

And we find present in our experience the sense that who we are (who each of us is) is constituted to a great extent by our rela-tionships with those others. Heidegger calls this aspect of human existence *Mitsein*, being-with,[18] meaning that the self (uncapital-ized) always finds itself related to others.

Self and Soul

When we are talking about what is most intimately oneself we often use the term "soul." That term also has various mean-ings, which must be made clear. Sometimes in general parlance in English the term "soul" refers to the human being generally (as in "twenty souls were lost in the disaster"). Often, particular-ly in a religious or spiritual context, the term refers to some inde-finable substance that is alleged to be the essence of the human and that persists after death. In the latter sense people debate whether animals have souls, and atheists deny that even humans have souls. In many languages the word for soul is related to the word for breath, so the soul is that which makes us breathe, that which gives us life. But what is the soul in itself?

I shall use the term "soul" to mean just what I mean by "self." Uncapitalized, "soul" means the interiority of a being, a coher-ence of private experience. Capitalized, "Soul" means the Tran-scendental Self, the unobservable center around which experi-ence is organized and from which action emanates.

Given these definitions of "Soul" and "soul," we can approach some of the ongoing questions about the nature of the soul. Is the soul unchanging? Does it survive after death? Is it eternal?

In the sense of coherence of interiority, the soul is certainly not unchanging; our inner experience changes constantly, and it takes some effort at meditation to quiet it down even briefly.

To say that the Soul as unobservable center is unchanging is more plausible. All things change, but the Soul is no observable thing. Thus, in our experience it does not change. But our experi-ence may not be all there is to the Soul. Perhaps we can observe its effects and thereby infer something about it. If it has effects, it must change. The argument is this:

> All things that have effects are changeable.
> The Soul has effects.
>
> ---
>
> Therefore the Soul is changeable.

But what are the effects of the Soul? I allude to this in my chapters on the Quantum level of reality. When one is at the cusp of a decision, the alternatives of which have approximately equal weight, one considers the alternatives, and then one of them is chosen. But who chooses? Perhaps it is the Soul. Or perhaps it is The God. Or perhaps these are the same. As Advaita Vedanta says, Atman is Brahman, the Soul is The God. One of the effects of the Soul is choice, or decision, so the Soul changes.

To me, this question is the great mystery, to which I shall return. For now, let's leave it open.

Does the soul in the sense of interiority survive the death of the physical body? I have limited personal experience in this regard, but there are plenty of stories indicating that it does, or at least can. And if coherence of interiority persists, then the unobservable center must persist as well, else there would be no coherence.

Whether the soul or the Soul is eternal, however, is completely speculative. "Eternal" means never-ending, perpetual, existing at all times. Our experience has not yet ended, but it might, so we cannot say for sure that it will never end. We have memories of the past in our lifetime, and some of us seem to have memories of past lives prior to this lifetime; but nobody, to my knowledge, has memories of the entire past, so it seems that a soul as coherence of interiority must have had a beginning, and hence has not existed at all times. Or maybe it has, but we lack memory of it. Such speculations are what the Buddha called "questions which tend not to edification."[19]

* * *

OK, with that behind us, let's look at the larger picture. What does the nature of the Self or Soul mean for the assertion that not only is everything connected to everything else but that all is one?

Chapter 11, All is One

As we look around the world, it is apparent that the world is composed of many things. The Chinese refer to this aspect of reality poetically as the "ten thousand things."[20] The mystics, however, tell us that reality is actually one and that the ten thousand things are, depending on the variety of mysticism, illusory or an aspect of the One. How can many things be one?

We have seen hints that many things can be one in the biological world and in the quantum world. These hints are based on observations from the outside, from the public, objective point of view. The unity of all that exists can be also understood from the inside. We can say that the One is that which is conscious and active in everything, in every event. What appears to be many from the outside is in fact the manifestation of one underlying reality. What I am saying is this: *the Transcendental Self of each of us is the same as the Transcendental Self of all of reality*. In other words, *there is one universal interiority*, which incorporates the interiority of all the separate constituents of reality into one unity of experience, one coherence of interiority.

I am making a metaphysical assertion. The discussions so far, of the biological world, the quantum world and the world of our own experience, do not logically mandate this assertion, but they suggest that it might be true, and they make sense within its framework. Let's examine in some detail what this framework is all about.

One Universal Interiority

One of the earliest of our world's great mystical writings is the set of treatises called the Upanishads, from India. The Upanishads say that Atman, the Transcendental Self of each one of us and (by virtue of the doctrine of Panpsychism) of every living and nonliving thing, is the same as Brahman, the universal Self of the entire universe: "This Self is Brahman indeed" say the scriptures.[21] Brahman is the supreme reality, which I call The One, The All or The God. The God is that which is conscious of and which animates everything from the inside.

This universal Self is known by many names in many different spiritual traditions: Brahman, the Void, the One, God, the All, the Spirit-that-moves-in-all-things, the Tao and many more. I prefer to say "The God" instead of just "God" to emphasize the unique singularity of this being. Lots of people have an idea of "God," but I don't want to get mixed up with lots of people's ideas. If I say "The God," I hope it will be unfamiliar enough to make you stop and think rather than assume that I am talking about your concept.

The God is the inside of everything. This insight is expressed in the Bhagavad Gita, Chapter 13, verses 1 and 2, in which Krishna, The God, speaks to Arjuna, a human:

> 1   *This body, Arjuna, is called the field. He who knows this is called the knower of the field.*
> 2   *Know that I am the knower in all the fields of my creation.*[22]

The God looks out through our eyes, hears through our ears, feels through our fingers and skin, smells through our nose and tastes through our tongue. (By "our" I mean each of us, individually.) The God thinks through our mind, feels through our emotions, and actualizes intentions through our will.

This process is rather like divine telepathy. Picture an octopus with an eye on the end of each tentacle. Each eye corresponds to a self. Imagine being at the end of a tentacle, looking out of the eye. That is, figuratively speaking, the condition of a separate self, looking out at the world. Now imagine being in the center of the octopus, being able to see out of all the eyes. That is, figuratively speaking, the condition of a higher-level coherence of interiority, a higher-level self, which we might term a god with a lowercase "g" or a spirit. We get an inkling of this condition when we see a whole flock of birds or a herd of animals turn and move as one; it is as if the flock or herd is one being, animated by one soul. Now picture a super-octopus, which is composed of all the separate octopi. This super-octopus can see through all the eyes of all the octopi. Viewed from the outside, this super-octopus is the universe, the entirety of all that exists. Viewed from the inside, this super-octopus is The God, with an uppercase "G."

This metaphor is visual, but we could just as well use an auditory or a tactile one. The point is, regardless of which metaphor we choose, a self is conscious of the world (from the outside) and of itself (from the inside), and a god would be conscious of many selves from the inside. The God is that which is conscious of all selves from the inside.

The God is that which "peers through the eyes," so to speak, of every self: animal, vegetable or mineral. Each self sees (or hears, or feels, etc.) the inside of itself and the outside of things in its surroundings. The God, being the knower in every field, as the Bhagavad Gita says, experiences the inside of every self and the outside of everything of which each self is conscious. Together they constitute the whole of reality. Therefore The God knows (is conscious of) everything.

Mystical philosophy, such as that found in the Upanishads and Bhagavad Gita, as well as in some Sufi writings, has emphasized the conscious, knowing aspect of The God. However, The God is not only that which knows, but also that which acts, the source of activity in every being. The God is not only conscious, but animating. Phenomenologically, the Transcendental Self is both the unobservable experiencer and the unobservable actor. We could call it a spirit. A spirit, as we perceive it from the outside, is a locus of animation. From the inside it is a point of view. The God is the Spirit-that-moves-in-all-things.

The God is that in every being from which activity emerges. From the inside, we experience that some of our activities arise from within us, not as a result of something from the outside, but spontaneously, of our own doing. Some of our activities are things that we do, our actions. (The term "activities" includes activities caused from outside of oneself and activities caused by oneself. I use the term "actions" to mean activities caused by oneself. Actions are a subset of activities.) The God is the source of all actions in every self. The God is the Self in all selves, animating all beings.

Here is a picture showing hierarchical levels or degrees of interiority, which we might call selfhood or soulness:

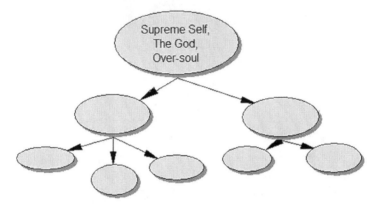

The term "Over-soul" is Ralph Waldo Emerson's translation of the Sanskrit term *Paramatman*, Supreme Self or Supreme Soul.[23] In this picture the smallest ovals at the bottom represent individuals such as human beings, and the intermediate ovals represent larger coherences of interiority, such as the spirit of a place or time or community in which one can participate, or spirit beings such as angels or gods. Or, since the whole thing is fractal in nature, the intermediary ovals can represent human beings, and the lowest-level ovals can represent organs or cells. The idea that there are intermediary levels of soul above the human is my own speculation. Of course, this discussion is all speculation, as there is no objective, third-party evidence for any of it. But it does not contradict objective, third-party findings either. It is, like all metaphysical theories, a conceptual framework within which to interpret the totality of our experience, including objective, scientific fact and subjective, private, personal fact.

How Do We Know?

The last point is important, because it provides a justification for asserting the mystical doctrine that all is one. Not all evidence is public, and not all facts are physical. Evidence can be private, or subjective, and facts can be mental. You can perceive the effects of something you may call God in your own life, and indeed we humans are prone to do so. Some examples of such evidence are the following:

- We may perceive portents and signs, patterns of synchronicity that seem to have greater significance than mere randomness.
- We may experience the presence of God as a result of practices that alter experience, such as meditation, chanting, fasting, ceremony and ritual, ingestion of certain substances, etc.
- We may experience responses to prayer and hence have a sense of a personal relationship with God.

If we adopt a stance of relating to our idea of God as if God exists and is person-like, and we can plausibly interpret events as embodying the actions of that person-like being responding to us, and particularly if those actions are to our benefit, then we do have compelling evidence.

None of these types of evidence prove the existence of God publicly, but if others report experiencing them as well, as many do, then they have more weight. In the absence of scientific proof, we may choose to believe in God on the basis of subjective evidence. If the effects of such belief are beneficial—if, for instance, we are happier and function better as a result of such belief than without it—then we are justified in that belief.

The Nature of The God

I want to note a potential equivocation here. I have used the term "The God" to refer to the highest (or, since it is all a metaphor, the deepest), most inclusive level of coherence of interiority. And I have just used the term "God," without the definite article, to refer to something like a person, with whom one can have a personal relationship. The two senses refer to the same thing but they are not the same.

The way we access the former is from the inside, through meditative practices that bring our attention to deeper and deeper levels of our own interiority, our own self. The way we access the latter is from the outside, through prayer and other forms of communion, rather like talking to and interacting with another person. These two modalities are not contradictory. Since everything has an inside and an outside, we can indeed relate to the All from the outside, as if it were a person. The All is for practical purposes infinite, meaning that as we experience it, we never come to its end. As such, the All can relate to us in an unlimited number of ways and can certainly be experienced by the limited self as a Thou.

So when I use the term "God," without the definite article, I am referring to that aspect of the One, the All, that we experience as personal, as a being with whom we are in relation. And when I use the term "The God," with the definite article, I am referring to that aspect of the One, the All, that each of us is in our inmost interiority. These are two aspects of the same thing. (Except that the One is not a thing.)

The God is not an object or living being in the world, one among many but much bigger or grander or more powerful. The God is the interiority of the totality of all that is. Since interiority is not separate from exteriority—both are aspects, one private, one public, of the same thing—then The God is the totality of all that is. In this sense, the doctrine I am espousing is Pantheism, from the Greek *pan*, meaning "all" and *theos*, meaning "God." All is The God. And I am saying that Pantheism is Panpsychism: the *theos* is the *psyche* of all; The God is the Soul of All.

I say "*The* God" because there is only one. Nothing exists apart from the universe as we know it. (If we suppose that something did exist entirely apart from the universe, then it would have no causal effect on us and, in practice, would be no different from not existing at all.)

Divine Influence

This doctrine, that The God is the interiority of everything, explains how the divine can influence the mundane. We need not suppose that an entity external to physical reality somehow intervenes. Instead The God perceives the inside of all the elements of physical reality that are interacting with each other and can put attention on places of interest. Especially if divine attention is placed on living beings with highly evolved nervous systems, we can imagine that The God could influence what those beings do by adjusting the probabilities at the quantum level of neural functioning.

We know that the synapses in the human brain are small enough that quantum indeterminacy operates there (see *Chapter 8, The Quantum World: Agency*), so we cannot predict whether any given neuron will fire or not. Neural firings are correlated with emotion, thought and decision—all the aspects of mentality. Hence, we cannot fully predict what a human being will think, say or do. This does not mean that the neural firings are merely random. As each dot in a pointillist painting is an element in a larger whole which gives it significance, so each individual neural event is an element in a larger whole as well. And that's how The God influences the world, through the larger whole.

What appears to be the random firing of a neuron may in fact be part of a larger pattern that extends through space and time, a pattern that exhibits consciousness and agency. And since The God is the ultimate interiority, that which senses everything from the inside, the pattern can span things that appear to us to be separate. In this view, The God is what creates and propagates the pattern. The God adjusts the probabilities at the quantum level to effect coordination of events on the macro level. I am not saying The God makes everything happen, although some theologies assert exactly that. I am saying that if there is a place where nonphysical[viii] reality exerts an effect on physical reality, it is in submicroscopic quantum spaces, in particular the interstices

---

[viii] By "nonphysical" in this context I mean "other than what is detectable by ordinary perception" (which may be amplified by scientific instrumentation). Metaphysically nothing is entirely nonphysical, just as nothing is entirely nonmental.

of the neurons; and I am saying that it is The God that exerts that effect.[ix]

What The God does is make disparate things move so as to express a common interiority, a common agency. They become a common locus of animation. The God is the Spirit-that-moves-in-all-things. This idea would make sense of a lot of things, from signs and portents in the outer world to the mysterious source of inspiration in the inner. The common interiority is the means by which The God gives us inspiration and guidance. By our prayers and our practices, we attract benevolent interest.

(Of course, in any given case it might not be The God moving disparate things as one. It might be a being or conflux of mentality that is greater than a person but not the entirety of The God. Such a being would be a god (lower-case "g"), an angel, a spirit, some greater pattern, some greater coherence of interiority than the individual human, but less than the entirety. But if it is such a thing, The God is behind or within it, as The God is behind or within all things.)

The mystic ascribes agential causality to The God. There is no way to prove or disprove this theory scientifically, but we can choose to believe it on other grounds, such as its internal consistency, its coherence with the other things we know and its practicality for achieving our ends.

[ix] The God adjusts probabilities. Ordinary causality consists of overwhelmingly probable sequences of events. In the realm of the personal, one's habits of action, thought and feeling are just very probable sequences. Where the influence of The God can be detected most easily (at least in retrospect) is in situations of choice whose alternatives have approximately equal weight. One considers the alternatives, and then one or the other alternative is chosen. But who chooses? There is no thing, no object of consciousness, that is the chooser. Perhaps The God chooses. The God appears to favor tiny interventions, as evidenced by the Jewish and Christian Bible's mention of the "still, small voice" of the Lord (I Kings 19: 11–12). It seems to require less effort, so to speak, to make a choice among approximately equal alternatives than to make a choice that goes against a habit.

Again, these thoughts are speculation, but they provide an explanation of one possible means by which divine benevolence can affect human life.

* * *

I have now laid out the basic metaphysical framework, that all is One. In the next chapter I speculate in a bit more detail about the nature of that One.

Chapter 12, Aspects of The One

All is One, and that One is a magnificently huge living organism. It has consciousness, will, intention and agency. It resembles a human being, but is much vaster, grander and more powerful than any of us. Its mind is the unified coherence of the interiority of all that exists. Its body is the physical matter of all that exists. Both are aspects of the same Being. In this chapter I consider various ways the One makes itself known to us.

The One Expresses Itself In Activity And Repose

The Tao Te Ching says,

> *The ten thousand things are born of being.*
> *Being is born of not being.*[24]

Inherent in nature are two contrasting principles, activity and stasis. Pattern is the key to understanding both.

The two poles of existence are difference and sameness. They both come out of the Nameless. You can't have one without the other.

Sheer difference would be completely chaotic and random, no pattern at all. Sheer sameness would be dead. In either case there would be no pattern.

Sheer difference and sheer sameness thus would be identical, i.e. completely without pattern. They would both be the same. This observation implies that sameness is fundamental. Difference comes from breaking up sameness into chunks. Eve came out of Adam's rib. Ultimately the question is meaningless, however, as we never experience pure difference or pure sameness.

The fundamental thing that makes reality is pulsation. Sameness gets broken up. Then pulses happen in variations of rhythm, more and more elaborate. The fundamental thing is pattern. Pattern is made up of sameness and difference. Difference keeps adding new variations to the pattern. Metaphorically, each time it gets a groove going, it adds something else.

The One Is Infinitely Wise

The whole, of which each of us is a part, is infinitely wise; it's not just a collection of stuff. The God, being the inside of everything, sees all and knows all. The God perceives the outside of each thing and event through the experience of every other thing and event. The mentality of such a huge interior inspires awe.

There are different metaphors for God. One is that God is at a distance, that God sees all from afar. This is a notion of God as one object among many, although in some way a much greater object than any of the others, being their creator. Another metaphor is that God is very close to us, so close as to be our friend and our lover and beloved. Another metaphor is that God is so close to us as to be identical with us, that God is our very self.

None of these metaphors are incorrect. They are ways that limited beings such as ourselves can think of and understand the totality, which is too grand for us to fully comprehend. The metaphor of God as our very self is, I believe, more useful than the metaphor of God as being at a distance.

The notion of God as separate from God's creation leads to the notion that God can do miracles that violate the laws of physics. This notion pits religious believers against the findings of modern science, which has no place for miracles. But if we understand the world as alive and God as that which is conscious of everything from the inside, we understand that God does not have to intervene from the outside. Does God intervene in the world? Of course, all the time. But from the inside of all the pieces that are interacting, not from the outside. God can put attention on places of interest and act through the various pieces of reality that are there.

It Is Useful To Pay Attention To The One

By our prayers and our practices, we attract benevolent interest. By tuning into the One, we get (each one of us gets) guidance, we feel part of something larger, we become the beneficiary of the divine benevolence, and in certain states we feel quite blissful.

When we pay attention to the divine, we pay attention to people's humanity and their connection with the divine, and we overlook the differences between our self and the others. Doing so promotes peace and harmony, to the benefit of all concerned.

Think of each lifetime as a pulse. Imagine a sheet of water pulsing up and down, not necessarily in waves, but in discrete pulses like the upward surge of water after something drops in, such as a raindrop or a pebble. If each lifetime is a pulse, some are higher than others. The higher ones can see out farther, see more of the pattern. The highest ones can see the broadest pattern. The higher the pulse, the more conscious it is. Paying attention to The God is a way of being more conscious, that is, of being able to pay attention to more of reality.

Those of us who are conscious in this way are like the responsible adults of the universe. It is up to us to see that things go well. We are leaders, bodhisattvas.

"Responsible" in this case means "able to respond," to respond with understanding and compassion.

Responsibility does not mean duty or compulsion. We are not obliged to see that things go well and we are not punished by anyone if we don't. (By "see that things go well" I mean to create a harmonious pattern.) If we don't see that things go well, we suffer the consequences. It's like being punished for not doing our duty, except nobody is doing the punishing. Duty is somebody telling you what to do. What I am talking about is just paying attention to consequences and choosing the consequences you want. The higher the pulse, the more consciousness there is—i.e., the broader the range of things we are conscious of—and the more effective we are at choosing harmonious and interesting patterns.

Reality Is Good

There is no absolute good. Goodness is always in relation to something else. To be good is to be good for something or good at something. Reality is good for giving us something to push against. By this I mean that reality gives us some stability, some predictability, in our experience. Reality provides a framework within which to act. Reality helps us learn how to actualize intentions.

We Are All Connected

From the mystical point of view, we are all connected in that we are all manifestations of the One. That is a fundamental premise of the Goodness Ethic and now we have further evidence for it.

* * *

If we assume that all these things are true—that everything has an inside as well as an outside, that all is one, that reality is good and that we are all connected—then there are implications for how to live our life, to which I turn in the next chapter.

Chapter 13, A Mystical Perspective

From a mystical perspective, each of us is an expression of the One, the All, al-Lah,[x] the Tao, Brahman, the Supreme Self, The God. The God lives in and through us, as it does through all reality. Hence, each one of us is part and parcel of the Whole. As Ram Dass says, there is only one of us.[25] We are connected, not only by virtue of living in an environment that provides physical nurturance, but also by virtue of being part of the Whole from the inside, from the interiority that is the most private aspect of each of us.

The Goodness Ethic and Divine Guidance

The mystical perspective reinforces the fundamental premise of the Goodness Ethic, that all things are connected. It makes sense to work for the good of all things because in doing so we are working for our own benefit as an integral part and expression of everything there is. We can think of ourselves as being part of a larger organism, like cells in a living body, but cells that have consciousness and will. The world as a whole is a living entity; and The God is the Soul, the observer and animator of it all. We need to fit in with the larger patterns of which each of us is an organic part in an appropriate way, a good way. By promoting the health of the larger organism we promote our own health. And by promoting our own health we enhance our ability to nour-

---

[x] I hyphenate the word commonly written in English as "Allah" to emphasize that the literal meaning is The God, rather than a personal name.

ish the organism of which we are a part, which in turn nourishes us.

In any event, we certainly do not want to harm the being we are part of because that would be harming ourselves. Any action or attitude that ignores or diminishes anyone's value is harmful. It harms not only that person but the person taking the action or holding the attitude. Because we are all connected, any harm done to someone harms the person doing it as well.

So we try to benefit the whole. We are aided in this effort by divine guidance. The Goodness Ethic advises us to figure out how to benefit all concerned in a given situation, but without the excessive calculation that Utilitarianism seems to require. We should just do the best we can, given the time and information we have. In engaging the mystical point of view, we have an ally in this effort; we have more resources for figuring out what to do. The vast intelligence of The God is at our disposal; or, to be more precise, we are at its disposal if we allow ourselves to be. By becoming still, quieting our chattering mind, we become more attuned to the "still, small voice"[26] of God.

This suggests another implication for conduct: that to function optimally we should cultivate the ability to listen for and heed the voice of God. The phrase "voice of God" is a metaphor; the means by which divine guidance comes is different for each of us, and each of us must find his or her own way to become open to it. For some it is indeed a voice that they hear; for others, a nonverbal sense or feeling or intuition. For some it comes as a vision; for others, a simple outcome of acting with no-thought, no-action. For some it comes as a revelation from inspiring words of scripture; for others, a sense of organic appropriateness from the patterns of nature. In all these ways and more, the pinnacle of human virtue is to align ourselves with the will of God. In doing so we find our best and deepest happiness.

Living for the benefit of the whole, in the sense of wanting to benefit each part of the whole, is part of the story. In addition we can benefit the Whole as such, the Only Being itself.

I have defined "soul" as the interiority of a being, recognizing that there are degrees of interior complexity that correspond to degrees of physical, or exterior, complexity. The soul in this sense is *coherence of interiority*. The more coherent and the more complex, integrative and harmonious our experience, the higher degree of soulness we (any of us, each one of us) have. The higher degree of soulness we have, the richer is The God's experience of the All, because The God experiences everything that we experience. The Sufi mystic speaks of the need for cultivation of our souls, which means to make the coherence of our interiority beautiful and productive. When we attain beauty and harmony in ourselves—which necessarily entails creating beauty and harmony in our world, because that is what we experience—we provide beauty and harmony to The God. It is the goal of everything, from the tiniest quantum event to the total unity of the All, to acquire satisfaction, to experience well-being. When we achieve some degree of harmony within ourselves we contribute to a higher harmony and are of service to The God.

Spiritual practice is doubly beneficial. It is beneficial for us, certainly, because it enables us more clearly to hear the voice of God, and it provides us a sense of peace, harmony and bliss. But it is also beneficial to The God. The God feels that peace, harmony and bliss. By doing our practices we send nourishment upstream, as it were, to higher levels of coherence of interiority, perhaps to souls that are larger and more inclusive than our separate selves, all the way up to the One Soul that enlivens us all.

The Purpose of Life

It would be presumptuous to guess at the purpose of The God, but if the highest virtue for human beings is excellence at second-order thinking, self-reflective knowledge (see *Chapter 20, The Human Virtue*), then by analogy the highest virtue for The God, the One of which we are all an expression, is its own self-reflective knowledge. And that knowledge comes about through the efforts of each one of us to achieve not just an intellectual understanding of our unity with the All, not just a belief in it, but a living experience of that unity. That is why a great many of the mystic traditions assert that the ultimate purpose of human life is to become conscious of ourselves as divine, as the eyes and ears of the Only Being. Our function in the scheme of things is to participate and do our part, consciously and deliberately, in the divine unfolding from ignorance to self-knowledge.

The purpose of existence is that The God may become more fully conscious of itself. Human existence is the culmination, the most advanced expression of that divine purpose. The function of the human being, what we are good at and good for, is to live in harmony with the purpose of the universe, which is to become increasingly self-conscious. The purpose of human existence is to live in the knowledge and awareness of the presence of The God, to know ourselves as divine. The Only Being is evolving from unselfconscious absorption in the One toward completely self-conscious knowledge of the All, and it is our great privilege and blessing to be able to participate in that unfolding.

Loving God

Many religions enjoin us to love God. This can mean two things. One is that we enjoy God's presence and feel good and nurtured by being around God and want to be with God a lot, even all the time. Another is that we want to do something for God, to be of service in some way. If we think of The God as the totality of all there is and in addition think of The God as that which is conscious of all there is from the inside, then whenever there is an opportunity to reduce the amount of distress, pain and hatred that someone experiences and increase the amount of love, joy and peace that they experience—regardless of who it is, oneself or someone else—then the loving thing is to take that opportunity. Doing so benefits God; it does good to God; it is of service to God. It increases the joy and harmony that God experiences, and if we love God we will want to do just that.

Alignment with Divine Will

Unlike other animals, we humans have the capacity for second-order thinking, the ability to reflect on ourselves, to think about ourselves and our place in the world; and this capacity gives us a sense of separation from the world, of standing apart from it. It gives us a sense of freedom (and indeed more than just a sense), but also a sense of disconnection, of alienation. We don't just organically move and act in the world as other beings do. We foresee events, think about goals and strategies, make plans. It is easy to think of ourselves as beings apart from, above, better than the rest of nature.

There is a germ of truth in the religious doctrines of sin. By virtue of our capacity to think ahead and think about ourselves as well as our world, we are able to go our own way, which might not be the most fitting and appropriate way for the whole. In religious terms, we elevate our own will above the will of God and become fallen from a state of grace. It is no accident that much of religious teaching exhorts us to become simpler, to become as little children (Christianity), to act with no-action (Taoism), to overcome ego (Hinduism, Buddhism), to submit to the will of Allah (Islam).

We find ourselves thrust into the world, and we believe ourselves to be isolated, separate entities. To alleviate this sense of isolation it does not work very well to stifle the ability for second-order thought, whether the means be mind-numbing drugs, devotion to a religious leader or succumbing to existential despair. Instead, we can achieve a higher synthesis by deliberately and consciously aligning our intention with the intention of the greater whole of which we are a part.

If it suits us to think of that whole in agential terms, as something like a human person with desire and intention, then we can strive to align our will with the will of God. If it suits us to think of that whole in impersonal terms, then we can cultivate mindfulness—careful observation of our immediate experience— in order to allow the Void or the Tao to move through us. In any case, by deliberately attuning to a greater wisdom in full knowledge that we are doing so, we can achieve a greater coherence of interiority, a greater sense of satisfaction arising from the harmonious placement and interaction of all elements of our experience, than by staying in the illusion of separation.

Duality of Good and Evil

The God contains and is the interior of everything, good and bad, beneficial and harmful. If this is so, you might ask why you should align yourself only with the good and not with the bad as well. Aligning only with the good seems a bit one-sided.

Perhaps from the point of view of perfect enlightenment it is, but very few of us are perfectly enlightened. Aligning ourselves with the good gives us a better chance of experiencing our unity with the whole than not doing so, and it gives us an especially better chance than aligning ourselves with the bad. What is good is analogous to light; and what is bad, or harmful, is analogous to darkness. If you live in darkness, you can't see very well; your strategies are limited because of lack of information. They may be brutally effective for a while, but are ultimately self-defeating. It is more efficacious in the long run to live in the light, and it is much more pleasant as well. Light and dark endlessly alternate, it is true, and the alternation is all part of the whole. If you live in that knowledge, then you are enlightened. If you don't, then turning toward the light will make it more likely that you will come to that realization.

God's Goodness

We are investigating how human beings can be fulfilled by discovering their function, what they are good for or at. If we are an expression of The One, then, we should want to discover the function of The One, what The One is good for or good at. But The One, encompassing everything that is, is beyond categories of good and bad. The One is not good for anything beyond itself because there is nothing beyond The One. From an absolute point of view The One is neither good nor bad. (Except we cannot take an absolute point of view, we can only imagine taking such a view. If we were to take such a point of view, we could say nothing about it.)

There is a sense in which The One is good, however, and that is the same sense in which the harmonious functioning of one's body is good for each part of the body. God (let us now take the One in its personal aspect) is good for human beings. In fact, God is the best for human beings. If you turn your life to God, all will be well for you. You can rely on God, for God is generous and merciful. The One has vast intelligence which it directs for the welfare of anyone who calls on it. That vast intelligence knows better than our limited minds what is good for us. God might lead us through pain and suffering, but all will ultimately turn out for the best.

I invite you to view the world as if The One, the Spirit-that-moves-in-all-things, is in fact moving in and through you and is operating to your benefit and the benefit of your surroundings and of all things. Find practices that enable you to actually experience this state of affairs rather than merely thinking about it or believing it. See what difference the experience makes in your life. Observe what happens when you take this stance, and then decide whether to continue taking it.

Part III: Facets of Human Nature

Chapter 14, What Are We Capable Of?

So far this inquiry has been a bit abstract even though derived in part from that which is most concrete, our own experience. I have asserted, I hope plausibly, that the world is one, that
each of us is united with the One as an organ is united with the
organism of which it is a part and that we are all manifestations
of one unified center of consciousness and awareness. Each of us
is a means through which The God views the world and acts in it.
Consequently it makes sense for us to work for the good in all
things because doing so benefits us.

But how shall we do that? To return to the original question,
what are the unique human gifts or abilities that will provide us
a fulfilling life if we exercise them? That is what this section is
about. The goal is to find out what human nature consists of in
order to determine what is good for humans and hence what
would constitute a fulfilling life. We shall now change the focal
length of the lens, as it were, and view human nature through a
different set of categories. We'll look for strategies for being in
the world in a healthy way, and in order to find them, we'll see
what objective, third-party knowledge tells us.

The chapters in this section look at human nature from a
public, scientific and third-person point of view, a point of view
that any competent observer could adopt in order to confirm or
disconfirm its assertions. First I compare humans to our closest
genetic cousins, the great apes. Then I examine what we have
learned from evolutionary psychology. There are certainly other
quite useful perspectives one could take—anthropology comes to
mind—but for now these two approaches are what I have been
able to produce.

Chapter 15, Humans as Apes

If you want to master your life, it helps to know your material. Think of yourself as an artist or a designer or a builder whose goal is to make of your life something both highly functional and aesthetically pleasing. You need to know what you have to work with. A good place for us to start is by comparing ourselves with our fellow hominins, the great apes, specifically chimpanzees and bonobos. These two form a sort of caricature in which we see aspects of ourselves in sharp relief, aspects which in some cases may give us cause for fear and in others may give us cause for hope.

The biological order Primates is a large one, including lemurs, monkeys and apes as well as humans.[27] Within it humans, chimpanzees and bonobos are all members of the family Hominidae, subfamily Homininae.[28] ("Hominin" means, somewhat unhelpfully, human-like.) Hominins have 97% of their DNA in common. DNA research indicates that humans diverged from the line of primates to become a separate species about 5.5 million years ago. More recently, about 2.5 million years ago, chimps and bonobos diverged from each other; they are our closest genetic relatives.

Chimps are found in Central and West Africa, north of the Congo River, where the habitat is relatively dry and open. Bonobos are found only south of the Congo River, in dense, humid forests. Bonobo territory is much richer in food—large, fruiting trees and high-quality herbs—than that of the chimps.[29] Since neither can swim, the river seems to have served as a barrier that enabled the bonobo to evolve into a separate species. Or perhaps it is chimps and humans that evolved away from the ancient species

from which all three are descended, and bonobos, having stayed
in the ancestral habitat, are closest to that ancient precursor. In
any case, the bonobo habitat seems like a primeval paradise: a
pleasant forest environment with lots of food in which the inhab-
itants find congenial sociality. The chimp habitat, by contrast, is
outside the gates of Eden; those who live there have to work
much harder for their sustenance.

Chimps, bonobos and humans exhibit many similarities. All
are social and inquisitive; all use tools; all exhibit cooperation,
empathy and altruism (helping others at some cost to oneself)
within their groups. There are many significant differences as
well. The most obvious is that humans are far more intelligent
and exhibit a much broader range of behavior than the others.
The most notorious difference between chimps and bonobos is
that chimps are patriarchal, violent and aggressive; and bonobos
are matriarchal, peaceful and sexual.

Chimps have the reputation of being "killer apes." Their society is extremely hierarchical, with much jockeying among males
for the top position and frequent scuffles, a few quite bloody,
among them. Political machinations are incessant because high
rank provides sexual mates and food for males; females forage for
themselves but sometimes trade sex for food. The dominance hierarchy is male. Female chimps form networks of affiliative
friendships.[30]

Conflicts among males are solved through violence and aggression. The hair of a male chimp stands on end at the slightest
provocation. He will pick up a stick and challenge anyone perceived as weaker. Chimps in the wild are highly territorial.
Chimp males patrol their borders and murder intruders from
other bands. Bands of males engage in lethal aggression against
their neighbors. Brutal violence is part of the chimp's natural
makeup.

Interestingly, shrewd skill at social manipulation is also part
of the chimp's natural makeup. Frans de Waal's classic *Chimpanzee Politics* relates a tale worthy of a Machiavelli. Old Yeroen,
the alpha male, is deposed over the course of several months by
the younger Luit. Luit engages in battle with Yeroen several
times and eventually wins, but his victory is due as much to his

campaigning and currying favor among the rest of the tribe, particularly the females, as to his physical prowess. Yeroen is defeated but allies himself with Nikkie, another youngster on his way up. Eventually Nikkie, backed by Yeroen, deposes Luit, again not through physical combat alone but by gaining the support of others as well. Nikkie reigns supreme. But Yeroen gets more sex than either of the other two![31] "It was almost impossible," says de Waal, "not to think of Yeroen as the brain and Nikkie as the brawn of the coalition between them."[32]

Chimps exhibit gentleness, play and cooperation among the in-group, but in-group conflicts are resolved through domination. Sometimes a dominant male will step in and break up a fight, and sometimes a dominant female or group of females will; in all cases, it is a matter of threatening violence. After a fight, however, the parties reconcile with each other, by hugging, kissing and grooming. Reconciliation is as important as conflict, because without it the group would disband. Like humans, chimps require group living for survival; and like most mammals, they are soothed by physical touch.

Sexual contact is sporadic among chimps because it happens only when the female is in heat and her genitals swell visibly. Dominant males get to mate far more often than subordinates, and the male will sometimes kill infants that are clearly not his offspring, for instance when taking in a female from a different tribe. Once his own infants are born, the male spends little time and energy nurturing them; chimps show low male parental investment.

We humans tend to think of ourselves as special, but chimps have some decidedly human-like capabilities: empathy and theory of mind. By "empathy" I mean the ability to be affected by the emotional state of another individual. "Theory of mind" refers to the ability to recognize the mental states of others. It means that one individual has an idea, a theory, about what another individual believes, perceives or intends to accomplish. In order to have that theory, of course, the individual has to have some sense of himself or herself as a separate entity. Chimps have all these traits. They console others in distress; they know what others know and can take another's viewpoint; they recognize themselves in a mirror; and they give aid tailored to another's needs, a behavior called "targeted helping," which requires a distinction between self and other, recognition of the other's need and sympathy for the other's distress.

Here is an example: In the Arnhem zoo the keepers had hosed out all the rubber tires in the enclosure and left them hanging on a horizontal pole. When the apes were released into the enclosure, one of them, Krom, tried to get a tire that still had some water in it, so she could get a drink. But it was several tires back and was blocked by the ones hanging in front of it. She could not figure out how to get to it. After Krom gave up, Jakie, an adolescent whom Krom had cared for as an infant, came up and pushed the tires off the pole one by one. When he reached the one with water in it, he carefully removed it so no water was spilled and carried it to his "auntie" and placed it upright in front of her so she could reach in and get the water. Clearly, he knew what she wanted and came to her aid.[33]

Chimps have a primitive sense of time. They are focused on the present but can remember past grievances and favors and avenge the former and reward the latter. They are able to anticipate the future and make plans as well. For instance:

> An adult male may spend minutes searching for the heaviest stone on his side of the island, far away from the rest of the group ... . He then carries the stone he has selected to the island's other side, where he begins—with all his hair on end—an intimidation display in front of his rival. Since stones serve as weapons (chimpanzees throw fairly accurately), we may assume that the male knew all along that he was going to challenge the other. This is the impression chimpanzees give in almost everything they do: they are thinking beings just as we are.[34]

Given this picture, it seems that chimps and humans are a lot alike, except that humans, being more intelligent, do what chimps do even better. We can plan further into the future and remember and document a greater range of the past. We have a much more ample capacity to understand what others are thinking and feeling and to understand ourselves. And, of course, we have much greater language abilities as well, giving us the ability to learn through history and culture. We have much better tools. And we can use them to kill each other much more effectively.

Some say that we are fundamentally aggressive and warlike, just like chimps, and the reason we have not killed each other off is that we have somehow managed to acquire a veneer of morality that holds these primitive urges in check.[35] That would seem plausible if all we knew about our genetic relatives were the chimps. But chimps are not the whole story. We are genetically related to bonobos as well.

Among bonobos females dominate, not males; there is no deadly warfare; and they enjoy enormous amounts of sex. This may well have to do with their richer supply of food; there is far less need for competition for it. Bonobos have lots of sexual contact with each other, in all combinations of genders. There is more of it in captivity, but frequent sexual activity has been observed in the wild as well. Females are sexually receptive for long periods of time, much longer than female chimpanzees. When different bands meet there is initial tension, but no vicious fighting; instead, individuals have sex with each other.[36] Sex seems to be a way to defuse tension in advance of potential conflict, particularly over food. But anything, not just food, that arouses the interest of more than one bonobo at a time tends to result in sexual contact. After a flurry of sex, the apes settle down to eat or investigate whatever has piqued their interest. Bonobos are not "sex-crazed apes" as the popular press would have it. For bonobos, sex is just a natural and common part of life.

Bonobo bands are hierarchical, but the hierarchies are dominated by females, who enforce their status non-aggressively by cultivating alliances. High rank provides food for the females and their families, males included. Males derive status from their mothers. There is no competition among males for sex, as it is plentifully available.

Bonobos, like chimps, show empathy, theory of mind and targeted helping. Once, when the two-meter moat in front of the bonobo enclosure in the San Diego zoo had been drained for cleaning, several youngsters climbed down into it. When the keepers went to turn on the valve to refill the moat with water, an old male, Kakowet, came to their window screaming and frantically waving his arms. He knew the routine and knew that the children were in danger (bonobos cannot swim). The keepers went to see what was wrong and rescued the youngsters.[37] Clearly, Kakowet had envisioned what was about to happen and cared enough to try to stop it. Fortunately, he succeeded.

Apart from the obvious superiority of human intellect, including language and culture, humans differ from both chimps and bonobos in reproductive strategy. Only the dominant chimp males get to reproduce, and the male sometimes enforces his own lineage through infanticide. Among bonobos all males reproduce, but there is no way to tell who the father of any given child is. Infanticide is unknown, probably for that very reason. Children are enjoyed and cared for by the whole tribe.

Humans have quite a different strategy for reproduction. We bond in pairs, creating a nuclear family that ensures resources for children, and the father is very much involved in child care: humans have high male parental investment. Sexual exclusivity ensures that every man has the potential to reproduce and that he knows which children are his. This arrangement allows males to cooperate in groups away from the females without fear of being cuckolded. There is some plausible speculation that this arrangement is fairly recent, arising only when humans adopted the technology of agriculture.[38] Quite possibly our pre-agriculture hunter-gatherer ancestors were more like bonobos, having multiple sexual partners.

Bonobos were recognized as a separate species less than 100 years ago and began to be fully documented less than 50 years ago. Before that time, many ethologists and anthropologists believed that humans were innately violent and aggressive. Morality, it was thought, was a veneer of cooperative sociality on an underlying bestial nature. Now that we know about bonobos, the range of human behavioral potential seems to have expanded. We recognize that we too have the capacity to live in peace and to defuse conflict proactively with pleasure. In addition, male dominance seemed a natural part of things until the discovery of bonobos; now we see that dominance by females may be equally natural.

Two things stand out from this comparison of species. First, our difference from chimps and bonobos is a matter of degree, not kind. There are few, if any, uniquely human traits that chimps or bonobos do not have to a lesser degree. We are embedded in nature and are not a species unique and special. The one trait that seems most unique is the cultural, not biological, innovation of nuclear family pair bonding. If we think of concern for others as a fundamental building block of morality (another is a sense of fairness in reciprocity), it is clear that even morality is not a unique feature of our species but an outgrowth of capabilities that have far older evolutionary roots. So when we observe our fellow humans jockeying and posing to gain status, or consoling each other when they are in trouble, or forgiving each other after a dispute, or throwing a party, or sharing food to build bonds and defuse tension, or being suspicious of those who are different, or vilifying an enemy, or generously giving aid to the unfortunate, or hundreds of other hominin behaviors, we should realize that these are not uniquely human practices but are instead embedded in a great chain of life that stretches back many millions of years.

Second, humans have the capacity to amplify the characteristics found in our sibling species. Humans have greater brain size and intelligence, so we can do more effectively all the things our siblings can. Our use of tools and technologies enables us to produce food in more variety and abundance. In fact, there is some plausible speculation that learning to cook was a turning point in our evolution, as cooked food provides more calories than raw, calories that could support the growth of larger brains.[39] Our use of language enables us to communicate more effectively and to perpetuate what we learn through culture and art. Chimps and bonobos seem to be able to conceptualize that something not happening in the present will happen later, but humans have a greatly enhanced ability to visualize and anticipate the future.

Disputes among humans often take the form of wars and feuds, but we are capable of sophisticated negotiation and diplomacy as well. And we can avoid conflict through proactive peacemaking and compassionate communication. We are better able to cooperate with others outside our own group than are chimps or bonobos. Says de Waal, "Humans share intergroup behavior with both chimps and bonobos. When relations between human societies are bad, they are worse than between chimps, but when they are good, they are better than between bonobos."[40]

We humans can be more aggressive but also more peaceful, more competitive but also more cooperative. We are more flexible and have more options than our fellow creatures. We have a great variety of possible behaviors, possible ways of being. And, through our ability to anticipate the future, we have a choice as to which of these we will actualize.

Being related genetically to both chimps, who settle sexual issues through conflict, and bonobos, who settle conflict issues through sex, we have the capacity for both. Being humans, with bigger brains, much richer culture and much wider repertoire of behavior, we get to choose our strategies.

Chapter 16, Evolution

If we want to know what human nature is—and we do, as that will tell us how to live a fulfilling and happy life—then we have to understand evolution. The theory of evolution describes how generations of living organisms change over time. Humans are living organisms. We are subject to and products of the same evolutionary pressures as all other living things. Understanding how we got to be as we are gives us insight into how we function. Knowing that, we can adjust our actions so as to function well. We'll consider various aspects of how we function in the following chapters, but first we'll take a look at the theory of evolution.

It is called the theory of evolution, but "theory" does not mean conjecture, speculation or mere opinion. The term in its scientific sense means a well-supported body of interconnected statements that explains observations and can be used to make testable predictions. The theory of evolution has been confirmed over and over again.[41] No serious biologist takes it as anything but fully established. In the words of Theodosius Dobzhansky, author of a major work on evolution and genetics, "Nothing in biology makes sense except in the light of evolution. ... Seen in the light of evolution, biology is ... the most satisfying and inspiring science. Without that light it becomes a pile of sundry facts, some of them interesting or curious but making no meaningful picture as a whole."[42]

It is unfortunate that religious fundamentalists, misusing the term "theory," regard evolution as unproven. Some go so far as to say that all the evidence that leads us to believe in the immense age of the universe and the proliferation of species over time, as opposed to instantaneous creation some 6000 years ago, was planted by the creator merely to give the appearance of great antiquity. Dobzhansky, a Christian, has this retort: "It is easy to see the fatal flaw in all such notions. They are blasphemies, accusing God of absurd deceitfulness. This is as revolting as it is uncalled for."[43]

The religious believer may view evolution as God's way of creating the world. The pantheist mystic may view evolution as the One Being's way of unfolding and coming to know Itself over time. The secularist, the atheist or the merely agnostic may view evolution as the way living beings have propagated themselves, blindly and without foresight, in increasing diversity and complexity. Regardless of your opinion on the ultimate purpose of it all, it is important to understand how evolution works because the theory reflects reality, and basing your actions on reality works out much better than not. So the rest of this chapter is a summary of the theory of evolution.[44]

The term "evolution" in a general sense means a process of change or growth, often taken as a process of continual change from a simpler to a more complex state. In biology, the term refers to two things:

- The observed fact that the distribution of inherited traits in a population of organisms can change from generation to generation.
- The theory that the various types of animals and plants we find around us, including ourselves, originated in earlier types and that their differences are due to modifications in successive generations.

The basic concept of biological evolution as we understand it today is surprisingly simple. Charles Darwin, its originator, called it "descent with modification." The concept is this:

- An organism's offspring may vary slightly from the organism itself. Offspring may have slightly different traits from the parents or the same traits in different degrees.
- Organisms typically produce more offspring than can survive and reproduce, given the resources available such

as food, shelter, sexual mates, etc. Hence, there is competition for such resources.

- In the competition for resources, some variations have an advantage over others. For example, one child's beak may be slightly better at picking up small seeds than another's, or one child may have slightly better eyesight than the other and hence be better able to find food and avoid predators.
- The individuals with advantageous variations have more offspring than those without.
- Since traits are heritable (are inherited from parent to child), this causes the population, over time, to contain more of the favorable variations and fewer of the unfavorable ones.

Darwin called this process *"natural selection,"* as opposed to artificial selection, the intentional breeding for certain traits that produces such differences in the same species as the Great Dane and the Chihuahua. The underlying mechanism is the same in both kinds of selection: certain individuals have more offspring than others, so their traits become more widespread in the population of that type of organism. A subset of natural selection called *"sexual selection"* is a result of competition for mates. In order to have offspring, an individual must not only survive but reproduce. Competition for mates, most often among males for females, selects for traits that enable males to dominate other males, such as horns and antlers, and for traits that attract females, such as plumage and other adornments.

This process happens slowly but inexorably. The variation between parent and offspring is most often minuscule, but over enough generations large changes result. A series of small, incremental changes can, given enough time, produce the extraordinary variety of speciation we find around us.[xi]

[xi] There are three sources of variation: mutation, gene flow and genetic shuffling through sexual reproduction. *Mutation* happens when environmental influences cause tiny changes in the chemical structure of genes, altering their functioning, or when cells divide and imperfectly replicate their DNA. By far the majority of mutations are destructive, degrading the gene's ability to do its job of directing the growth of organs

This process is not purposive.[xii] No organism intends to produce a better beak or a better eye. It is merely a fact of life that those with favorable variations tend to have more offspring than those without, each of which in turn has the favorable variation. Among that generation's offspring, those that further amplify the favorable variation have more offspring, and so on for generations. Conversely, unfavorable variations tend to die out over time. We should not take phrases such as "designed by natural selection" as implying a conscious, deliberate designer.

What is inherited is a *trait*, a feature of an organism such as eye color. Traits are passed from generation to generation as discrete units. Gregor Mendel conducted a famous study in which he mated pea plants, some of which had purple blossoms and some of which had white. The offspring did not have pale purple blossoms, but rather some had purple and some white, in distinct proportions.

What passes these discrete traits from generation to generation is the *gene*, the fundamental physical and functional unit of heredity. A gene is a segment of nucleic acid that, taken as a whole, specifies a trait. Genes are contained in chromosomes, which are composed of DNA (deoxyribonucleic acid), a polymeric molecule found in cells of the body. DNA governs the production, growth and reproduction of the cells of the body. The current understanding of biological evolution, developed since Darwin's

---

and characteristics, but some enhance that ability, or change it so that the result is advantageous. *Gene flow* refers to the transfer of genes between populations of an organism. Individuals from one population mate with individuals of another and transfer genes between them. *Genetic shuffling through sexual reproduction* causes the combination of genes in each child to differ from that of its parents. In species that reproduce sexually, each individual has two copies of every gene (specifically, each has two strands of DNA, each of which contains chromosomes, which contain genes). In sexual reproduction, the child gets some genes from the mother and some from the father, and the combinations vary with each child.

[xii] Religious or mystical thinkers may postulate a divine purpose that guides the process of evolution, but the science of biological evolution does not need that hypothesis to explain the process.

time, recognizes the gene as a fundamental, if not *the* fundamental, unit of natural selection.

Functionally, genes pass traits from generation to generation. They do this by replicating themselves from parent to child. Physiologically, the same chemical structure appears in the child as was found in the parent. In combination with other genes and triggered by environmental influences, the genes cause the parent's traits to appear in the child. The term "trait" includes physical forms, such as bone density and eye color, behaviors such as sounding mating calls in certain seasons, and mental abilities or talents such as stereoscopic vision, empathy and language.

Genes are not the only replicators. Ideas, symbols, behaviors and other elements of culture replicate as well. Geneticist Richard Dawkins has coined the term *"meme"* to mean a unit of cultural transmission, similar to the gene, which is a unit of biological evolution.[45] Genes replicate from generation to generation; memes, their cultural analogues, replicate from mind to mind through writing, speech, gestures, rituals and the like. The principles of evolution apply the same: like a gene, a meme is a replicator, except memes replicate contemporaneously between minds rather than historically between bodies. Just as genes are subject to competition—the ones that replicate to the next generation are those that help their host bodies to survive and reproduce—so also are memes: only those that are catchy enough to secure attention in human minds replicate from mind to mind. What makes a meme catchy can be something as trivial as a memorable tune or limerick or something that has continuing usefulness, such as ideas that hold cultures together.

* * *

So there is an abbreviated account of evolution. What does it mean for understanding human nature? To know what we are, we must understand where we have come from. It is not just in our physical form that we have evolved but in our mental capacities and in our cultures as well. Are we, then, merely products of our evolutionary heritage, unable to change? No, but in our attempts to change, it certainly helps to understand what we have to work with. Understanding that inherited traits are the result of natural selection can help put in context findings about how we humans actually function in the world, a topic to which I turn in the following chapters.

Chapter 17, Ways of Knowing: Cognition and Emotion

Each age has a metaphor for how humans work. In the 17th century it was mechanical: the heart was a pump, the lungs were bellows and the muscles and bones were like pulleys and levers. In the 21st century the metaphor is electronic computing: the brain is a computer, and our minds are composed of mental modules, much like software modules, each of which does a job and interacts with others to get things done.

There is some truth to these metaphors. The heart really does pump liquid, and the lungs really do draw in and expel air. Similarly, brain research has discovered specific portions of the brain that are active when we discriminate colors and shapes or think about a mathematical problem or respond to moral problems. The convergence of brain research, information theory, cognitive science and behavioral psychology provides insights into how our minds work. In particular, cognitive science explains how thought and emotion work in terms of information and computation, and evolutionary biology explains the complex design of living things as the product of evolutionary selection. Evolutionary psychology combines the two.

Evolutionary Psychology

Evolutionary psychology takes the mind to be an organ, a bit like the kidney or the stomach. It provides a theory of how our minds evolved to have the functions that they do.[46] It does not so much discover facts about human nature as provide a framework within which to understand facts found experimentally by other branches of psychology. It also suggests experimentally verifiable hypotheses about how the mind works. Many such hypotheses have been corroborated, thus lending credence to its concepts.[47]

Evolutionary psychology explains how various mental modules evolved in response to challenges humans encountered in the environment of evolutionary adaptedness (EEA), the environment in which our ancestors lived for hundreds of thousands of years.[48] Between the invention of writing, agriculture and cities and the present (early twenty-first century A.D.) humans lived about 500 generations. The time before that, the Pleistocene epoch, when proto-humans evolved into the humans we know today, was about 80,000 generations, 160 times as long. Although human culture has advanced significantly in the past 500 generations, it is built on mental capacities that are evolutionarily designed for a much different environment.

The environment of the Pleistocene varied physically, but much of it was probably open savannah, with rolling hills and occasional forest. People all over the world are drawn to images of that type of landscape regardless of the environment they actually live in.[49] More important was the social environment: small bands of humans numbering from 20 up to a maximum of about 150, in which each person had to cooperate with the others to provide sustenance and survival but also had to compete with others to acquire food, status and sexual mates. These early bands of humans were probably much like the hunter-gatherers found today in the remote forests of the Amazon or the jungles of Africa or Indonesia. Now such bands have been pushed to the margins of habitable lands by the advance of industrial society, but in the past our ancestors lived, no doubt, in much richer and lusher surroundings. Their lifestyle has been called "a camping trip that lasts a lifetime."[50]

The mental abilities we find today in humans all over the world evolved to solve adaptive problems faced by our hunter-gatherer ancestors. Those mental abilities, oriented toward action in the world, are both cognitive and emotional.

Cognition

The central premise of evolutionary psychology is that the human mind is a system of mental modules—"organs of computation"[51]—that enabled our ancestors to survive and reproduce in the EEA. Leda Cosmides and John Tooby, pioneers in the field, point out that the single resource most limiting to reproduction is not food or safety or access to mates, but information, the information required for making behavioral choices that lead to survival and reproduction.[52] The mind as we know it today is the result of a long series of cognitive successes, successes in acquiring and processing information.

The mind, embodied in the circuitry of the brain and nervous system, is not a single organ but is composed of many faculties that solve different adaptive problems. An "adaptive problem" is a cluster of conditions that recurred over evolutionary time and that constituted either an opportunity for or an obstacle to reproduction.[53] For example, the arrival of a potential mate—which happened countless times over 80,000 generations—is an opportunity for reproduction. How the mind recognizes and responds to a person of the opposite sex is a function of algorithms embedded in the mind as a result of how successfully our ancestors responded to similar situations. In order to recognize a person of the opposite sex, of course, you must first perceive that person. On a level closer to physical as opposed to social reality, how human visual perception works is in part a function of mental algorithms evolved to respond to the properties of reflected light. (Another part is the structure of the eye itself.) Examples of obstacles to reproduction are such things as the speed of a prey animal and the actions of a sexual rival. In these cases and many others, the way the human mind processes information is a result of how our ancestors solved such adaptive problems and survived to pass on their abilities to their offspring.

We can view the current state of the mind as the result of a very long process of testing randomly generated alternative designs for coping with the physical and social environment—each of which embodied different assumptions about the nature of the world—and retaining those that succeeded most effectively, that is, those that reflected most closely the actual structure of the ancestral world.[xiii]

Cognition in this sense is not necessarily or even primarily a conscious process, one available to introspective attention. Conscious, voluntary and deliberative thinking—called "cold cognition" by Cosmides and Tooby,[54] the kind of thinking we do when we work out a math problem, for instance—is only one kind. Much more prevalent is the information processing that takes place unreflectively in everyday life, in perceptual judgments, in forming immediate responses to situations and in guiding our activities. When a child gauges the intensity of his or her parents' annoyance or approval, the child is not going through a conscious thought process. Instead the child is using an algorithm or computer-like program that is built in to the mind, a capability or faculty that is already available for use. The mind is not a blank slate, written upon by experience. It is a collection of modules capable of solving specific problems. When a problem for which it is suited arises, the relevant modules are activated and guide our responses, immediately and intuitively.

In this model, the mind is a set of capabilities for problem-solving and for guiding behavior. The capabilities are a result of the evolution of the human race, but the specific content of how the problems are solved or how the behavior is manifested depends on the circumstances of one's life. For instance, all humans have the capacity for language, but which language or languages you speak depends on the culture and community in which you are raised. Similarly, all humans have the capacity for moral intuition regarding how one should behave in a social context, but the specific set of moral rules you find compelling depends on the society in which you live.

[xiii] Obviously this view entails a realist ontology, the assumption that there is a real world other than our private experience to which our mentality adapts. More interesting is the implied connection between adaptive success and truth. What we depend on, what we assume to be true, is what has worked to help humans survive, thrive and reproduce.

Emotion

Cosmides and Tooby call the mind "multimodular," composed of "domain-specific expert systems." The human mind is "a diverse collection of inference systems, including specializations for reasoning about objects, physical causality, number, language, the biological world, the beliefs and motivations of other individuals, and social interactions."[55] These inference systems get coordinated through emotion.

Domain-specific expert systems such as those for regulation of sleep or detection of predators need a context in which to operate. If it is dark and you are tired, you should sleep; but if a predator is nearby, you should stay alert in case you need to flee or fight. (By "should" I mean merely that these are the typical activating conditions for the expert systems.) What causes an individual organism to activate alertness when danger might be nearby at night? The answer is emotion, in this example the emotion of fear. Cosmides and Tooby assert that emotions are actually a type of cognition, cognitions writ large as it were. They are high-level programs that orchestrate the activation of many subordinate programs:

> Each emotion entrains various other adaptive programs—deactivating some, activating others, and adjusting the modifiable parameters of still others—so that the whole system operates in a particularly harmonious and efficacious way when the individual is confronting certain kinds of triggering conditions or situations.[56]

Psychologist Steven Pinker says it more succinctly:

> The emotions are mechanisms that set the brain's highest-level goals. Once triggered by a propitious moment, an emotion triggers the cascade of subgoals and sub-subgoals that we call thinking and acting.[57]

That's not what we usually think of when we think of emotion. We usually think of a felt quality such as fear or anger or elation. Evolutionary psychology says these are indeed aspects of emotion, but not their defining characteristic. What defines an emotion—in fact, what defines any evolved capacity—is its function. And the function of emotion is to coordinate multiple subsystems such that an organism reacts appropriately to a stimulus, where "appropriately" means in a way that caused its ancestors to survive in the presence of similar stimuli.

It is instructive to look at Cosmides and Tooby's specific examples of emotion:

> cooperation, sexual attraction, jealousy, aggression, parental love, friendship, romantic love, the aesthetics of landscape preferences, coalitional aggression, incest avoidance, disgust, predator avoidance, kinship and family relations, grief, playfulness, fascination, guilt, depression, feeling triumphant, disgust, sexual jealousy, fear of predators, rage, grief, happiness, joy, sadness, excitement, anxiety, playfulness, homesickness, anger, hunger, being worried, loneliness, predatoriness (an emotion pertaining to hunting), gratitude, fear, boredom, approval, disapproval, shame[58]

Not all of these are what common usage calls emotion. Some of them—fear, anger, joy, guilt and the like—certainly are, in the sense of being felt qualities or states. Others, such as coalitional aggression and predator avoidance, seem like strategies rather than emotions. Many, such as fear of predators, being worried about something, and sexual attraction, are primarily ways of being oriented to an external object or person, to something or someone other than oneself. Others, such as guilt, shame and pride, are oriented to ourselves as we imagine others feel about us. All of them have in common that they coordinate a large number of separate cognitive subsystems. Cosmides and Tooby provide an extensive list:

> perception; attention; inference; learning; memory; goal choice; motivational priorities; categorization and conceptual frameworks; physiological reactions (such as heart rate, endocrine function, immune function, gamete release); reflexes; behavioral decision rules; motor systems; communication processes; energy level and effort allocation; affective coloration of events and stimuli; recalibration of probability estimates, situation assess-

ments, values, and regulatory variables (e.g., self-esteem, estimations of relative formidability, relative value of alternative goal states, efficacy discount rate); and so on.[59]

Every emotion has four aspects: [60]

- Physiology—what happens in our bodies when we are feeling or are under the influence of the emotion.
- Behavioral inclination—what the emotion disposes us to do.
- Cognitive appraisal—what the emotion tells us about what it is directed towards.
- Feeling state—how the emotion feels to us.

An emotion is not reducible to any one of these four; it includes them all. Pinker says "No sharp line divides thinking from feeling, nor does thinking inevitably precede feeling or vice versa."[61]

Of these four, the most fundamental is behavioral inclination. Evolutionary theory is all about life perpetuating itself, about what we will do, how we will act, in different situations.

Implications

Several things are interesting philosophically about this view of cognition and emotions:

- Despite a long history of thinking of ourselves as the "rational animal," much of our cognition is not rational, in the sense of being thought through as we might think through a proof in geometry. Only a small part of our thinking is cold cognition. Most of it is hot cognition: quick, intuitive flashes of judgment.
- These intuitive flashes of judgment are also emotional. The emotional component impels us to action.
- We can feel or be under the influence of an emotion without knowing it.
- Emotions (in the sense of feeling state) have a cognitive component. All emotion has some element of judgment or interpretation. Emotions are ways we know ourselves and our world.

- All emotions have an intentional structure.[xiv] They are oriented toward something; they have an object. The broader emotions, which we call moods, are oriented toward the world in general; specific emotions such as fear are focused on specific real or imagined things or events. Some of the specific emotions—fear and disgust, for example—are about the physical world. Others, such as trust, sympathy, gratitude, guilt, anger and humor, pertain to the social and moral worlds.[62]

- Every emotion has implications for action and has an effect on our readiness for or actual undertaking of an activity or a course of action.

These assertions about emotion can be verified by phenomenological analysis. Existential philosopher Robert Solomon, coming at the issue from an entirely different perspective, says that "emotions [are] our own judgments" and "the very source of our interests and our purposes."[63] You can, if you like, corroborate this by examining your own experience.

In sum: There is a lot going on in our lives to which we mostly don't pay attention, and we are far less rational than we like to think.

[xiv] By "intentional" I do not mean the ordinary usage of planning to make something happen. "Intentionality" is a technical term meaning the "ofness" or "aboutness" inherent in experience. Being conscious always entails being conscious *of* something; you are never just conscious without an object. The term comes from a Latin phrase, *intendere arcum in*, which means to aim a bow and arrow at (something). This image of aiming or directedness is central in most philosophical discussions of consciousness.

Chapter 18, Intelligence

Cognition is how we acquire knowledge. Intelligence is what we do with our knowledge. Human intelligence—and, I assume, the intelligence of some other species such as apes, dolphins and whales—consists in the ability to entertain in thought something that is not happening at the moment and consequently—by comparing what is happening now to what happened or might happen at another time—to tailor behavior to the specific features and nuances of a particular situation. Less intelligent animals have far less flexibility.

A gazelle on the plains of Africa has, we can imagine, quite a vivid appreciation of its surroundings. What looks to us like uniform grasslands is to it a rich tapestry of differentiated food patches. In this sense its visual cognition is rich. But it has only a limited repertoire of what do with that richness, a repertoire evolved to be universal to the species and applicable uniformly across the environment in which it lives. By contrast, a bushman hunting the gazelle uses arrows that are tipped with a poison found only on the larvae of a certain beetle. Cosmides and Tooby say "Whatever the neural adaptations that underlie this behavior, they were not designed specifically for beetles and arrows, but exploit these local, contingent facts as part of a computational structure that treats them as instances of a more general class."[64]

In contrast to nonhuman animals, we have the ability to improvise our behavior in response to local, contingent facts, facts most likely not true for all humans and in all the environments in which humans find themselves. Eskimos hunting seals have no knowledge of poisonous beetles.

The capacity of other animals to process information is limited. It has evolved to handle features of the world that were true across the species' range and throughout many generations, enough that they selected for the adaptations we find in such animals today. "These constraints narrowly limit the kinds of information that such adaptations can be designed to use: the set of properties that had a predictable relationship to features of the species' world that held widely in space and time is a very restricted one." [65]

We humans, in contrast, can recognize and respond to a far greater set of environmental cues. We can envision far more possibilities and are far more flexible in our behavior. In short, humans can plan. Humans, say Tooby and Cosmides, are "intelligent, cultural, conscious, planning animals."[66] "By planning," they say, "we mean creating cognitive representations of past, present and future states of the world, evaluating alternative courses of action by representing consequences and matching these against goals."[67]

More succinctly, Pinker gives this definition of intelligence: "The ability to attain goals in the face of obstacles by means of decisions based on rational (truth-obeying) rules."[68]

Intelligence requires three things:

- A goal or goals to be obtained.
- Knowledge about how the world works, beliefs that turn out to be true and workable in practice. Such beliefs provide rules of inference that guide thinking.
- The ability to apply the knowledge in flexible ways, depending on circumstances, to reach the goals.

Planning—the application of intelligence—is an evolved adaptation for improvising novel sequences of behavior to reach targeted goals. Human intelligence widens the range of environments in which we can survive and reproduce.

The Scope Problem

Planning involves imagining different scenarios and, importantly, the ability to distinguish imagined, remembered and anticipated scenarios from what is actually happening in the present situation. Cosmides and Tooby call this the "scope problem," how to distinguish facts and valid inferences that are true within a certain imagined scenario from those that are true in other scenarios or in the actual world.[69] In the language of computation, this means

> the capacity to carry out inferential operations on ... suppositions or propositions of conditionally unevaluated truth value, while keeping their computational products isolated from other knowledge stores until the truth or utility of the suppositions is decided, and the outputs are either integrated or discarded. [70]

Our ability to keep things separate in this way enables all sorts of advanced behavior:

> This capacity is essential to planning, interpreting communication, employing the information communication brings, evaluating others' claims, mind-reading [the ability to understand others' beliefs, intentions and desires], pretense, detecting or perpetrating deception, using inference to triangulate information about past or hidden causal relations, and much else that makes the human mind so distinctive.[71]

Cosmides and Tooby postulate a capacity they call "scope representation," the ability to identify under what conditions information can be treated as accurate and inferences as valid.[72] Because we can represent their scope independently, we do not confuse our considerations of possible strategies, memories of past situations, anticipations of the future and imaginings of possible scenarios with the actual conditions we find ourselves in. Those who do confuse these things we readily identify as aberrant. Schizophrenia can be interpreted as a failure of mental boundaries in which, for example, a person experiences the desire to do something as a command to do it.[73]

The capacity to represent the scope of our plans, perceptions and imaginations separately is at the foundation of literature, and of story-telling generally. Humans in all cultures love stories. In stories we can mentally rehearse or represent various social situations without actually having to encounter them. We can find out how others—the characters in the stories—handle these situations and, hence, learn successful and unsuccessful strategies for ourselves. As Cosmides and Tooby put it, "individuals are no longer limited by the slow and erratic flow of actual experience compared to the rapid rate of vicarious, contrived, or imagined experience."[74]

This ability to decouple various scope representations enables quite a number of human faculties, including the following:

- Theory of mind [see below] and prediction of behavior, the ability to guess with some accuracy what another person is thinking or feeling and to anticipate correctly what they will do: Motives, feelings, beliefs and perceptions imputed to the other are decoupled from our own.[75]
- Representation of goals: The goal state is decoupled from the present state of affairs.[76]
- Making plans to accomplish goals: Plans for the future are decoupled from the present.[77]
- Simulating the physical world: Simulations are decoupled from the actual world.[78]
- Creating and enjoying fiction: The fictional world is decoupled from the real world.[79]
- Remembering episodes of our own past and maintaining a sense of our identity through time: Memories are decoupled from our present experience of the actual world, and personal memories are decoupled from general knowledge gained through other means.[80]

Theory of Mind

Of these faculties, theory of mind is one of the most interesting because it entails much that is strikingly human. Humans have been called "ultrasocial"[81] and "obligatorily gregarious."[82] We live in large cooperative societies in which hundreds or thousands of people enjoy the benefits of division of labor. We must have ongoing and extensive contact with our fellows in order to survive and thrive. To succeed at living together we must understand our fellow humans as having subjectivity like our own. The term "Theory of Mind" refers to the ability to attribute mental states—beliefs, intentions, desires, pretense, knowledge, etc.—to ourselves and others and to understand that others have beliefs, desires and intentions that are different from our own.[83]

We do this all the time. We see someone striding purposefully and assume they are going somewhere to do something they consider important. We see a smile and assume the person is pleased, or a scowl and assume they are displeased. We see someone cross the street to avoid a barking dog, and we understand that they do so precisely in order to avoid the dog. We assume that the salesperson in the store will sell us the goods we want, and that other people walking on the sidewalk with us will generally stay on the sidewalk. Depending on context, we view the offer of candy as friendly or a threat.

Philosophers may ponder how we can have knowledge of other people's mental states, to which we have no direct access; but in fact we assume such knowledge all the time, and life together would be impossible without it. Of course we can be mistaken or deceived, but mistakes and deception would not be possible without familiar assumptions that most often turn out to be correct.

Researchers have found several stages in the development of theory of mind in infants and young children as well as in animals.[84]

- If something appears to move on its own, our minds interpret it as an agent.
- If it appears to move toward something, we take that thing to be its goal.
- If it changes direction flexibly in response to what is happening in its environment, we take it to have some degree of rationality or intention (in the sense of intending to accomplish something).
- If its action is followed closely in time by another object's action, we take the second action to be a socially contingent response to the first.
- And if something is a goal-directed agent that shows some degree of flexible response, then we know that it can cause harm or comfort to other agents and possibly to ourselves.

These judgments are automatic, a form of hot cognition, not something we stop to think about. They form the basis of our well-developed ability to get along in groups of others like us. We, like all social animals, have the skills to detect who cooperates and who cheats, who is kind and who is dangerous, who is dominant and who is submissive. Humans have these skills to a greater degree and have the ability to fine-tune them with greater precision than other animals do.

Where chimps and bonobos can understand that individual A knows where some food is hidden and individual B doesn't and consequently expect different behavior from the two,[85] humans can easily grasp much more complicated scenarios. We quite understand that when Hermia loves Lysander but has been commanded to wed Demetrius; and Demetrius wants Hermia; and Helena, Hermia's friend, wants Demetrius; but a magic potion causes Lysander to fall in love with Helena rather than Hermia, then much hilarious confusion can ensue.[86] No ape could possibly keep up.

* * *

We are awfully intelligent. But we are not always rational: our intelligence does not always function as well as it could. In the next chapter we'll see why that is and what we can do about it.

Chapter 19, The Overlooked Adaptation

Human beings have greater intelligence than other animals, but sometimes we don't act like it. We've all had the experience of having our buttons pushed, so to speak: of reacting with anger at something that doesn't really warrant it, or being afraid in certain situations without knowing why, or finding it hard to think about certain topics. In such cases our intelligence does not function as well as it could; something interferes with it.

Fortunately we also have a self-corrective mechanism that enables us to recover our intelligence when it is interfered with.[87] What interferes with intelligence is the activation of certain painful emotions, emotions that put into place (or are the felt component of) strategies for coping with situations that threaten our survival or well-being. Chief among these emotions are the following:

- Grief or sadness, typically activated by separation from others of our kind or the loss of or injury to someone close to us.
- Fear, typically activated by the presence, real or imagined, of a threat.
- Embarrassment, typically activated by the possibility of disapproval by other people because we have violated a social norm. Embarrassment is a kind of fear, fear of social condemnation.
- Anger, typically activated by interference with our attempt to accomplish a goal.
- Boredom, activated by lack of sufficient environmental stimulus to fruitfully occupy our mind.

We can speculate about the evolutionary origins of these emotional strategies. Fear can inhibit movement or induce an urge to flee; and no doubt our ancestors who became immobile when a predator was nearby or who ran away, and thereby avoided being detected and eaten, lived to have offspring with a similar strategy. Anger usually entails forceful exertion and vigorous movement, and no doubt such exertion enabled our ancestors to overcome obstacles or fight off predators and rivals so they could acquire food and sexual mates in adverse conditions. Embarrassment, a form of fear, entails inhibition of talking and further embarrassing behavior. Those who avoided group disapproval garnered the benefits of living in a group—it is easier to acquire food, shelter and a mate in a group than to do so alone—and lived to pass that kind of behavior on to their offspring.

These strategies all have a similar effect on our intelligence. When they arise, they produce mental "noise" that prevents or at least diminishes our ability to plan, to consider alternatives to what is currently happening and envision and choose a workable course of action to bring about envisioned goals. It is as if we are too preoccupied with instinctive responses to the triggering situation to be able to think clearly. Afterwards, if not healed, the diminishment of intelligence remains.

Evolution has provided us with ways to heal the painful emotion and recover our intelligence. (The proto-humans long ago who were able to heal in this way and recover and augment their intelligence had more offspring than those who did not.) The healing mechanisms involve physical release or discharge of the tension provoked by the triggering situation and one's emotional response to it. Chief among these healing discharges are the following.[88]

- Grief or sadness is healed by crying, by tears and sobbing.
- Fear is healed by shaking and trembling, chattering of teeth and cold perspiration. After sufficient shaking, the remainder of the fear is healed by intense laughter.
- Embarrassment, a less intense form of fear, is healed by laughter.

- Anger is healed by vigorous and abrupt movements and loud noises accompanied by warm perspiration. This is called "throwing a tantrum" or "blowing your top."
- Boredom is healed by nonrepetitive talking and laughter.

If not interfered with, these discharges take place during the triggering situation or as soon as it is feasible to do so after the situation is over. In many current cultures, however, some or all of these discharges are interfered with. Boys are told it is unmanly to cry. Girls are told it is unladylike to get angry. The more warlike or militant the culture, the more trembling and shaking are discouraged. People who interfere often mean well. They want to help the sad or fearful or angry person feel better but mistakenly think the discharge is the hurt rather than the healing of the hurt.

In our culture [late twentieth-century USA], tears are usually taken to mean grief. Trembling is taken to mean terror. Angry shouting is taken to mean anger. Therefore, it is thought that to shut off these discharges is to free a person from the emotion. "If you can stop them from crying, they won't feel bad." This is fundamentally backward.

The profound process of discharge of which tears are the outward indication is the getting over of grief. Tears indicate freeing oneself from grief. Crying never occurs unless a person needs to do it. In the same way, trembling and cold perspiration indicate the *release* of terror. Laughter accompanies becoming un-afraid or un-irritated. Shouting and violent movement accompany becoming un-furious.[89]

If not rectified by emotional discharge, the effects of the painful emotion last after the triggering situation is over, causing a long-term impairment of intelligence. When a situation arises that reminds us of the triggering situation, we respond as we did in the original situation, whether or not that response is appropriate or workable in the current situation. This phenomenon is easy to observe once you know what to look for. Here are some examples:

- A person who was once frightened by a dog and was not permitted to discharge the fear is uneasy around any dog, whether or not it is acting menacingly.

- A boy who was not permitted to cry when someone acted mean to him grows up to be a man who is emotionally distant, unable to express his feelings and, hence, unable to enjoy deep intimacy with another person. (Compounding the inhibition of grief is the residue of fear brought on by having been forced not to show the tears and, most likely, not to show any outward manifestation of fear either.)

- A girl who was not permitted to be outwardly angry acts nice, accommodating and polite but at times is cutting and brutal with words or unable to assert herself clearly and directly. She may undermine and undercut other women.

- Children who are bored in school because the instruction modality does not suit their learning style and who are not permitted to heal the boredom by talking and laughing grow up to be less inquisitive than they would otherwise be.

The phenomenon of reacting to a current situation as one did to an earlier, painful situation—reacting as if the current situation were the same as the earlier situation—is called "restimulation." The current situation reminds us of the earlier situation, the painful effects of which were not discharged. In the present, we are unable to think clearly, and we react as we did in the earlier situation. We act, as it were, mechanically instead of organically. In this case we are said to be restimulated, rather than merely being reminded. The technical term for such a repetitive and inflexible response to a situation in which a person is restimulated is "distress pattern." This term is derived from the general word "pattern," which means repeated regularity, such as a decorative design or a model to be followed in making things, like a pattern for clothing or other artifacts. A distress pattern is a model that guides our responses to restimulating situations but does so repetitively and inflexibly.

Discharge has a threefold effect: cognitive, behavioral and emotional. Cognitively, we are freed from rigid ways of thinking and interpreting the world. We re-evaluate our beliefs (hence the name of the organized movement that embraces this practice) and come to a clearer understanding of ourselves, the world and the past and current situations. Behaviorally, we act with greater flexibility and effectiveness in the present and are freed from rigid, distressed patterns of behavior. More and more, we are able to decide to act differently from the old, suboptimal patterns and act creatively instead of repetitively. Emotionally, we are freed from painful emotion and enjoy a happier, more zestful feeling tone.

We do not know what happens neurologically before, during and after the discharge process because the needed research has not been done. Nor do we know precisely what happens in the brain when discharge is inhibited and the person is left vulnerable to restimulation. It is as if information were stored in an unusable fashion, as a recording of the entire painful situation as a whole, rather than usefully, as discrete bits of data that can be rearranged and thought about separately. A synonym for "distress pattern" is "distress recording," to reflect this theory about how information is recorded during an emotionally painful situation.[90] What we do know is that emotional discharge can heal the emotional pain and relieve the person of distress patterns even long after the original painful incident took place. We can recover our intelligence and become less vulnerable to restimulation through the process of emotional discharge.

It is beyond the scope of this chapter to go into the techniques of encouraging emotional discharge, but the fundamental process is easy: take turns listening. Discharge tends to occur spontaneously when we are in the presence of a sympathetic listener who pays attention as we remember and talk about distressing experiences. What makes it difficult for a person to listen well is that they get restimulated by the story they are hearing or are too caught up in their own distress to listen in the first place. To alleviate that restimulation and distress, they need to be listened to as well. By taking turns listening, any two people can assist each other to discharge distress and recover intelligence.

I call this the overlooked adaptation because it is not widely known and practiced in current technologically advanced cultures. That is unfortunate, as we need all the intelligence we can muster to solve the pressing problems of the day. The cause of its being overlooked seems to be a matter of human culture changing more rapidly than human physiology. Certainly the physiological responses are still intact; folklore and common sense know the value of, for instance, a good cry to make you feel better or a good laugh to relieve social tension.

It is possible that the systematic inhibition of emotional discharge is a factor in the development of societies in which some classes of people gain advantage at the expense of others. Dominance hierarchies are a feature of quite a number of species, and humans are no exception. What is unique about human dominance hierarchies is the greater extent and sophistication of the mechanisms by which classes of individuals maintain and enhance their status and material advantage. Inhibition of discharge reduces the flexible intelligence that subordinates might use to criticize or even change the social structure and thereby enhance their material well-being. They become docile and resigned to their position. What is doubly unfortunate is that even those at the top of the hierarchy suffer from reduced intelligence, although their distress patterns differ from the distress patterns of those further down. The rigidity of the class structure prevents those in dominant positions from, for instance, having close emotional contact with others, especially those of other classes, and instills quite a bit of fear. It may well be that for overall well-being those at the top would be better off with more closeness and less dominance.

A byproduct of the relative ignorance of the function of emotional discharge is the lack of rigorous research on the topic. Given that lack, how do we know that this account is correct? We know because thousands, perhaps millions, of people have used the techniques of mutual listening and encouragement of discharge to recover their intelligence and have found out what works and what doesn't in this effort. The situation is analogous to a scientific experiment writ large. The hypothesis is that emotional discharge enhances one's ability to think creatively and flexibly and that failure to discharge the tension arising from distressing situations inhibits that ability. The prediction is that in specific cases, after people discharge they will tend to act more rationally. The test is to engage both as listener (counselor) and one listened to (client) and to elicit such discharge. So far the results have been overwhelmingly in support of the hypothesis. People do in fact regain intelligence, get restimulated less often and increasingly make their lives better. The knowledge gained is both observational and first-person. You see changes in behavior in other people, sometimes quite dramatic changes, after they discharge. And you find yourself increasingly able to think more clearly and make better choices.

Traits of Undistressed Humans

The theory of how emotional discharge works includes some remarkable assertions about human nature: that we are all connected, which is probably not controversial, but also that we are inherently capable of being far more intelligent, loving, powerful and enthusiastic about life than most of us imagine.

The evidence for these assertions is not from observing all humans and drawing inferences, or at least not entirely, because all humans are damaged, some more than others. By "damaged" I mean that our intelligence has been impaired as explained above. It is as if all the people we knew had broken ankles and were unable to run. We would then conclude that humans were bad at running, but in fact undamaged humans are good at running. To see these facets of human nature clearly, we need to look at undamaged humans. Unfortunately, there aren't any undamaged adults, but we have some clues: (1) Babies are, by and large, undamaged, so we can get a glimpse of human nature by looking at them. (2) An increasing number of people are recovering from their damage through the process of discharge, reevaluation and decision. We can get an idea of human nature by looking at them, particularly at the ones who have carried out the process the furthest.

Let's look in detail at each of these claims about human nature.

Fundamental to all humans, damaged or not, is that we are all *connected* to each other and to the world in which we live. We are connected in the following ways:

- We are part of nature, the universe. Biologically we are embedded in the natural world and could not live or function without it.
- We are social animals. We are descended from a long line of highly social ancestors and have always been interdependent and bonded. Zoologists would classify the human species as obligatorily gregarious.[91] Consider also the following:
  - We share language and can understand each other. Language in isolation is inconceivable; the essence of language is to communicate with others.
  - Without other people, human babies would not be able to survive.
  - Solitary confinement is the harshest penalty we can inflict short of death.
- We have the capability or capacity to imagine another's point of view, to experience things as they do, and it is fulfilling to do so. (See *Theory of Mind*, above.)

Beyond the claim of the fundamental connectedness of all humans are claims of characteristics of undistressed humans, characteristics that any clear-thinking person would want to emulate.

First and foremost, we have the capacity to be *intelligent*. We are the most intelligent beings we know of. We have the ability to think rapidly and accurately and to come up with an appropriate response to every situation, a response that achieves our goals in the face of changing circumstances. At the lowest level such intelligence is instinctual. We blink our eyes without thinking when an insect flies near our face and thereby preserve our ability to see. At higher levels intelligence is learned and habitual. Adults can walk over uneven terrain and navigate around obstacles to get where they are going without giving much conscious thought to the process, having learned the skill as small children. At the highest level intelligence is conscious and deliberate. Faced with a difficult ascent, a rock climber carefully considers different possible routes before trying them out. That is the aspect of intelligence that humans have to a greater degree than any other species, so far as we know. Part of our intelligence consists in our ability to know, to detect and understand the universe surrounding us to whatever level of precision we need or desire.

Second, we have the capacity to be *loving and cooperative*. Humans are social beings; as babies we would die in isolation, and as children and adults we thrive in the company of others like us. We are inherently connected with other people. Our natural way of feeling about those close to us is love, and our natural way of interacting with those close to us is to cooperate to accomplish our chosen goals.

Third, we have, potentially, great *personal power* and the ability to decide at any moment how to approach life and what actions to take. By "power" I mean simply the ability to get things done, to accomplish what we have decided to do. We can say to life's challenges "I can" and "I will," and the more we discharge away our distress patterns, the more we do exactly that.

Fourth, we can be *enthusiastic and zestful* about life. When we are free of distress, we feel vibrantly alive and take great delight in enjoying and mastering our environment.

These things may not seem obviously true. Many of us do not act this way, and the reason we don't is that we suffer from distress patterns. Emotional hurts that have not been healed impair our ability to think clearly, love and cooperate with each other, act powerfully and enjoy life.

I want to be precise here. Although Re-evaluation Counseling, from which the foregoing assertions are taken, says that people *are inherently or naturally* this way, that humans have a "basic loving, cooperative, intelligent, and zestful nature,"[92] I am claiming merely that humans undeniably *have the capacity* to be that way. Purely descriptively, the assertion that humans are inherently loving and cooperative is only a partial truth. We certainly are that way, particularly with people in our family, clan, tribe or ingroup; but we are also inherently aggressive, brutal and competitive, especially toward those not in our group. Both behaviors have been and are found throughout humanity. To assert that we are loving and cooperative without asserting that we are also aggressive and competitive is to disguise a recommendation or prescription as a declarative fact. That said, it is certainly more useful to remind ourselves of the possibility of the former than to dwell on the latter. And it is undeniable that we are far more capable of being loving, cooperative, zestful, powerful and intelligent than most of us have realized.

Humans are Good

On a related note, Re-evaluation Counseling claims that humans are inherently good. The claim as stated is meaningless, as nothing is inherently good; things are only good *for* something or someone or good *at* something. The only goodness is instrumental. But the claim is heuristically useful, and there are a number of ways in which humans are in fact fundamentally good instrumentally.

The heuristic value of the claim is obvious. Telling someone they are good is useful as a contradiction of emotionally distressing messages that they were bad as children—that they were naughty or did not live up to parental expectations or did not do what adult authorities wanted them to do—or are bad as adults, that they deserve disapproval. In this sense "good" means "worthy of approval by others" and "bad" means "deserving of disapproval by others." It is very useful to tell someone they are good in this sense because doing so often facilitates emotional discharge and results in that person being released, wholly or partially, from harmful patterns of thought, feeling and behavior. And it is more useful for each of us to think of ourselves as good than as bad because doing so leads to better results and better functioning. Such good results do not in themselves prove that the claim is true, but strongly suggest that it may be true, in that true claims are more likely to be useful than falsehoods.

But the fundamental question is "What are humans good for?" And is there a way that all humans are good for something such that it makes sense to say that they are good without qualification?

That, of course, is the question this whole work is attempting to answer. At this point we can say that it is clear that human beings are valuable to themselves and other human beings. We possess the most complicated intelligence and the greatest capacity for mastery of the environment of any organism we know of.

The only thing sufficiently complex to engage the human intelligence for a long period of time is another human intelligence. It is good for us to engage each other in that it exercises our facilities for understanding and mutual delight. We are good in that we have the ability to be good for each other.

Chapter 20, The Human Virtue

So far we have seen that humans are like other animals, but amplified significantly. We have greater intelligence and hence greater technology, greater culture and greater ability to keep track of and get along with others of our species. We've seen how cognition and emotion work and what intelligence consists of; and it is certainly plausible to think that other animals have rudimentary forms of the same. Our primate cousins, chimps and bonobos, resemble us in many ways. But we are more than just super-apes.

We humans have an ability that goes well beyond what any other animal can do: we can turn our attention to ourselves. Even more than our mighty intelligence, the capacity for self-reflection—that we are able to turn our attention to our own experience, to take ourselves as an object of thought and perception—is what makes us uniquely human.

We have seen in the previous chapters that humans have far greater intelligence than other animals, that we are the species that makes plans, that imagines states of affairs not immediately present and targets our behavior to reach envisaged goals. When this intelligence is directed at affairs in the world, I call it *first-order thinking*. It can range from the very simple, such as jotting down a grocery list, to the very complex, such as planning a multi-year project encompassing thousands of interrelated tasks. Not only do we make plans, we execute them and accomplish our goals, making corrections along the way to overcome obstacles and take into account changing circumstances. When this kind of observation, planning and execution is directed at ourselves, I call it *second-order thinking*. Others have called it self-knowledge, self-awareness or self-reflection (as one examines one's reflected image in a mirror).

I am using "thinking" in a very broad sense to mean mental—that is, private or subjective—acts of all kinds: thought, imagination, desire, aversion, volition (intending in the ordinary sense, planning and acting), direct perception and so forth. Second-order thinking occurs when we direct these activities toward ourselves. This work is an example: a human being thinking about being human. Another example is self-knowledge, such as knowing your strengths and weaknesses. Another is paying attention to yourself, whether that be in the awkwardness of social embarrassment or in the focus of learning a new skill. Another is remembering how you interacted with others or mentally rehearsing how you will interact with them in the future. In these and many other ways we take ourselves as objects of our own cognition.

These forms of self-reflection enable *self-transcendence*. By this I mean that in "seeing" ourselves as an object, we take a position, as it were, outside of ourselves, and that enables us to alter the self that is "seen."[xv] Of course the self that is "seen" is not different from the self that "sees," in that both are the interior of the same physical body. But in another sense, the self that "sees" is different. It has a larger vantage point and is not caught up, or at least not entirely caught up, in the life of the self that is "seen." By taking a position outside yourself, you can alter yourself.

Harry Frankfurt describes this self-reflective structure of the self in his essay "Freedom of the Will."[93] Humans, along with all other living beings, have first-order desires, desires to do or to have something. Some animals—chimps and bonobos are good examples, and possibly dolphins and whales—even appear to have the rudimentary ability to anticipate the future and make decisions based on prior thought. But only humans have "the capacity for reflective self-evaluation that is manifested in the for-

---

[xv] "See" and its variants are in quotes because the experience is not entirely and not merely visual. We experience ourselves in many modalities.

mation of second-order desires,"[94] desires to have certain desires. The second-order self wants the first-order self to want something, typically something different from what the first-order self actually wants. For example, suppose you have a craving for a certain food—something sweet and sugary, say, or full of fat and salt—that tastes good but is not healthy. Realizing that, you may feel bad about the craving and *want to want* something else to eat. That is a second-order desire.

An even stronger form is second-order volition, where you want a certain desire to be your will. By "will" Frankfurt means a desire that is strong enough to move you to action.[95] In this example, you would not only want to want to eat something healthy and want not to want the unhealthy food, but would also want the desire to eat healthily to overrule the craving, to be the desire that actually results in action so that you end up eating the healthy food. Frankfurt regards the capacity for second-order volition to be the essential characteristic of being a person.[96] I regard it as an aspect of the second-order thinking that is uniquely human.[xvi] For Frankfurt, freedom of the will consists in being able to make second-order volitions effective; that is, to have the second-order volition actually govern the first order such that the preferred first-order desire is what results in action. When that happens, we judge that our will is free. "It is in securing the conformity of his will to his second-order volitions ... that a person exercises freedom of the will. ... The unwilling addict's will is not free."[97]

Having a free will in this sense is an example of our second-order thinking functioning well. Like any human activity, second-order thinking can be done poorly or skillfully. When we are unable to see the whole picture, when we have false ideas about ourselves, distorted by ignorance or painful emotion, we are doing it poorly. When we are able to observe ourselves carefully over time, identifying and removing preconceptions, we are doing it

---

[xvi] The distinction between "human" and "person" is just terminological at this point, but if we discover that some non-humans—whales, say, or beings from another planet—have the same capacity for second-order thinking that we do, then, with Frankfurt, we should speak of persons rather than humans.

better. When we have true ideas about ourselves but are unable
to act on them, we are doing it poorly. (This is Frankfurt's unfree
will.) When we are able to use what we find out about ourselves
to change for the better how we behave and hence what kind of
person we become, we are doing it excellently.

Our capacity for second-order thinking is subject to excess
and deficiency. It is excessive when we are too embarrassed to
function well socially or too self-conscious to be able to, for instance, swing a golf club properly or do some other task that
takes physical skill. It is deficient when we fail to learn from experience. It is deficient when we lose ourselves in what
Heidegger calls "the publicness of the 'they,'"[98] when we just go
along with the crowd without thinking about what we are doing.
It is deficient in quite a brutal way when we see that we are
caught in a repetitive and painful pattern of behavior but lack
the skill to get out of it. But we always have the possibility of doing better. A failure of second-order thinking is a case of failure
of intelligence generally, and there are ways to overcome such
failures. I'll return to that topic in later chapters.

What I am suggesting is this: *Second-order thinking is the
peculiarly human virtue*, what we do that other beings don't. We
are all capable of it, and when we do it well we function optimally
and are most fulfilled. It is what enables us to achieve the goals
we set for ourselves. Second-order thinking gives us mastery because it enables us to tune the instrument, so to speak, by means
of which we exert first-order influence on the world.

Second-order thinking gives us the peculiar sense of self that
is expressed in the poem *Invictus*: "I am the master of my fate: / I
am the captain of my soul."[99] The *I* to which the poet refers is the
coherence of interiority of second-order thinking, the ongoing inner life of how it feels to be operating at that second-order level.
We each (unless we are damaged) have a first-order sense of ourselves as continuous and ongoing entities, as being the same person through time, a sense that comes from familiarity with a
point of view, from being within that point of view and seeing the
world from it. Within our interior landscape, so to speak, there
are certain familiar features—habitual thoughts, feelings, emotions, attitudes and ways of behaving—that are present all or

most of the time. These comprise a sense of how it feels to be oneself. Much of the self-sense no doubt comes from the experience of being in our body, a particular body that has a particular vantage point on the world. The body changes over time but gradually enough that we have a sense of continuity. The sense of self is the unity over time of interior background feeling tone; and the sense of self arising from second-order thinking is the same, except it seems more vivid, somehow more real or efficacious. That is because it *is* more efficacious: you exert control not only over your world but over yourself as well.

And the point of this whole philosophical inquiry is to be able to do exactly that: to command yourself so as to live well.

Chapter 21, Our Sense of Morality

In order to command anyone well—that is, to get them to do what you order them to do—it helps to know whom you are commanding, what sorts of inducements they respond to, what sorts of things inhibit their ability to respond and what sorts of things shape their responses. One striking feature of humans in general is that we have a sense of morality, a sense that—no matter what someone, even ourselves, may tell us to do—some things are forbidden, others are allowed but not required, and others are mandatory. Hence if we are to command ourselves successfully, we need to understand our own moral impulses.

We all have a sense of morality. The details of what conduct is prohibited, allowed and required by the moral code vary from culture to culture, but all cultures have sets of rules, whether stated explicitly or not, that specify how people are to act. And people in every culture—which is to say all people, as we never find humans in isolation—have internalized the moral code of their culture and have a conscience, a sense of right and wrong.

Morality differs from social convention, and moral judgments differ from other kinds of evaluative judgments.[100] Consider the following:

- "Murder is wrong"—a moral judgment
- "Brussels sprouts taste terrible"—a personal aesthetic judgment
- "Bell-bottom pants are old-fashioned"—a social aesthetic judgment
- "You should not scratch a poison ivy rash"—advice, a judgment of prudence

The moral judgment has specific cognitive, behavioral and emotional characteristics. Cognitively, the rules it evokes are taken to apply without exception. Prohibitions against rape and murder are believed to be universal and objective, not matters of local custom; and people who violate the rules are deemed to deserve punishment. Behaviorally, we do in fact punish moral offenders and praise those who obey the law in ways that do not apply to, for instance, people who merely wear unstylish clothes. Emotionally, when our sense of morality is triggered, we feel a glow of righteousness when we abide by the rules, guilt when we don't, a sense of anger or resentment at those who violate the rules and a desire to recruit others to allegiance to the rules.[101]

Moral Intuition

Philosophers have long debated the rational basis for moral judgments, but in fact most of our moral judgments are not made rationally. They are not carefully thought out; instead, they are the result of intuition.

Consider the so-called "trolley problem."[102] Imagine that you are on a trolley traveling at high speed toward a switch in the track. On the main track are five people who cannot get off because the banks on each side are very steep. They will die if the trolley hits them. On the side track is one person who also cannot get off the track. The engineer has passed out and has no control of the trolley, but you do. By remote control, you can throw the switch. Should you throw it and shunt the trolley to the side track, thereby saving five at the expense of one?

Now imagine that you are standing on a bridge above the track. Again, five people will die if the trolley continues. This time the only way to stop the trolley would be to throw a massive object onto the track. But the only massive object available is a very large man standing next to you. Should you throw him onto the track, thereby saving five at the expense of one? (Ignore, for the moment, the small chance that the mass of the man would actually stop the trolley, or that you would have sufficient strength to throw him down.)

Stop for a moment and consider your responses. Why did you respond as you did?

Most people say Yes in the first case and No in the second even though the consequences are the same, sacrificing one life to save five. Evidently, calculation of consequences is not the deciding factor. And most people have trouble coming up with a reason for their choice. This thought experiment has been administered to over 200,000 people from 100 countries. "A difference between the acceptability of switch-pulling and man-heaving, and an inability to justify the choice, was found in respondents from Europe, Asia and North and South America; among men and women, blacks and whites, teenagers and octogenarians, Hindus, Muslims, Buddhists, Christians, Jews and atheists; people with elementary-school educations and people with Ph.D.'s."[103]

The key point here is "inability to justify the choice." People make the choice first and think of reasons later, if at all. We have a moral instinct that prompts us to make snap judgments regarding, in this case, prevention of harm to others.

Here is another example.[104] (Bear with me for a moment until we get to the moral implications.) Imagine a set of cards, each with a letter on one side and a number on the other. You are asked to test whether the following rule is true: "If a card has a D on one side, it has a 3 on the other." You are shown four cards:

D	F	3	7

Which cards should you turn over to see whether the rule is true? Most people have trouble with this.[xvii]

Now imagine you are a bouncer in a bar and you have to enforce the rule that a person must be eighteen or older to drink beer. You can check what people are drinking and you can check how old they are. Which of the following do you have to check: a

---

[xvii] The correct answer is D and 7. Turn over the D to see if it has something other than 3 on the back, and turn over the 7 to see if it has a D. The 3 is irrelevant, because the rule does not say that only Ds have a 3 on the other side.

beer drinker, a coke drinker, a twenty-five-year-old, a sixteen-year-old? Most people get this one right away. You have to check the age of the beer drinker and you have to check what the sixteen-year-old is drinking.

But logically these are the same problem! Beer-drinking implies being old enough, just as D implies 3. Being too young implies not drinking beer, just as 7 implies that the letter is not a D. Why is the first one hard and the second one easy?

What's different about the second one is that it is set in a social context in which cheating is a possibility, and you are asked to find the cheaters. The experiment has been replicated numerous times. When the rule to be tested is a contract, an exchange of benefits, then finding that the rule is false is equivalent to detecting a cheater, one who takes a benefit without paying the price. When the rule does not involve a contract—for instance when the rule is "If a person eats hot chili peppers, then he or she drinks cold beer"—it is just as hard to solve as the card puzzle.

We seem to have an inbuilt cheater-detection mechanism which sometimes overlaps with logic but is not the same. It is not extensible, as logic is, but is confined to the realm of social exchange. Using that mechanism we make snap judgments in the area of fairness and reciprocity.

There are many more experiments and empirical findings that indicate that humans make moral judgments rapidly without deliberative thought, that we have instincts for morals, a moral sense that seems to be built in. And it is not merely a matter of social convention. If it were, we would expect that different societies might provide different answers to the trolley problem, but they don't. The sense of morals shows up at an early age. Four-year-olds say that it is not OK to wear pajamas to school (a convention) and also not OK to hit a little girl for no reason (a moral principle). But when asked whether these actions would be OK if the teacher allowed them, most of the children say that wearing pajamas would now be fine but that hitting a little girl still would not be.[105]

Most moral judgments are not the result of conscious deliberation (cold cognition). Instead they are intuitions, snap judgments made instantly and automatically. People rely on gut reactions to tell right from wrong and then employ reason afterwards to justify their intuitions. *Intuitions* are "the judgments, solutions, and ideas that pop into consciousness without our being aware of the mental processes that led to them."[106] *Moral intuitions* are a subset: "Feelings of approval or disapproval pop into awareness as we see or hear about something someone did, or as we consider choices for ourselves."[107]

> The adult mind is full of moral intuitions, which are like little bits of input-output programming connecting the perception of a pattern in the social world (often a virtue or vice) to an evaluation and in many cases a specific moral emotion (e.g., anger, contempt, admiration). When people think, gossip, and argue about moral issues, the playing field is not affectively flat and open to any kind of reason; it is more like a minefield or pinball machine where flash after flash of affectively laden intuition bounces around one's attention and pushes one toward specific conclusions.[108]

This behavior is not unique to morality. Our minds do most of their work by automatic pattern matching. We do not pay attention, for instance, to how our visual system and our knowledge of the world translate excitation of receptor cells on the back of the eyes to recognition of objects and people; instead we just recognize things. Similarly, most of our social cognition occurs rapidly and automatically. We very rapidly appraise people we meet as attractive or not, friendly or threatening, male or female, higher or lower in status than we are, etc.[109] Moral intuitions are a form of social cognition. Human beings "come equipped with an intuitive ethics, an innate preparedness to feel flashes of approval or disapproval toward certain patterns of events involving other human beings."[110]

Six Moral Domains

We have seen examples of instinctive moral judgment in two areas: caring and prevention of harm is one, and fairness and reciprocity is another. Social psychologist Jonathan Haidt has found that there are at least four more: loyalty to one's ingroup, respect for authority, concern for purity and sanctity, and a desire for liberty in the face of oppression. These six domains—he calls them "Moral Foundations"—are areas in which people have moral intuitions. Each is found in human populations throughout the world, although to different degrees in different cultures, and each has a plausible evolutionary explanation of how it came to be. Here is a list of them and their characteristics.[111]

Caring and the Prevention of Harm

The Care/Harm domain is the impulse to care for people who are needy, vulnerable or less fortunate. Why do people have a sense of compassion? Because our ancestors, like all mammals, needed to care for vulnerable young or kin, and those who developed an instinct for doing so had more offspring than those who didn't. The proper domain—meaning the range of stimuli that the intuition evolved to detect—is suffering, present or foreseen, of one's kin. The actual domain—meaning the range of stimuli that in fact actuate the intuition in the present—includes lots of things that are not intrinsic to the proper domain. If we see suffering by or harm to any child-like entity, we are triggered; a good example is pictures of baby seals being clubbed by large men. The emotion triggered by the stimulus is compassion, and we instill compassion in our young people by exemplary stories of people who are caring and kind. We admire those who show the virtues of caring and kindness and condemn those who are cruel.

Fairness and Reciprocity

Fairness and reciprocity have to do with exchanges with others. We have evolved to reap the gains of reciprocal altruism with people who are not our kin or may be only distantly related. In order to be successful at this, our ancestors had to develop a finely tuned intuitive sense of when someone was cheating, getting a benefit without giving something in return. We want to make sure that people get what they deserve and don't get away with more. Today that sense can be triggered by a vending machine that takes our money without dispensing the goods. We feel angry when we are cheated, grateful when we get a fair exchange, and guilty when we are caught cheating. We instill virtues such as fairness, honesty and trustworthiness, and we condemn vices such as dishonesty.

Ingroup Loyalty

Humans aggregate into tribes, gangs and teams that compete. We evolved as members of such small groups, and are keenly attentive to threats or challenges to the group. Our ultra-sociality is a reason for our success as a species. "Mutual dependence is key. Human societies are support systems within which weakness does not automatically spell death."[112] Hence, "Evolution has equipped us with genuinely cooperative impulses and inhibitions against acts that might harm the group on which we depend."[113] A corollary is that we are indifferent or hostile to outsiders, members of other groups. Originally adapted for small groups of hunter-gatherers, the sense of in-group loyalty is now triggered by other things like sports teams. We feel proud to be a member of our group and are enraged by traitors. We admire and expound virtues such as loyalty and self-sacrifice and are morally offended by treason and cowardice, which undermine the group.

Authority and Respect

This foundation of morality is the impulse to show respect to persons of higher rank and to treat subordinates protectively. Humans, like other primates and many other species, live within dominance hierarchies. The hierarchy may be based on brute force or something more rational, like demonstrated competence at a task. The art of politics is all about negotiation within such hierarchies, and we have evolved emotions of respect and fear—and, from the point of view of the superiors, something like parental benevolence—to guide us. In the environment of evolutionary adaptedness, such emotional reactions were triggered by displays of dominance and submission. In the present, the signs of dominance are more subtle, and we pay deference to authorities and professionals—think of the doctor in his white coat—who have no real ability to compel our behavior. The relevant virtues of the subordinate are obedience and deference, and we condemn the vices of disobedience and disrespect. But superiors are expected to exhibit virtues as well: impartiality, magnanimity and parent-like concern.

Purity and Sanctity

The concern for purity is the impulse to avoid contact with things or people we view as unclean or impure. Unlike the others, whose adaptive challenge was social, the concern for purity arose because of our ancestors' omnivorous food strategy. We can eat just about anything, and we live in groups or tribes that are larger than those of other primates. That means we risk being exposed to disease-causing organisms that spread by physical contact. "Humans (but no other animals) therefore developed a suite of cognitive and emotional adaptations related to disgust that makes us wary but flexible about the kinds of things we eat, and about the contact histories of the things we eat."[114] Originally directed at putrid meat, waste products and diseased people, the emotion of disgust that we direct at what is perceived as unclean now gets attached to doctrines and social groups that seem to threaten our ingroup. Some of the most maladapted behavior is seen in the confluence of Ingroup and Purity intuitions that lead to violence and oppression toward those not in the group, such as ethnic cleansing, segregation and apartheid. The drive toward purity has gotten attached to religious doctrine, and may explain ideas about "keeping religious objects set apart from pollutants and profane objects, and about overcoming carnal desires and treating the body as a temple."[115] Purity-related virtues are chastity, self-restraint and cleanliness. Corresponding vices include lust and intemperance.

Liberty and Oppression

This one is about the visceral revulsion we have to those who dominate and misuse others.[116] As primates we have a long evolutionary history of living in dominance hierarchies, and the impulse to respect authority is an outgrowth of that. But the earliest "authorities," the alpha males that acted as chimpanzee alphas still do, were not so much leaders as bullies: they took what they wanted through sheer physical force. About five hundred thousand years ago humans got good at making weapons, and once all the members of the tribe had weapons, they could stand up to the bullying alpha. Nomadic hunter-gatherers, equipped with tools and weapons, are all egalitarian. (Only with development of agriculture and its attendant food surpluses, about ten thousand years ago, did hierarchy re-enter the picture.) In hunter-gatherer cultures—which lasted long enough that the impulse to cooperate with others to resist dominance became adaptive and hence selected for—people could unite against an oppressive dominator and take him down. Early humans not only had weapons, they had language, and they gossiped about moral violations. They could unite in order to shame, ostracize or ultimately kill anyone whose behavior threatened the rest of the group. This was the beginning, anthropologists believe, of moral communities. Today the impulse to resist oppression is found on the political left in the drive for social justice and on the right in the drive to reduce the power of government over the individual. A typical virtue is heroic resistance to authority, and the corresponding vice is craven submission. Another virtue is being good at politics, the ability to talk to people, listen to their concerns and persuade them to unite in a common purpose.

Analogues in Other Species

Precursors to these moral instincts are found in our primate relatives as well as in other animals. Frans de Waal puts it nicely:

> Survival often depends on how animals fare within their group, both in a cooperative sense (e.g., concerted action, information transfer) and in a competitive sense (e.g., dominance strategies, deception). It is in the *social* domain, therefore, that one expects the highest cognitive achievements. Selection must have favored mechanisms to evaluate the emotional states of others and quickly respond to them.[117]

Concern for harm and care is evidenced in numerous examples of ape empathy and targeted helping. A mother chimp helps her whimpering youngster climb from one tree to another by draping herself between them.[118] A youngster puts his arms around an adult male chimp who has been bested in combat to console him.[119] An adult bonobo screams and pounds on a window to attract the attention of a human who is about to let water into a moat where juveniles are playing. Bonobos cannot swim, so this action is obviously a warning.[120]

Alertness to fairness and reciprocity is found not only in apes but in less complex animals as well. When experimenters gave chimpanzees and capuchin monkeys differential rewards—a grape (valued highly) or a cucumber (valued less)—for the same effort, the one who got the cucumber was sometimes so angry that she threw it away. "Overall, both species were less likely to engage in an exchange or accept the reward when their partner got the better deal."[121] Chimps have a sense of gratitude; they are more likely to share food with individuals who have groomed them earlier.[122] This sense of inequity is the evolutionary precursor to the full-blown human sense of fairness.

Authority and respect are hallmarks of the dominance hierarchies found in all but the simplest of animal societies. de Waal devotes a whole book, *Chimpanzee Politics*, to the strategies chimps employ to gain rank in their very hierarchical communities.

Ingroup loyalty is found in numerous species; animals direct helping behavior toward members of the group and hostility to outsiders. de Waal calls this "community concern." It is shown when individuals encourage former combatants to reconcile after a fight, or a high-ranking male breaks up a fight.[123] He notes that "the most potent force to bring out a sense of community is enmity toward outsiders."[124] Chimpanzees are a notorious example. Within the group there is violence in the service of establishing dominance in the social hierarchy, but the degree of violence shown toward outsiders is far greater, more targeted and coordinated. Bands of males patrol the borders of the group's territory and attack and murder males of other groups.[125] One community in Gombe, Africa, grew large and split over the years into two groups, a southern and a northern community. "These chimpanzees had played and groomed together, reconciled after squabbles, shared meat and lived in harmony. But the factions began to fight nonetheless. Shocked researchers watched as former friends now drank each other's blood."[126] Says de Waal:

> The profound irony is that our noblest achievement—morality—has evolutionary ties to our basest behavior—warfare. The sense of community required by the former was provided by the latter. When we passed the tipping point between conflicting individual interests and shared interests, we ratcheted up the social pressure to make sure everyone contributed to the common good.[127]

These examples indicate that the roots of human morality are found in the social instincts we share with other animals. Morality, says de Waal, is "neither unique to us nor a conscious decision taken at a specific point in time; it is the product of social evolution."[128]

Chapter 22, Ways to Say "Should"

A central theme of this book is the value of the Goodness paradigm to guide our behavior. We are now in a position to understand the alternative, which I call the Rightness paradigm. By that term I mean a set of concepts revolving around moral rules and duties. What is morally right, in this view, is what conforms to moral rules, and we have a duty to obey those rules. This way of thinking is called "deontological," from a Greek word, *deon*, that means "duty."

According to this approach, an action is justified, regardless of its consequences, on the basis of a quality or characteristic of the act itself, its conformance to a rule. Morality is concerned with identifying and obeying moral rules. It is right—indeed, it is mandatory—to obey the rules and wrong to disobey them. Any particular act can be judged right or wrong according to whether and to what extent it conforms to the moral rules. A central concern, then, is to identify the rules so you can make sure you obey them.

The problem, of course, is how to determine what those moral rules are. I'll return to that issue shortly.

How the Mind Works Morally

It is undeniable that we have moral intuitions, that we have a sense of right and wrong. The six domains of moral intuition listed in the previous chapter are innate, meaning "organized in advance of experience."[129] Children do not have to learn from scratch all the rules of caring for others, being fair, being loyal, being respectful, being pure and resenting bullies. They have inbuilt mental mechanisms that allow them to learn the ways their culture activates the pre-existing moral inclinations.

There is some debate about whether the mind is composed of many little modules or a few big ones or something in between. By "module" evolutionary psychologists mean a computational mechanism that is "innate, fast, informationally encapsulated, [and] functionally specialized."[130] Is the mind a Swiss Army knife of many little mechanisms? Are there only a few such mechanisms, having to do with sense perception and language acquisition? Perhaps what is innate is the capacity to learn how to deal with things found in the ancestral environment, including the social world that engenders moral sentiments and judgments; and the specifics of what is learned vary from culture to culture. Haidt and Joseph think the latter hypothesis is most plausible. "For example, if there is an innate learning module for fairness, it generates a host of culture-specific unfairness-detection modules, such as a 'cutting-in-line detector' in cultures where people queue up, but not in cultures where they don't ... ."[131]

For the purposes of this chapter it does not matter what the mind is composed of. What does matter is that we now have an explanation for why people have a moral sense: because our ancestors faced specific adaptive problems in the social realm and, over thousands of generations, evolved mental mechanisms to handle them. We evolved this way because humans have to live with other humans in order to survive, and moral rules regulate how we get along together. A shared sense of morals makes for group cohesion, and those who are members of cohesive groups survive and reproduce better than those who aren't.

Philosophical Implications

That explanation is descriptive, not prescriptive. It tells us where the moral sense comes from, but not what to do in any given situation or what kind of person to try to become. We certainly have moral intuitions, but we still have to decide whether or not it makes sense to act on them. In making that decision we need to look at more than where they come from. We need to look at the consequences of our proposed actions and whether we expect them to have a good effect.

Moral norms have two functions according to Duke professor David Wong, interpersonal and intrapersonal: "The interpersonal function is to promote and regulate social cooperation. The intrapersonal function is to foster a degree of ordering among potentially conflicting motivational propensities, including self- and other-regarding motivations. This ordering serves to encourage people to become constructive participants in the cooperative life."[132]

In order to understand these two functions, it is helpful to take a closer look at the various types of moral judgments and what they entail for our behavior. Here is an illustration:[133]

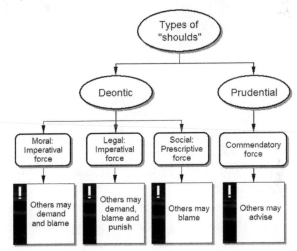

Moral and ethical judgments are all ways of saying "should:" telling someone what he or she should do (or refrain from doing) or should have done, or telling ourselves the same.[xviii] Moral rules are in the branch labeled "deontic." But the deontic is not the only type of "should;" another type is prudential. In deontic cases the "should" is a prescription or even a command. In the prudential case it is a recommendation. The force of our prescription or

---

[xviii] I do not distinguish between "moral" and "ethical," although some philosophers do, reserving the former for the Rightness paradigm of rights and obligations, and the latter for any situation in which advice or command is appropriate.

recommendation depends on the category in which the "should" is presented.

The first category is moral law (Deontic/Moral in the illustration). An example is "Thou shalt not steal" ("should" being stated in its strongest form, "shall"). In this case we feel justified in demanding that people obey the "should" and blaming them if they don't. The imperative provokes in us feelings of moral righteousness and indignation. And the imperative has a sense of universality, that it applies to everyone. This is the domain of what I call the Rightness paradigm.

The second category is legal law (Deontic/Legal in the illustration), such as defining misdemeanor or felony theft. In this case we feel justified in demanding that people obey and not only blaming but punishing them if they don't. The imperative has force, however, only within the context of the laws of a given political community.

The third category is social convention (Deontic/Social). An example is the rule that if one attends a wedding, one should bring a gift. In this case we may not demand obedience (you can't demand a gift) but we do feel justified in assigning blame for failure to comply, if not to the offender's face then in gossiping to others. Such a rule is clearly a matter of social agreement, not universal law, and applies only within a given community.

The fourth category is prudential evaluation (Prudential/ Commendatory), for example, that for good health one should eat lots of vegetables. In this case we may not demand but may certainly advise adherence to such a "should." And we may not blame or punish someone for failure to comply but may say the choice is foolish. This kind of judgment is in the Goodness paradigm, one of the features of which is that such judgments are objectively verifiable. We can study the effects of diet on health and discover factual evidence, so the recommendation is not just someone's opinion. The scope of applicability is interesting. Potentially such a judgment could be universal, but in practice it depends on context. Perhaps for a malnourished vegan, eating lots of vegetables would not be good, and instead he or she should try some meat. I claim that there is nothing that is good in itself.[134] When you are speaking about goodness, if you want to avoid confusion always ask "Good for whom? Good for what and under what circumstances?"

This taxonomy gives us some insights into the nature of rights and duties, the objects of moral judgment. There is a quite a large body of literature on the ontological status of moral entities, meaning the manner of their existence. They seem to be real, in that many people recognize them, but they can't be touched or felt or measured as physical objects can. Do they exist objectively, independent of our perception of them, as physical reality does? Are they merely social conventions? Are they somewhere in between?

There is good reason to believe that moral entities do not exist objectively because it is a matter of empirical fact that people disagree about them in a way that they do not disagree about physical reality. A study asked respondents in the United States and in India whether it would be morally wrong to steal a train ticket in order to attend a best friend's wedding. People in the US said it would be wrong to steal; people in India said it would be wrong *not* to steal, if that were the only way you could get to the wedding![135] This disagreement is clearly in a completely different category from, say, whether water always boils at the same temperature regardless of atmospheric pressure. You can observe and measure water boiling and come to a decisive answer, regardless of where you live. Cultural differences play no role at all in your answer about physical reality, but they do in your answer about moral reality.

This leads some to deny any reality to moral entities at all, and to label all moral judgments as false because they refer to fictional entities. This position, known as "moral error theory,"[136] goes a bit too far, I think, as it ignores our indubitable intuitions of right and wrong. (Not that the content of such intuitions is indubitable, but that we do have them is not to be doubted at all.) We could say that moral entities are just social conventions, but that statement is not strong enough. We do not get together and decide what we shall regard as right and wrong in the same way as we decide when to have tea every day. We really do seem to recognize something that exists independently of whether or not we agree that it exists.

My take on it is this: Moral entities are realities that are *intersubjectively constituted* within a community of practice, a social group, a culture or a society. By that I mean that within such a community or society, everybody agrees (more or less) on what they are, everybody treats them the same way and everybody acts as if they are real. So, for members of such a community, they *are* real.

The term "constitute" comes from the phenomenological insight, verified by cognitive psychology, that in large part our minds concoct what we perceive. We don't just see physical things; we make up what we see, based on sensory input that we do not make up. There is a large cognitive component in our experience, which we mostly overlook, but which sometimes becomes startlingly obvious.

Here is an example: A woman I know was walking across her ranch one day and stepped over a hose. Then she thought "That's odd. What is a hose doing here?" She turned and looked and saw that it was a snake. (Fortunately, she was wearing boots.) Before she recognized that it was a snake, she had constituted it as a hose. Was it really a hose? No. Did she really see a hose the first time? Yes, she did.

Similarly, we really do intuit that some things are right and others wrong, that some deeds are obligatory and others forbidden, that some actions can be demanded of us and others cannot, that some behavior is blameworthy, some praiseworthy and some neither. And considering the effects of honoring those intuitions or not—namely, the reactions of others in the community—the objects of our moral intuitions really do have reality.

Does that mean we are stuck with the morals our society constitutes for us? Not at all. Now that we recognize the true nature of moral entities, we can choose what to do about them.

But how shall we choose? This question actually presents a bit of a conundrum. Rationally, the sense of what is right and wrong, of what is our duty, loses its obligatory force. Constructed socially, moral entities are real but do not constrain our actions as physical reality does. When we recognize this state of affairs, a sort of spell is broken, and we do not see our world the same way as before; we are no longer taken in by moral reality. We are able to choose, within the constraints of our emotional and social conditioning, which duties to obey, or even whether to obey any at all. And we have this freedom even if we would rather not have it. You can't go back; you can't undo a realization about how the world works. As the existentialists say, we are condemned to be free.[137] Second-order thinking, our ability to consider in thought and imagination not just the world around us but ourselves as well, can seem like a burden because emotionally we still feel the force of these moral intuitions. We may know intellectually that it is not always wrong to steal a train ticket, but we still cringe at the thought of doing so. We seek a way to reconcile the antinomy of freedom and facticity.

Here is where the Goodness paradigm becomes useful. Since sensitivity to moral concerns is a part of our biological inheritance, it is difficult to imagine that we could ever get rid of it even if we wanted to. And we might not want to; moral intuitions enable us to live with others without having to think what to do all the time. So it behooves us to choose wisely what duties and rules to live by. And the way to choose wisely is by considering the effects of our choices.

Consider the injunction against stealing. Even though there could be some short-term gain for the thief, it is in a person's long-term interest to live in a society where people are honest. And being honest produces in us a greater internal harmony of feeling than being dishonest. There are benefits to playing by the rules. An honest person will be better off in the long run, even though in certain instances it might seem disadvantageous.

So if you are wise, you will notice the moral urge to be honest, the call of conscience, and decide to accept it. Even though it is a triggered response, you will let that response happen. You will adopt a policy of accepting such responses, of refraining from taking what is not yours even if the opportunity arises, and you will enjoy a happier life as a result.

Recall the function of moral norms: to promote social cooperation and well-being. Moral rules that promote well-being are worth following; moral rules that don't, aren't.

A Universal Morality

There are, however, some aspects of reality that make certain kinds of moral intuitions plausible as candidates for a universal morality. One of the hallmarks of moral judgments is that they are taken to be universal, applicable to everyone. If there are universal aspects of reality relevant to morality, then the claim that certain moral principles should always be observed and obeyed would make more sense. Three of these are empathy, nonzero-sum games and the nature of persuasive discourse.

Empathy

Humans have the capacity to feel what others feel, not telepathically, but in the sense that one person's emotions tend to arouse matching emotions in other people, much like sympathetic vibration of strings on a musical instrument. Physiologically, this effect is due to mirror neurons. "A mirror neuron is a neuron that fires both when an animal acts and when the animal observes the same action performed by another. Thus, the neuron 'mirrors' the behavior of the other, as though the observer were itself acting. Such neurons have been directly observed in primates and are believed to occur in humans, [where] brain activity consistent with that of mirror neurons has been found in the premotor cortex and the inferior parietal cortex."[138] Empathy is not a uniquely human capacity although it is more highly developed in humans than in other species. Ape researcher Frans de Waal says "Empathy is widespread among animals. It runs from body mimicry—yawning when others yawn—to emotional contagion in which the self resonates with fear or joy when it picks up fear or joy in others. At the highest level we find sympathy and targeted helping."[139] (Targeted helping is giving aid tailored to another's needs; it requires a distinction between self and other, recognition of the other's need and sympathy for the other's distress.)

Empathy is the foundation of compassion, but unfortunately the mere capacity for empathy does not ensure that virtue. Just as a saint is motivated by empathy to alleviate suffering, a fiend can use empathy as way of getting feedback on how effective his torture is. If we want to encourage compassion, we need to make a case for it.

The normative case for a morality based on compassion (as opposed to the descriptive assertion that humans do in fact feel moral impulses to care for and prevent harm to others) is that it makes sense for us to try to alleviate the suffering of others because to do so alleviates our own suffering. When someone is in distress, we feel it and are to some degree in distress ourselves. There two ways to alleviate that distress in ourselves. One is to ignore the other's suffering and our own discomfort. That may work for a time, but does not address the root cause; the discomfort, both theirs and ours, is likely to arise again. The other is to do something to alleviate the other person's distress. That is both more likely to fix the problem so it does not arise again and more fulfilling: in doing so we are exercising an innate capacity, we are functioning well. And when we function well, we experience happiness, fulfillment, *eudaimonia*.

Nonzero-sum games

There are many situations in which cooperation and fairness benefit all parties. These are called "nonzero-sum games," exchanges which produce wins for all parties rather than a win for some and a loss for others. As Steven Pinker observes,

> In many arenas of life, two parties are objectively better off if they both act in a nonselfish way than if each of them acts selfishly. You and I are both better off if we share our surpluses, rescue each other's children in danger and refrain from shooting at each other ... . Granted, I might be a bit better off if I acted selfishly at your expense and you played the sucker, but the same is true for you with me, so if each of us tried for these advantages, we'd both end up worse off. Any neutral observer, and you and I if we could talk it over rationally, would have to conclude that the state we should aim for is the one in which we both are unselfish.[140]

This is a purely pragmatic, prudential assessment, and like all such assessments, it has the advantage of being rooted in reality. Fairness, cooperation, caring and avoidance of harm are not only the results of evolutionary adaptation but are also good ideas for how to conduct ourselves in the present.

Rational persuasion

Pinker makes an interesting observation about the nature of attempts to convince or persuade someone to do something. In order to do so, we have to appeal to some sense of universality.

> [Rationality] cannot depend on the egocentric vantage point of the reasoner. If I appeal to you to do anything that affects me—to get off my foot, or tell me the time or not run me over with your car—then I can't do it in a way that privileges my interests over yours (say, retaining my right to run you over with my car) if I want you to take me seriously. Unless I am Galactic Overlord, I have to state my case in a way that would force me to treat you in kind. I can't act as if my interests are special just because I'm me and you're not.[141]

Appeals to general rules are more apt to be successful than citing special privilege. No doubt this is why many of humanity's moral philosophies, from the Golden Rule to the Categorical Imperative and beyond, have at their core the interchangeability of perspectives. To be just and fair, a moral rule should apply to two people in the same way if they were to trade places.

Need for reason

The sense of morality is easily subverted by maladaptive triggers. What was useful to guard against disease from tainted food is not useful when it leads us to view persons of another race as unclean or another religion as impure and evil. If we are to live well—that is, harmoniously and in a way that exercises our abilities in good way—we need to examine our intuitions critically, not just blindly follow them. Once we have decided what kinds of moral intuitions we want to obey and in what circumstances— that is, what kind of person we want to be—we can certainly rely on those intuitions so we do not have to deliberate tediously about every situation we face. But we do have to do the careful thinking in order to make such decisions, or else live a life prone to emotional tripwires that subvert us. Socrates said the unexamined life is not worth living. I would not go that far, but I do say that the examined life is far more likely to be satisfying.

And if you feel the need for an overarching duty, a sort of highest principle, let me suggest this: The best duty is the commitment to find ways to live that promote the well-being of yourself, your community and your environment. The highest and noblest endeavor, which we are free to regard as a duty if we wish, is to work for the good in all things.

Chapter 23, Religion

It can be a bit daunting to draw philosophical conclusions from the state of scientific belief. Scientific theories change with the addition of new evidence. Different theorists sometimes disagree, and the informed but non-expert onlooker does not know which to take as grounds for philosophizing. And the issue is particularly vexing in the social sciences, which do not lend themselves as easily as the physical sciences to experimental verification. Case in point: the evolutionary origins of religion.

That humans are religious is indisputable. Like morality, religion in one form or another seems to be a universal aspect of human culture. By "religion" I mean any form of socially organized relationship to what we might call an unseen realm of disembodied agency, including ancestors who are no longer living in the flesh; totemic spirits associated with places or objects; genies, angels and demons; deities such as the gods of the Greek pantheon; the all-knowing, all-powerful and eternal God of monotheism; and the All or Universal Soul of advanced mysticism.[xix] An intimate social relationship between living people and supernatural beings of some sort is characteristic of human societies everywhere.[142] The question for evolutionary psychology is twofold: how did religion come to be, and what advantages did it provide to our ancestors?

[xix] Buddhism and Taoism, arguably nontheistic religions, nevertheless stress the importance of something nonphysical that influences human affairs, which can be understood as an attenuated form of more-than-human agency.

The advantages seem straightforward. One aspect of religion is social cohesion; it "served as an extra cohesive force, besides the bonds of kinship, to hold societies together for such purposes as punishing freeloaders and miscreants or uniting in war."[143] Evolutionary theorists are divided on the historical causes of this effect. Does the explanation require the controversial notion of group selection, that genes can become fixed or spread in a population because of the benefits they bestow on groups, regardless of their effect on the fitness of individuals within that group?[144] Or is it instead merely that all humans benefit by being members of groups, and exhibit genetic or cultural traits that have evolved to enhance the ability to function well in a group, any group? In either case religion, like language and sensitivity to norms, may well be one such adaptation.

Another advantage is a sense of hope or confidence in the face of adverse circumstances. When confronted with danger or something fearsome, the believer does not succumb to despair and hopelessness. (Those who did, who gave up, did not survive to produce offspring.) Instead he or she calls on God—or the ancestors or the gods or guardian spirits, etc.—for help. As a person feels that help, he or she carries on, survives and thrives. This is the case regardless of whether the entity called on actually exists or not. Here is an example: (The author has found out he needs open-heart surgery.)

> My wife was raised Catholic, and though she's been a student of Buddhism for years, she still has an ability to pray aloud and unselfconsciously. The practice is alien to me, with my secular Jewish upbringing, as palm trees are to Kansas. But over the years, a tiny part of her ease in addressing the central mystery had rubbed off on me. That night, when she started praying, I joined her. As soon as I said the word *God* aloud, a fierce longing took hold of me, and I called out, in full voice, to something that had no face, no shape, no name. I called out for the faith I did not have. And, paradoxically, the act of calling out was its own answer. A trust in *something*—some strength that might get me through what was coming—

was kindled by the friction of my doubt rubbing up against my undeniable need. I had called out in the night, unashamed.[145]

It is a survival characteristic to feel that God is with you.

But how did this characteristic evolve in the first place? We can only speculate as there is little archeological evidence.

The so-called "New Atheists"—those who invoke science to denigrate religion with much the same fervor as some believers defend their faith—view religious beliefs not as useful adaptations, but as parasitic memes that have embedded themselves in human minds. (Recall that a *meme* is an idea, behavior or style that replicates from person to person within a culture much like genes replicate from generation to generation of living organisms.[146]) Such beliefs started out as mistakes but then took on a life of their own, they say.

Daniel Dennett, one such atheist, believes the origin of religion had to do with an extension of our species' aptitude for theory of mind, the ability to attribute mental states like our own to others. Humans have such an advanced capacity for what he calls the "intentional stance," the propensity to attribute beliefs, desires and a certain amount of cunning to anything that moves and seems to do so with intention, that we find it hard to turn it off.[147] Citing other researchers, Dennett calls this capacity a "hyperactive agency detection device," a term that is widely used to mean a cognitive module that readily—perhaps too readily—ascribes events in the environment to the behavior of agents. Such a tendency confers a survival benefit: it is better to avoid an imaginary predator than be killed by a real one.[148] We are the descendants of those whose agency detectors were overly, not insufficiently, vigilant.

Dennett's argument, in brief is this:

- When a person died, our ancestors got rid of the body, but had the persistent memory of the living person, so they thought of him or her as still existing as a ghost or spirit.[149] That is the hyperactive agency detector at work.
- Then they started asking the deceased or the spirits for advice.[150]

- From there it is short step to divination—ceremonies and rituals to find out what the gods know—and then to appeasement and prayer, to try to influence the gods to be good to us.[151]
- Finally we get self-serving shamans and priests who promote belief in their authority as ways to enhance their own self-esteem, power and wealth.[152]

At this point humans are treating the gods not just as disembodied beings who know things, but as agents who do things, who cause things to happen to us, both calamities and good fortune. Philosopher and researcher Robert Wright observes that the notion of causality was probably originally rooted in agency:[xx]

> People reared in modern scientific societies may consider it only natural to ponder some feature of the world—the weather, say—and try to come up with a mechanistic explanation couched in the abstract language of natural law. But evolutionary psychology suggests that a much more *natural* way to explain *anything* is to attribute it to a humanlike agent. This is the way we're "designed" by natural selection to explain things. Our brain's capacity to think about causality—to ask why something happened and come up with theories that help us predict what will happen in the future—evolved in a specific context: other brains. When our distant ancestors first asked "Why," they weren't asking about the behavior of water or weather or illness; they were asking about the behavior of their peers. ... To answer a "why" question—such as "Why did the thunderstorm come just as that baby was being born?"—with anything *other* than a humanlike creature would have been kind of strange.[153]

With this observation, we are moving from away from genetics alone. We may be genetically endowed with a mental module for understanding other minds—the agency detection device[154]—but the way that module plays out into beliefs about gods and

---

[xx] In philosophical terms, the belief in agent causality preceded the belief in physical causality. See Meacham, "Do Humans Have Free Will?"

supernatural spirits goes beyond genetics. Religion is a cultural phenomenon, not a genetic one. The evolutionary analysis continues to be relevant, however, because culture evolves much as biology does. Religious beliefs and practices are memes, and truth-value is not the only attribute that causes memes to jump from mind to mind. Memetic replication can paradoxically favor ideas that are hard to confirm.

The very idea of gods or a God is a catchy meme. As Wright puts it,

> We would expect the following kinds of memes to be survivors in the dog-eat-dog world of cultural evolution: claims that (a) are somewhat strange, surprising, counterintuitive; (b) illuminate sources of fortune and misfortune; (c) give people a sense that they can influence these sources; (d) are by their nature hard to test decisively. In this light, the birth of religion doesn't seem so mysterious.[155]

Once religion has been born, other mechanisms ensure its propagation. One is the natural tendency of people to believe what others in the group believe. "If you are surrounded by a small group of people on whom your survival depends, rejecting the beliefs that are most important to them will not help you live long enough to get your genes into the next generation."[156] Then, as belief systems become more complex and mysterious, self-serving motives of the priestly class contribute to their propagation. Shamans and priests promote belief in their authority as ways to enhance their own self-esteem, power and wealth.[157] And finally we get full-blown rationales such as that belief in God is the foundation of morality and in any case is important for its own sake.[158]

This story of the evolutionary origins of religion is, say the New Atheists, adequate to account for how it came to be. "Religion arose out of a hodgepodge of genetically based mental mechanisms designed by natural selection for thoroughly mundane purposes."[159] We do not need to postulate the actual existence of God—or gods or deities or spirit beings—to explain religion.

On this view, particularly in light of the sorry history of much of organized religion, religious beliefs and practices are outmoded and dangerous residues of our evolutionary heritage. If they ever did serve a useful purpose, that purpose has long been superseded, say the New Atheists. At best, God is a social hallucination or, to put it more kindly, something constituted intersubjectively. Belief in God is as mistaken as the belief in an external, objective morality.

But there is another view, equally steeped in evolutionary psychology, that says that religion has positive benefits.

Psychologist Jonathan Haidt, in his intellectually superb *The Righteous Mind*, claims that religion has been evolutionarily adaptive because it binds groups together in a way that enhances the survival prospects of their members. He observes that despite our innate tendency to favor ourselves, human beings are able at times to be quite unselfish in service to the group or groups of which they are a member. We are not only selfish, we are also *groupish*:

> We love to join teams, clubs, leagues, and fraternities. We take on group identities and work shoulder to shoulder with strangers toward common goals so enthusiastically that it seems as if our minds were designed for teamwork. ... Our minds contain a variety of mental mechanisms that make us adept at promoting our *group's* interest in competition with other groups. We are not saints, but we are sometimes good team players.[160]

He attributes this trait to group competition.

> Groups compete with groups, and that competition favors groups composed of team players—those who are willing to cooperate and work for the good of the group, even when they could do better by slacking, cheating, or leaving.[161]

He goes on to give a number of reasons for believing that the tendency to be a team player is not only cultural but has become a physical, genetic trait. This idea is a group selection theory: some groups fare better than others in the competition to turn resources into offspring,[162] and members of those groups come to have specific genetic traits that help the group survive, traits such as a tendency to be loyal to the group and feelings of sanctity toward what others in the group value. "Groups in which these traits are common will replace groups in which they are rare, even if those genes impose a small cost on their bearers (relative to those that lack them within each group)."[163]

Can group membership really influence the genetic makeup of its members? Consider this (one among several arguments that Haidt advances): If you want to increase egg output, you would breed only those chickens that lay the most eggs, right? Actually that doesn't work. In the egg industry, where chickens live in crowded cages, the best layers are also the most aggressive, and breeding such hens causes more aggression and fewer eggs. A geneticist tried a different approach:

> He worked with cages containing twelve hens each, and he simply picked the *cages* that produced the most eggs in each generation. The he bred *all* of the hens in those cages to produce the next generation. Within just three generations, aggression levels plummeted. ... Total eggs produced per hen jumped from 91 to 237 [after several more generations], mostly because the hens started living longer, but also because they laid more eggs per day. The group-selected hens were more productive than were those subjected to individual-level selection.[164]

Haidt claims humans have become adapted to group living in much the same way. Natural, not artificial, selection has caused us to be groupish as well as selfish. As Haidt puts it, we are 90 percent ape and ten percent bee.[165]

I am not going to adjudicate whether this phenomenon would best be called group selection, multi-level selection or "individual selection in the context of groups."[166] But it is undeniable that humans function best in groups, and it does seem plausible that natural selection has produced specific adaptations in us to serve that end. One of them is the propensity to submerge self-interest in favor of service to the group. Dennett, in fact, recognizes the same phenomenon, but chalks it up to cultural evolution—memes, not genes.[167]

What Haidt adds to the debate is the recognition that it is not just our behavior that inclines us to service to the group; it is our experience as well. It can be quite agreeable to lose our sense of individuality in a feeling of unity with something larger than ourselves. He gives a number of examples: the sense of well-being felt by soldiers when drilling in close order; the ecstasy of collective dancing; awe in nature; the effect of certain hallucinogenic drugs; and more.[168] He does not mention the rhythmic movements and breath practices of the Sufis, the chanting and hand-clapping of Hindu *bhajan* and *kirtan* (devotional singing and dancing), or the similar enthusiasm of certain evangelical Christians, but they certainly qualify as well. From the point of view of the phenomenology of lived experience, it seems that we thrive on ecstasy.

Haidt calls this experience being in a sort of hive mind, "a mind-set of 'one for all, all for one'" in which we are willing to work for the good of the group as a whole, not solely for our own advancement within it.[169] Just as evolution has caused sweets to taste good to us, it has caused the experience of being in harmony with others, of moving in unison and sensing that we are part of a larger whole, to be profoundly satisfying.

And religion is one of the ways we create that experience of being in harmony. This version of the story of the rise of religion starts in the same place as that of the New Atheists: our hyperactive agency detection device gave rise to belief in disembodied ancestors, spirits, gods and the like. But far from being memetic parasites, such beliefs served a positive benefit: the cohesion of the group. The gods condemn selfish and divisive behaviors, and the gods can see what you are doing. It is a fact verified by experiment that people act more ethically when they think somebody is watching and less ethically when they think nobody can see them. "Creating gods who can see everything, and who hate cheaters and oath-breakers, turns out to be a very good way to reduce cheating and oath breaking."[170] And if those gods are said to punish the group for its members' infractions, then people in the group will be more vigilant towards and gossipy about each other's behavior. "Angry gods make shame more effective as a means of social control."[171]

The upshot is this:

The very ritual practices that the New Atheists dismiss as costly, inefficient and irrational turn out to be a solution to one of the hardest problems humans face: cooperation without kinship.[172] Gods and religions ... are group-level adaptations for producing cohesiveness and trust.[173]

And there is evidence that religious people are more kind, generous and charitable than nonreligious people. This fact is true regardless of the specifics of the theology. What really matters is how enmeshed people are in relationships with their fellow religionists. It is religious belonging that matters for neighborliness, not religious believing.[174] The New Atheists have it wrong; certainly many religious beliefs are irrational, but that is not the point. The point is that religious belonging, regardless of belief, triggers altruism, although it is often a parochial altruism, aimed at members of the ingroup.[175]

Does this mean that religion is a good thing, and we should embrace it? Well, no, not necessarily. We need to be choosy. Evolution has equipped us with a desire for and a response to being subsumed in something greater than our individual selves. But that instinct can be triggered by all sorts of things: football games, social clubs, political movements, religious congregations, and more. The yearning to be absorbed in the hive can be exploited by a fascist rally as well as evoked by a mystical dance. Devotion to the ingroup can be seen in a mafia gang as well as a Quaker meeting. Given that we have an innate predilection to lose ourselves in something greater, it is up to us to decide where to place our allegiance.

There is no question that hideous things have been done in the name of religion: the slaughter of infidels; the abuse of children and women; lies, deceit and hypocrisy; arrogant exercise of domineering power. And there is no question that many beautiful and noble things have been done in the name of religion: feeding the hungry; clothing the naked; housing the homeless; comforting the afflicted; standing up for the oppressed against the abuses of the dominators. If you feel drawn to religion, you get to choose which it will be.

As Bob Dylan says, you're gonna have to serve somebody.[176] Will it be the monolith of a fascist state or the community of the faithful? Will it be the rigidity of a top-down institution or the living flexibility of a decentralized organism?

Best of all would be the fellowship of those committed to working for the good in all things.

Chapter 24, When Intelligence Fails

Fine-tuned and highly developed as it is, our intelligence—our ability to respond flexibly and adaptively to new situations—is not always accurate. We do not always perceive reality accurately, and not just because we make occasional mistakes. There are ways in which systematic susceptibility to illusion and error seem to be built in evolutionarily, and it is important to understand those ways in order to counteract them. This chapter explains several of these mechanisms of cognitive impairment.

Self-Deception

The basic evolutionary mechanism is propagation of replicators. The unit of biological replication is the gene, and what has shaped our cognitive capacities is what has enabled the survival and replication of the genes that govern their development and expression. Consequently, in most cases we are finely tuned for discovery of truth, but not always. We are certainly adapted for accurate perception of physical reality, because physical reality doesn't change, but the same is not true for social reality. How we treat physical reality does not change its properties; it will behave toward us as it always does. But how we treat others is a different story. Other people treat us differently depending on what they think of us, and we are evolved to induce them to think of us well because doing so increased our ancestors' ability to survive and reproduce. That may mean deceiving them, and one of the best ways to deceive others is to deceive yourself.

Such deception can be seen in three areas: sexual mating, reciprocal altruism and social hierarchy.

The Mating Game

Genetically it is in the interest of both parents that their off-spring survive, but males and females—of all species—have different strategies to accomplish this end.[177] The male's strategy is to impregnate as many females as possible. His biological investment is small; he contributes a tiny bit of sperm and then his job is over. His "essential role may end with copulation, which involves a negligible expenditure of energy and materials on his part, and only a momentary lapse of attention from matters of direct concern to his safety and well-being."[178] The female's strategy is to be choosy about which males she will mate with because her investment is much larger. She has to sit on the egg or carry the fetus much longer, and this constraint limits her chances for passing her genes to the next generation. For her "copulation may mean a commitment to a prolonged burden, in both the mechanical and physiological sense."[179] Females who picked the fittest males had more robust offspring, who in turn had a penchant for picking the fittest males, so females typically prefer males who exhibit signs of fitness, whether that be strength, speed, intelligence, big antlers, fancy feathers or some other quality.

Over eons of evolutionary time many species developed courtship, the male's advertisement of how fit he is and the female's discrimination among advertisers. In such a situation it would be in the genetic interest of males to advertise being more fit than they actually are—to become showoffs—and it would be in the interest of the females to become even more discriminating. Fast-forward to human society, with its elaborate culture born of language and big brains. With the development of parental care by the male (known technically as male parental investment), an aspect of the pair-bonding that is one of the things that distinguishes us from chimps, bonobos and other primates, the woman's choice of a mate is even more important. She wants (whether consciously or not; we are talking about genetic urges, not rational calculation) a man who will stick around and provide food and other resources for her offspring. Human females prefer men who have high social status, wealth, power, ambition and industry. More importantly (because those traits would also be desirable in species without high male parental investment), women look for men who are generous, trustworthy and who show enduring commitment, because those traits will ensure that he will nurture her offspring. Men in turn have no genetic interest in raising a child fathered by someone else, so when looking for a marriage partner (as opposed to a purely sexual liaison) they look for women who will be chaste and sexually faithful.

Hence, men learn to portray themselves as being emotionally committed; and females, for their part, tend to portray themselves as committed and virtuous as well. In both cases—and here is where self-deception comes in—it is much easier to portray yourself in a certain light if you believe that light to be true of yourself. Hence, both men and women sometimes deceive themselves. As Robert Wright says, "One effective way to deceive someone is to believe what you're saying. In this context that means being blinded by love."[180] "Men and women may mislead each other—and even, in the process, themselves—about the likely endurance of their commitment or about their likely fidelity."[181]

Reciprocal Altruism

The term "altruism" has a special meaning in evolutionary biology: "behavior that benefits another organism ... while being apparently detrimental to the organism performing the behavior, benefit and detriment being defined in terms of contribution to inclusive fitness."[182] ("Inclusive fitness" means the ability of an organism not only to produce and support its own offspring, but to support genetically related offspring as well, such as children, siblings, cousins, etc.[183]) There are two types, kin altruism and reciprocal altruism. Kin altruism occurs when an organism helps another to which it is genetically related; and the genetic mechanism is straightforward: "If an individual dies in order to save ten close relatives, one copy of the kin-altruism gene may be lost, but a larger number of copies of the same gene is saved."[184] The gene for such altruism will be carried forward to the next generation, hence continuing the behavior.

The other type is reciprocal altruism, which takes place when one individual expends energy to help another, genetically unrelated individual; and either at that time or later the latter does something to help the former. For instance, a man jumps in a river to save someone else, not his kin, putting himself in danger. Another example: certain fish clean parasites from other fish, even swimming into the other fish's mouth to do so, and the other fish does not eat the one that is cleaning. Robert Trivers, in a classic and much-cited paper, says "under certain conditions natural selection favors these altruistic behaviors because in the long run they benefit the organisms performing them."[185] In other words, reciprocal altruism is selected for because there are benefits to the altruist. In the case of the fish, the cleaning fish gets food and the cleaned fish gets rid of parasites. In the case of the rescuer, the benefit is that in a society where saving people is regarded as noble or heroic, someone would in turn save him if he were in a similar plight.

Trivers defines several conditions under which altruistic behavior evolves. The first is that the cost to the giver is less than the benefit to the recipient, where cost and benefit are defined as decrease or increase in the chances of the relevant genes propagating to the next generation. He uses the term "altruistic situation" to refer to such a circumstance and says that altruistic behavior would be selected for under three conditions: (1) that there are many such altruistic situations in the life of the altruist; (2) that a given altruist repeatedly interacts with the same small set of individuals; and (3) that pairs of altruists are put in symmetrical altruistic situations, such that one can help the other roughly as much as the other can help the one.[186] All three of these conditions obtained in the environment of evolutionary adaptedness, so it is not surprising that we have an urge to be altruistic.

Imagine living in a Neolithic band of hunters. On any given day you might have a forty percent chance of catching some game. When you did, you would give some to others who were not so lucky; and when you didn't, they would give some to you. This assures you of a steady supply of food regardless of your own daily catch. Everybody would benefit; and, more to the point, the genes for such altruistic behavior would get passed to the next generation. Such behavior applies, by the way, to foods whose supply is erratic but not to foods whose supply is relatively fixed, like the products of gardening or agriculture. In the latter case giving away food would be pointless, because there would be no need to assure a future supply. Anthropologists studying foraging cultures have indeed found that "High-variance foods are shared, low-variance foods are hoarded."[187]

Sometimes it pays an individual to cheat. "Cheating" means simply "failure to reciprocate; no conscious intent or moral connotation is implied."[188] If an individual receives a benefit but then fails to reciprocate, then it has come out ahead. So genes for that behavior will proliferate. But then other individuals will start to detect cheaters and refuse to provide benefits. Their genes will proliferate more than the genes of those who give to cheaters without return. Then some individuals will learn how to cheat more effectively. Then others will get more sophisticated about detecting cheaters; and we end up with a sort of arms race—over many generations—in which members of the species get very good both at cheating and at detecting cheaters. Cheating may be gross—failure to reciprocate at all—or subtle, "always attempting to give less than one was given or ... to give less than the partner would give if the situation were reversed."[189] In either case, there is selection pressure both to get better at cheating and to get better at detecting cheaters.

In humans the ability to detect cheaters is taken to an extreme. Not only do people remember who has reciprocated and who hasn't, but they learn from others. We get a reputation based on gossip in the community. Perhaps one of the things that drove humans to develop such large brains and cognitive capacities was the increasing need to keep track of all the relationships in the tribe and compute who owes what to whom, who can be trusted and who can't, and so forth.

Everybody wants to be known as a trustworthy reciprocal altruist, not a cheater. Whether or not the desire is conscious, everyone has an interest in having a good reputation, because that is the way to acquire resources to sustain life and have offspring. One of the ways we tell whether someone is trustworthy, particularly whether they might be a subtle cheater, is by assessing their motives and the depth and sincerity of their emotions.

Emotions play a key role. The emotion of gratitude probably arose to regulate response to altruistic acts and the emotion of sympathy arose to motivate altruism as a function of the plight of the recipient.[190] The emotion of guilt probably arose "to motivate the cheater to compensate [for] his misdeed and to behave reciprocally in the future, and thus to prevent the rupture of reciprocal relationships."[191] Liking (the emotion of affection) is what initiates and maintains an altruistic partnership, and anger—in this context—protects someone who has been cheated from falling for it again.[192] We do not have much deliberate control over our emotions, so if someone shows these emotions genuinely, we trust them. But if they seem cold and calculating in doing something altruistic, it is likely that under different circumstances they might not be so helpful. We can't count on them.

Now we can understand the selection pressure for self-deception. It enables a person to be more believable when showing deceitful emotion. Wright says "We deceive ourselves in order to deceive others better."[193] Trivers says if "deceit is fundamental to animal communication, then there must be strong selection to spot deception and this ought, in turn, to select for a degree of self-deception, rendering some facts and emotions unconscious so as not to betray—by the subtle signs of self-knowledge—the deception being practiced."[194]

We are not to blame for this strategy. It is not something anybody deliberately cooked up. Indeed, it would not work if it were deliberate because it works only if it is unconscious. But it is part of our nature.

Social Hierarchy

In human society, as in many other species, the higher your social status, the greater the rewards, both for yourself and for the likelihood of passing your genes on to the next generation. We are highly attuned to status and prone to inflate our own accomplishments and good character and denigrate those of others. Robert Wright sums it up nicely:

> Status is a relative thing. Your gain is someone else's loss. And vice versa: someone else's loss is your gain ... . The best way to convince people of something ... is to believe what you're saying. One would therefore expect, in a

hierarchical species endowed with language, that the organisms would often play up their own feats, downplay the feats of others, and do both things with conviction.[195]

That's why when we win, we believe it is due to our skill and prowess, but when somebody else wins, it's because they got lucky.[196]

Summary of Self-Deception

In these and other ways, we are systematically blind to our own shortcomings and impure motives. Not completely, of course. We do have enough intelligence to be able to notice and think about ourselves and how we are thinking, feeling and behaving, but it requires some effort to do so. It helps to know something about the mechanisms and typical occasions for self-deception.

Maladaptation

Self-deception in the social realm is an evolved characteristic that is still—from a gene-centered point of view—applicable and effective today. But there are ways in which our cognitive machinery is not so useful today because conditions have changed since the time of the environment of evolutionary adaptedness (EEA). Our mental modules are evolved to handle the environment our Pleistocene ancestors lived in, but we don't live there anymore. In many ways the current environment does not match the EEA, so some of our behavior is maladapted to current conditions. Here are a few examples.

Road rage, the well-known condition in which we get irrationally angry at other drivers, can be viewed as an outgrowth of primitive theory of mind. We encounter a bunch of large, fast-moving objects and interpret them as agents with goals. When one comes up rapidly from behind, we see it as a threat. When one cuts in front of us we interpret it as hostility and get mad. We do not have the perceptual cues that we get from seeing people's faces that might meliorate our judgments, so we are left only with primitive, instinctual responses. It takes some effort of will and conscious, cold cognition to overcome them.

We are adapted to crave fatty, sweet and salty foods, which are nutrient-dense and were somewhat rare in the EEA. In modern times they are abundant, in part because people who manufacture them go to great pains to make them appeal to our primitive tastes,[197] but such manufactured foods are simpler and contain fewer nutrients than their naturally occurring analogues. Consequently in the developed nations many people are obese and unhealthy because they eat too much junk food and not enough healthy, natural foods. Again, it takes some effort of will and deliberate thought to overcome artificially reinforced cravings and form habits of healthy eating.

Advertising of expensive products appeals to an unconscious instinct that they will either enhance or signal our fitness, much as peacock feathers signal that the male displaying them is strong enough to afford such conspicuous waste and hence would be a good mate. In humans this instinct is left over from a time when we lived in small bands and rarely encountered strangers. But nowadays making such displays to strangers makes little sense. Evolutionary psychologist Dr. Geoffrey Miller says "We evolved as social primates who hardly ever encountered strangers in prehistory. So we instinctively treat all strangers as if they're potential mates or friends or enemies. But your happiness and survival today don't depend on your relationships with strangers. It doesn't matter whether you get a nanosecond of deference from a shopkeeper or a stranger in an airport."[198] Once again, it takes deliberate thought to overcome the instinctual, but unhelpful, appeal of certain kinds of advertising.

Modern warfare is an example of primitive instincts run amok with greatly exaggerated destructive potential. Many, many species, including chimpanzees, our closest genetic relatives, exhibit territoriality and hostile behavior to other members of the same species. Not surprisingly, humans do too. But we, with our big brains and greatly increased intelligence, have so augmented our ability to inflict harm that the potential exists to destroy life as we know it on our home planet. Careful, deliberate thought and attention are needed to inhibit instinctual aggressive reactions.

We are subject to sometimes disastrous surprises from phenomena known as "Black Swans." A Black Swan is a highly improbable event with massive consequences, so-called because for many years people thought all swans were white. Nassim Nicholas Taleb, successful securities trader and best-selling author, defines it as follows:

> What we call a Black Swan (and capitalize it) is an event with the following three attributes. First it is an outlier, as it lies outside the realm of regular expectations, because nothing in the past can convincingly point to its possibility. Second it carries an extreme impact. Third ... [we] concoct explanations for its occurrence after the fact.[199]

Examples of Black Swans abound (as of early 21st Century): The terrorist attack on New York City of September 11, 2001; the rise of the Internet; the demise of the Soviet bloc; the rise of Islamic fundamentalism; the Lebanese civil war of 1975-1990, which erupted unexpectedly after a thousand years of peace; and many more. None of these were anticipated before they happened. Taleb says they weren't anticipated because our minds are adapted to an earlier environment and now circumstances have changed. Some of his speculations are unlikely, but these seem plausible: "In a primitive environment, the relevant is the sensational ... [but now we are in] a world in which the relevant is often boring, nonsensational."[200] Furthermore, "Our emotional apparatus is designed for linear causality. ... We are too narrow-minded a species to consider the possibility of events straying from our mental projections."[201] But Black Swan events are precisely not the result of trends that can be predicted with ease. Taleb gives a number of tips for overcoming this maladaptation, all of which involve exerting some effort to break out of habitual modes of thought. Fortunately, he says "the logical part of our mind, that 'higher' one, which distinguishes us from animals, can override our animal instincts."[202] He is referring to what I call our capacity for second-order thinking.

Daniel Kahneman, a Nobel-prize-winning psychologist, has described at length many of the ways our cognitive apparatus fails to provide accurate results. What I have been calling hot and cold cognition, he names "System 1" and "System 2."

System 1 operates automatically and quickly with little or no effort and no sense of voluntary control.

System 2 allocates attention to the effortful mental activities that demand it, including complex computations. The operations of System 2 are often associated with the subjective experience of agency, choice, and concentration.[203]

System 2 requires far more effort than System 1, and because we have a limited amount of mental energy we often rely on System 1 even when careful reflection would reveal that it is wrong. Kahneman says "the idea of mental energy is more than a mere metaphor. The nervous system consumes more glucose than most other parts of the body, and effortful mental activity appears to be especially expensive."[204] Our thinking goes wrong when we fail to pay attention. "The often-used phrase 'pay attention' is apt: you dispose of a limited budget of attention that you can allocate to activities, and if you try to go beyond your budget, you will fail."[205] We are, in a sense, lazy, but this laziness has quite understandably sound evolutionary origins. Our ancestors were the ones who honed their System 1 capabilities to perfection, reserving scarce energy for System 2 thinking only when it was really needed.

Kahneman describes a surprisingly large array of cognitive biases with names such as "availability heuristic," "affect heuristic," "confirmation bias," "halo effect" and the like. His hope is that if we put names on them we will be more likely to spot them when they crop up. In other words, we can augment our capacity for second-order thinking, which is built on System 2 capabilities, by recognizing the patterns we find in ourselves that lead to hasty generalization.

There are numerous other examples of our inability to cognize with perfect accuracy—or even good-enough accuracy—the world we live in. Daniel Gilbert's *Stumbling on Happiness*, for instance, describes in some detail the difficulties we have in imagining our own future and predicting how happy we will be if certain things come to pass, things that we ourselves strive to achieve. The point is that we should not assume that all of our perceptions and judgments are accurate, since in many ways we no longer live in the environment in which our cognitive capacities evolved.

Afflictive Emotion

Recall that emotion in evolutionary psychology is more than just a felt quality such as fear or contentment. Emotion is an overarching cognitive program that sets an organism's highest-level goals. An emotion is, in effect, a strategy for coping with reality; and some strategies work better than others.

Buddhist psychology calls certain emotions "afflictive" or "destructive" or "obscuring," meaning not only that they are harmful to the person experiencing them and to others, but that they distort our perception of reality, which is itself a kind of harm.[206] Some of the obvious ones are hatred, attachment, pride, confusion and jealousy.[207] They all have the characteristic that they impair our judgment, they interfere with clear thinking. "Obscuring emotions impair one's freedom by chaining thoughts in a way that compels us to think, speak, and act in a biased way."[208]

In this respect, Buddhism recognized thousands of years ago the phenomenon of emotional restimulation. (See *Chapter 19, The Overlooked Adaptation*.) To recapitulate, restimulation is reacting without the benefit of careful thought to a current situation as one did to an earlier, painful situation. We are, as is it were, overcome with emotion. Hence, our reaction may not be effective in producing a beneficial outcome. (Some restimulations do not have an intense felt component, but they influence thought and behavior nevertheless. Emotions need not be conscious—that is, attended to—to be operative.) Afflictive emotion is one of the causes of cognitive failure to perceive reality accurately.

* * *

Obviously, failure to perceive reality accurately leads to impairment of our ability to cope with it. But even when we perceive reality accurately, we sometimes find ourselves acting in ways counter to what we intend. It is not only our cognition that fails but our will also. That failure is the subject of the next chapter.

Chapter 25, The Rider and the Elephant

Psychologist Jonathan Haidt has a wonderful metaphor for human existence: a rider on an elephant. We each have a two-fold nature. The rider part is how we like to think of ourselves, as rational beings in charge of our actions. The elephant part is the mass of instinctual desires and reactions that really, in a great many cases, determines what we do. Says Haidt,

> The image that I came up with ... was that I was a rider on the back of an elephant. I'm holding the reins in my hands, and by pulling one way or the other I can tell the elephant to turn, to stop, or to go. I can direct things, but only when the elephant doesn't have desires of his own. When the elephant really wants to do something, I'm no match for him.[209]

Evolution does not work in a straight line. New structures and capacities are built on the framework of what has gone before, and the old structures and capacities remain in place. This is true of the human mind and is an explanation of why our rational thinking, the rider, does not always successfully guide our behavior. Haidt cautions against believing that conscious verbal thinking has complete power to guide our decision-making. It certainly has some power, but so does the elephant, the automatic mental processes and emotional reactions that have a great influence on our behavior regardless of—and in many cases in opposition to—our conscious intent.

We have all had the experience of wanting to do something—say, refrain from eating something tasty but unhealthy, or do some unpleasant but needed task—but then not doing it. It is as

if our will has no power. (And this is one reason why some speculate that free will is an illusion.) Haidt gives a number of reasons
for this phenomenon.

The brain is not the only seat of mentality. Neural processing
occurs also in the intestine, which contains over 100 million neurons. This "gut brain" is largely autonomous from the conscious
mentality seated in the brain in our head.[210] Called the Enteric
Nervous System, it controls digestion but can also influence
moods and emotions.[211]

*The rational and verbal part of our brain can get divorced
from other parts.* The left hemisphere of the brain processes information differently from the right hemisphere. The left hemisphere is specialized for language and analysis; the right, for pattern recognition. Patients whose brain has been split by severing
the mass of nerves joining the two, the corpus callosum, show
surprising behavior. The left brain can come up with a verbal
explanation for a response to a stimulus given to the right brain
only and hidden from the left, but the explanation has nothing to
do with the true stimulus.[212] This process is called "confabula-
tion," and the condition is also found in people with intact brains
when they fill in gaps in memory and believe their memories to
be true.[213] Haidt says

> [Split-brain studies show that] the mind is a confed-
> eration of modules capable of working independently and
> even, sometimes, at cross-purposes. ... One of these mod-
> ules is good at inventing convincing explanations for your
> behavior, even when it has no knowledge of the causes of
> your behavior. [This] "interpreter module" is, essentially,
> the rider.[214]

*Various parts of the brain evolved at different times and have
different functions.* The oldest parts, in the center and bottom,
close to the spinal cord, connect it to the senses and to the rest of
the body, so perception of the world can guide behavior. A newer
part, the limbic system, surrounds the old brain and contains
sections that coordinate basic drives and motivations, memory
and emotional learning and response. The newest part, the neocortex, is the seat not only of conscious reasoning—the ability to

think, plan and decide what to do with some degree of freedom from immediate stimuli—but of sophisticated emotional processing as well. We have seen such processing in the discussion of moral emotions, and it applies in many other areas as well. Whenever the world presents us with the possibility of reward or punishment, of pleasure, pain, loss or gain, part of the neocortex becomes very active. "When you feel yourself drawn to a meal, a landscape or an attractive person, or repelled by a dead animal, [or] a bad song ..., your orbitofrontal cortex is working hard to give you an emotional feeling of *wanting* to approach or get away."[215]

We may think of ourselves as rational, thoughtful creatures, but it is hot cognition, driven by automatic, instinctual emotional reactions, that most often drives our behavior. And in fact such emotion is a crucial component of that cognition. Research has found that people with a damaged orbitofrontal cortex lose much of their ability to feel emotion, even though their ability to reason is intact. In that state they do not act solely on the basis of reasoned argument. Instead, they have trouble acting at all! They spend hours examining alternatives and are unable to make simple decisions or set goals.

> They must examine the pros and cons of every choice with their reasoning, but in the absence of feeling they see little reason to pick one or the other. When the rest of us look out at the world, our emotional brains have instantly and automatically appraised the possibilities. One ... usually jumps out at us as the best ... . We need only use reason to weigh the pros and cons when two or three possibilities seem equally good.[216]

This sophisticated emotionality comprises much of the elephant:

> Reason and emotion must both work together to create intelligent behavior, but emotion (a major part of the elephant) does most of the work. When the neocortex came along, it made the rider possible but it made the elephant much smarter, too.[217]

The upshot of all this is that *our brains function in two modes, controlled and automatic; and the automatic mode is far more pervasive.* The controlled mode is the mode of cold cognition, step-by-step reasoning to solve a problem that is new to us. The automatic mode is everything else: the "gut brain," hot cognition, emotional response, instant pattern recognition, intuition and genetically conditioned fundamental urges and drives. "It is no accident that we find carnal pleasures so rewarding" says Haidt. "Our brains, like rat brains, are wired so that food and sex give us little bursts of dopamine, the neurotransmitter that is the brain's way of making us enjoy the activities that are good for the survival of our genes."[218]

In evolutionary terms, the rider—the verbal, analytic, consciously rational part of us—evolved to serve the elephant. Those organisms (our ancestors) who developed the ability to foresee and plan, to think about things not immediately present, survived and reproduced better than those who didn't; but the point, from a gene-centered perspective, was to survive and reproduce, not to create art, civilization, morality and philosophy. So when our conscious thinking runs contrary to our instinctual urges, oftentimes conscious thinking loses. Much as we would like to think of ourselves as rational beings, in charge of our destiny, in fact "the rider is an advisor or servant; not a king, president, or charioteer with a firm grip on the reins."[219]

Haidt suggests that it is a mistake to think of ourselves primarily as rational beings: "Our minds are loose confederations of parts, but we identify and pay too much attention to one part: conscious verbal thinking."[220] The mistake is twofold, both conceptual and strategic. Conceptually, to identify ourselves with the rider is incorrect, for all the reasons listed in this chapter. Strategically, to do so just doesn't work. The non-automatic portion of our mind has relatively little power to cause behavior, at least by directly confronting the elephant and commanding it to do something. Instead, we need to learn how to guide and influence the elephant, a matter of self-knowledge and practical skill.

To Know The Good …

"To know the good is to do it." Socrates does not say these ex-act words in Plato's Dialogues, but it is a good summary of a cer-tain ancient Greek idea. "Good" means beneficial; what is good for someone is what is beneficial or helpful to that person and enables that person to be happy. Socratic scholar Laszlo Versenyi puts it this way:

> The good … is that which makes man happy by ful-filling his nature. One can go no further than this and ask why men want to be happy rather than miserable; to Socrates, and, indeed, to all Greeks, this is self-evident: "All men by nature desire to be happy and no one wants to be miserable" (*Symposium, Meno,* etc.). Happiness is the final goal of all desire and the ultimate end of human existence.[221]

Since nobody wants to be unhappy, surely the only reason people do things that don't bring happiness is that they don't know any better. Once a person finds out what makes them hap-py, what works to bring fulfillment, then they will do it. That is the argument. Of course, some things bring short-term pleasure but long-term misery, so we have to figure out what works in the long run. But having done so, we would then do what works in the long run and eschew the short-term pleasures. In this view, the only reason anybody does anything that does not bring them happiness is ignorance.

Haidt shows why this is only partially true: because our ver-bal, conceptual rationality has only a limited ability to influence our behavior. We need to distinguish two meanings of the term "know," knowing *that* and knowing *how*. We can know that cer-tain things are good for us, but that is not the same as knowing how to accomplish them. You may know that you would be better off abstaining from a rich dessert, but not know how to overcome the desire for it in the moment. In addition to theoretical knowledge, we need skills to handle the elephant. "The elephant and the rider each have their own intelligence, and when they work together well they enable the unique brilliance of human beings"[222] says Haidt. How to accomplish that brilliance is the subject of the next chapter.

Chapter 26, Being the Rider: Strategy

Prior chapters have talked quite a bit about aspects of the elephant, that mass of instinct, habit and emotional reaction that governs our lives much of the time. Most of our cognition is hot, consisting of intuitive flashes of judgment, colored by emotion, that cause us to pay attention to and value some things and not others without thinking about how these judgments come about. Without knowing quite how we do it, we see and understand and navigate our way around the physical world quite easily. Our capacity to understand the thoughts, feelings and motivations of others guides us through the complex maze of social reality. We have moral intuitions about what is right and wrong, admirable and despicable, that guide our actions even before we have given any thought to their rational grounds. We find comfort, social cohesion and the strength to carry on in religion, whether or not the theological tenets of our faith actually make sense. We have a powerful intelligence, but it is fallible. We are subject to disorders, such as self-deception, maladapted responses and afflictive emotions, that interfere with it.

We have talked about the rider as well. Intelligence, the capacity for rational, deliberate thought, is a core component of human nature; it enables us to "think about long-term goals and thereby escape the tyranny of the here and now."[223] We are able to envision things that are not present in experience, make plans to acquire or avoid them, execute those plans and revise our plans on the fly to accomplish our goals successfully. Through language and culture we learn from others and build upon prior discoveries to understand and master our world. We employ an impressive arsenal of cognitive tools to shape our world: the scientific method, logic, mathematics, visual art, music, literature and more.

What really sets the rider apart from the elephant, however, is our capacity for self-reflection, for second-order thinking. The rider, not the elephant, has the ability to aim that impressive arsenal of cognitive tools toward himself or herself.

So we are both rider and elephant. Now what? It is up to us— to each one of us—to make the best of our situation, and that means really being the rider, really exercising our capacity for second-order thinking. The elephant isn't going to do it for us. Like any capacity, second-order thinking can be done poorly or well. It behooves us to do it well so we can enjoy the benefits of living a fulfilling life.

Excellence at second-order thinking is an iterative process:

1. Observe yourself and your life carefully and, as much as possible, without bias. Find out what works to bring you the satisfaction of functioning well, and what doesn't. Observe the patterns, the regularities, in your life and note their effects. Find out which ones serve you and which don't.

This may well entail learning how to learn, learning how to observe accurately. You attempt to observe without bias your own life and your interactions with the world and others. You step back and observe yourself—both in the present moment and in recollection, both individually and in dialogue with others— without getting caught up in the story. For most of us it will probably take some repeated practice and discipline, because we have blind spots that prevent us from "seeing" ourselves accurately. Emotional discharge to remove painful rigidities of thought, feeling and behavior will help.

2. Act on what you find out. Such action requires two things:
   a. Plan to do something differently. Think of some way to improve the situation.
   b. Do it. Try it out.

Planning, of course, is one of the things we humans do well, better than other animals. But planning alone is insufficient. If we don't take action, nothing will change. If we do take action, things might change for the better or for worse, but in either case we will have more information, and that will help us make a better plan.

3. Perform this cycle repeatedly.
    a. Observe (step 1). Evaluate the results of your actions.
    b. Act (step 2). Change the plan if needed and try it again.

Once you have started an improvement plan, observe carefully to see whether and in what way it is working or not. Then change the plan if needed, and take additional action. If it is working, keep on with it; if not, try something else.

You may find that your actions work, and you may find that they don't. In this respect we need to become skillful riders of the elephant. Sometimes it doesn't work to confront the elephant directly and try to overcome its inertia by sheer force of will. For instance, if sheer willpower can't prevent you from indulging harmful cravings, you can try to outwit them instead. Don't put yourself into situations where the craving arises; instead get busy with something else. Get more exercise. Remove the addictive food from your house. Enlist the help of friends. Substitute something healthier when you get hungry. Clear up the emotional issues that underlie the craving. Form a habit of eating healthy food, keep it up, and notice how much better you feel. There are many possibilities, all of which tend to strengthen the rider—the part of us that exercises second-order thinking—and tame the elephant.

Finally, see what else in your life is working and what isn't (return to step 1) and take action to improve the areas that aren't.

This process bears a great deal of resemblance to process and quality improvement in industrial and engineering settings, in particular the Deming Cycle of Plan-Do-Check-Act.[224] In industry and engineering, people apply an iterative process much like this to manufacturing, product development and the like in order to improve the processes and their output. In that context it is all first-order thinking, looking at aspects of the world and changing them. Using second-order thinking, we can direct this process at our own lives.

Sometimes we take this capacity for granted, but it is really quite extraordinary. We can change who we are. We can activate latent capacities, overcome bad habits, cultivate virtues of character. Within limits we can reinvent ourselves, become whole new persons. This capacity provides the germ of truth in the existentialist claim that existence precedes essence, that human beings have no fixed nature but instead create themselves through their choices and actions.[225] In fact, as we have seen, there is quite a lot that is fixed about human nature, but within that fixity we have the freedom to reinvent ourselves; by virtue of second-order thinking, we are not fully constrained by the past.

(Do not mistake this for the New Age 101 doctrine that we create our reality, so it is our fault if we don't like it. It may well be that our past actions have determined not only where we find ourselves today but also what kind of person we are and how the world appears to us. But that does not mean we deliberately chose those actions. Maybe we did and maybe we didn't. The point is not to feel ashamed of the circumstances we find ourselves in, but to realize that now we have the capacity to do something different.)

The existentialists warn us about inauthenticity, which is knowing you have the capacity for second-order thinking and pretending to yourself that you don't. By contrast, an authentic stance toward life is to know that you have the capacity for second-order thinking and to cultivate that capacity and use it effectively. To do that is to achieve excellence at being human.

* * *

This chapter has given the method in the abstract. In the next chapter we'll look at how to apply the method in specific cases.

Chapter 27, Being the Rider: Tactics

In order to experience the fulfillment of functioning well, we must be able to think clearly, and our thinking must guide our actions. We need to avoid unthinking, inflexible behavior. (Unless we have previously chosen to allow it. Using cold cognition to guide everything we do would be tedious and unworkable.)

Inflexibility arises in four ways: habit; afflictive emotional responses to triggering events; distress patterns; and instinctual behavior. These are ways in which the elephant—the nonrational, or prerational, part of us—makes its influence known. Different methods are useful for dealing with each one.

Working with Habit

Habits are routines of behavior that take place regularly without conscious thought, and they are indispensable. If we had to think carefully about everything we do—tying our shoelaces, for instance, or getting the breakfast cereal from the cupboard— we would hardly get anything done. The problem is that we are prone to bad habits as well as good, things we do habitually that do not serve our long-term interests as well as those that do. We would like to shed bad habits and acquire good ones.

A classic and insightful exposition of habit is found in the work of psychologist and philosopher William James.[226] According to James, habit is a result of the plasticity of the brain and nervous system. The more we exercise a set of physical motions, the more that set is entrained in the brain and nerves. The virtue of habit is twofold: (1) It "simplifies the movements required to achieve a given result, makes them more accurate and diminishes fatigue;" and (2) it "diminishes the conscious attention with which our acts are performed."[227] His example is learning to play a musical instrument: in time what is difficult and tedious becomes easy and automatic, and after a while we do not need to pay attention to it at all. We play without thinking about physical technique and can concentrate instead on the music to be played, or even daydream about something else entirely.

In order to avoid bad habits and acquire good ones, it is best to substitute a good habit for a bad one. It is difficult to stop something habitual by sheer force of will. It is easier to start a new habit, because there is no elephantine inertia to overcome; so the workable strategy is to start a new habit as a substitute for the old. To accomplish this feat, James gives some useful advice: [228]

We must take care to *launch ourselves with as strong and decided an initiative as possible.* Accumulate all the possible circumstances which shall reinforce the right motives; put yourself assiduously in conditions that encourage the new way; make engagements incompatible with the old; take a public pledge, if the case allows; in short, envelop your resolution with every aid you know. This will give your new beginning such a momentum that the temptation to break down will not occur as soon as it otherwise might; and every day during which a breakdown is postponed adds to the chances of its not occurring at all. ...

Never suffer an exception to occur till the new habit is securely rooted in your life. ... The peculiarity of the moral habits, contradistinguishing them from the intellectual acquisitions, is the presence of two hostile powers, one to be gradually raised into the ascendant over the other. It is necessary above all things, in such a situation, never to lose a battle. Every gain on the wrong side undoes the effect of many conquests on the right. The essential precaution, therefore, is so to regulate the two opposing powers that the one may have a series of uninterrupted successes, until repetition has fortified it to such a degree as to enable it to cope with the opposition, under any circumstances. ...

Seize the very first possible opportunity to act on every resolution you make, and on every emotional prompting you may experience in the direction of the habits you aspire to gain. It is not in the moment of their forming, but in the moment of their producing motor effects, that resolves and aspirations communicate the new 'set' to the brain. ...

Keep the faculty of effort alive in you by a little gratuitous exercise every day. That is, be systematically heroic in little unnecessary points, do every day or two something for no other reason than its difficulty, so that, when the hour of dire need draws nigh, it may find you not unnerved and untrained to stand the test. Asceticism of this sort is like the insurance which a man pays on his house and goods. The tax does him no good at the time, and possibly may never bring him a return. But, if the fire does come, his having paid it will be his salvation from ruin. So with the man who has daily inured himself to habits of concentrated attention, energetic volition, and self-denial in unnecessary things. He will stand like a tower when everything rocks around him, and his softer fellow-mortals are winnowed like chaff in the blast.

These pieces of advice are tricks we can use to train the elephant to go along with the rider's will. They all rely on our capacity for second-order thinking.

Overcoming Afflictive Emotion

The great virtue of Buddhist psychology is that it not only identifies categories of cognitive and volitional impairment, but it suggests ways to overcome them as well. It is acutely grounded in self-observation and has been finely honed over years of assessment of reports of such self-observation. By observing our own experience, each one of us can in turn validate the Buddhist findings for ourselves. The Buddhist view has close parallels with Western psychological findings.

According to the Buddhists, there is a reliable pattern to the onslaught of an afflictive emotion, and knowledge of this pattern gives us the power to intervene and deflect its afflictive power. Such an emotion first arises from a perceptual trigger, a recognition that something is happening. Western psychologists call this an *appraisal*, because it is cognitive, a form of instant pattern recognition. For example, perhaps someone cuts in front of you in line. (In many Western cultures this is considered quite rude.) Your appraisal is that the person is being rude. Then, almost instantaneously, comes an emotional reaction—anger—and an accompanying impulse to action—to object sharply. The emotion rapidly grows in intensity and you are caught in a full-blown reaction, verbally berating the rude person. In this state you have virtually no power to think clearly or to stop what you are doing. The elephant is roaring full blast. Eventually the emotion subsides and you can reflect on what happened. [229]

There are three different choice points in this process: During the appraisal, during the reactive impulse and during the resulting action.[230] A fourth occurs after the emotional reaction has subsided.

In reverse order, the easiest point of intervention is after the emotion subsides. You can notice and reflect on what happened, see that it is an instance of a repetitive pattern, compare the effects of the afflictive emotion with other, more benevolent, emotions and resolve to do something different next time.[231]

The hardest point of intervention is during the emotional reaction. In that state you have little, if any, ability to think critically or to observe yourself. Fortunately this state need not last a long time. Neuroanatomist Jill Bolte Taylor notes that physiologically it takes less than 90 seconds for an emotional reaction to subside: "Within 90 seconds from the initial trigger, the chemical component of my anger has completely dissipated from my blood and my automatic response is over."[232] After that, you have a choice whether to continue in that state or not. With practice you can learn to simply allow the emotion to surge for 90 seconds and then choose not to continue it. You learn to shorten the duration of the reaction.

Another point of intervention is just as the emotion is arising, after the initial appraisal and before you act on the emotion. You pay attention to your own interior life. "The crucial point here is to free emotions at the moment they surge in one's mind, so that they don't trigger a chain of thoughts that proliferate and take over the mind, thus compelling one to act—to harm somebody else, for instance."[233] Western psychology calls this "impulse awareness,"[234] although I would prefer the term "impulse consciousness," and the goal is to insert a pause, to increase the time between impulse and action,[235] thereby creating the possibility of avoiding harmful action.

Finally, the most subtle point of intervention is at the point of the triggering perception itself, to increase the time between appraisal and impulse.[236] To do this, you must spot, at the moment of appraisal, the potential arousal of an afflictive emotional impulse, and head it off. Again, you pay attention to your own interior life. This requires much practice and familiarity with your own mind and the phenomenal nature of thoughts and emotions, how they arise, persist and fade away from the spotlight of attention. The uniquely Buddhist contribution to treatment of afflictive emotions is to recognize that such "appraisal awareness" is indeed possible.

All of these forms of dealing with afflictive emotion entail self-knowledge, what we might call emotional mindfulness, in one form or another. After the emotion has subsided, you can remember and think about what happened, including your own reactions and role in the affair. During the emotional storm it is very difficult to pay attention to yourself, but with practice it is possible. Both impulse awareness and appraisal awareness entail being conscious of yourself in the moment, paying attention to the subtleties of what is happening subjectively in one's experience. The more you practice such self-observation in times when you are not emotionally triggered, the more you have the capacity to engage in it when you are.

These too rely on the human capacity for second-order thinking, the ability to take oneself as an object of thought and perception.

Overcoming Distress Patterns

The modern recognition of the function of emotional discharge has added an important insight and an important strategy to the ancient Buddhist doctrine of afflictive emotions. (See *Chapter 19, The Overlooked Adaptation*.) There is a way to reduce the impact of the triggering event, such that it is less likely to spark a cascade of potentially harmful emotion and action: by discharging away the tension that causes it to be a trigger in the first place.

We can think of our susceptibility to restimulation, to being set off by a triggering event, as a button. The triggering event pushes the button and closes an electrical circuit; and the resulting appraisal, emotion and action then follow automatically. Emotional discharge removes the wire from the button. The triggering event happens from time to time, but the more you discharge, the less effect it has. Discharging the tension gives you more freedom at the very beginning of the process. You can cognitively reframe the triggering event, appraise it in a different way. You do not feel such a strong urge to incendiary emotion and action, so you can choose to act differently.

Emotional discharge is a way of preparing yourself in advance to handle triggering events. The practice of self-observation in order to intervene at critical points is a way of handling the events when they arise. Together, the two techniques provide a powerful way to free yourself from the unchosen, mechanical effects of restimulated afflictive emotion.

Another strategy for handling restimulating trigger events, of course, is to avoid them. If a certain person or type of person always seems to push your buttons, you can try to stay out of their way. If you can't seem to refrain from rich desserts, you can eat at home and not have them in the house. Such a strategy can work but has the disadvantage of restricting your range of activities. And, if you encounter the trigger event despite precautions, you have no defense. This strategy is best used in conjunction with the others, not as a sole remedy.

These methods also entail some self-knowledge, some second-order thinking, to know what to discharge about and what types of triggers to avoid. The more you discharge, the more you have the possibility of accurate self-knowledge.

Working with Instinct

Some repetitive and inflexible patterns of behavior are built in, as it were, part of our genetic inheritance. These are the hardest to counteract. Psychologist Paul Ekman gives an example:

> It is very unlikely that we could ever learn not to be emotional about certain events. If there is a sudden sense of free fall, such as occurs when you're flying and suddenly hit an air pocket, there is a fear response. I've talked to airline pilots, and they still have that fear response even though it happens every day. That is ... an emotion theme that is built into us; we're not going to get over it.[237]

There may be many more such instinctual reactions; it is hard to tell. Humans have such an enhanced ability, compared to other primates, to modify their own behavior, and such a susceptibility to distress patterns caused by undischarged painful emotion, that it is hard to know what is truly instinctual and what is not. But we have clues. If there is a plausible explanation of its evolutionary benefit and it does not yield to repeated discharge, a reaction or behavior pattern may well be instinctual. Even so, instinctual reactions may be mitigated by self-observation, the "appraisal awareness" and "impulse awareness" mentioned above.

Chapter 28, Summary: What Is It About Humans?

We started out Part III with a goal in mind: to find out what human nature consists of as viewed from an objective, scientific, third-person point of view. We wanted to find out in order to learn how to live well. We are now in a position to fulfill that goal and make some plausible assertions about human nature and what we need to do in order to experience the fulfillment of functioning well.

We are embedded in nature. Our differences from our closest genetic relatives are a matter of degree, not kind. We are not separate from the biological and physical world, not somehow divorced from the rest of reality, raised above it in some special way. Instead, we are connected to each other, to all life and to the entire universe. Our minds are adapted to the world we find ourselves in because we have co-evolved together with that world. Hence, we are completely at home here. The idea that this world is somehow a prison or a place of exile for a soul whose essential nature is to be disembodied is not in line with the findings of evolutionary psychology. One obvious implication is that there is no need to be ashamed of being embodied. Rather, it makes sense to enjoy being here and to take care of our bodies. Good health comes from spending time outdoors in natural settings, exercising and eating good food. Another implication is that for our well-being we need to take care of our environment, because our environment nourishes us. To do that we are better off when we work with nature instead of arrogantly against it. Doing so can take many forms: designing dwellings, gardens and landscapes to work like natural systems is just one example.

With our greater intelligence, *we amplify the characteristics of our sibling species.* We can be aggressive and competitive like chimps but also peaceful and cooperative like bonobos, and in either case we go to greater extremes. Modern weapons enable us to kill and maim far more effectively than any chimp, but we can also live peacefully and harmoniously in much larger groups than bonobos. It is up to us to choose which way to be. And it is not just that one is bad and the other good. There are obvious benefits to a peaceful way of life, but there are virtues to be found in the violent and aggressive side of our nature as well. A certain toughness enables us to overcome the hardship and adversity that comes in part from other humans and in part from the vicissitudes of nature.

We have a much greater intelligence than other animals, so much so that we can be called the species that makes plans. We can envision states of affairs not present and clearly distinguish what is here and now from what is only imagined. We can tailor our behavior to particulars of the present situation in order to reach targeted goals. Hence, it behooves us to keep that intelligence functioning well. I list some ways to do that in *Chapter 27, Being the Rider: Tactics.*

We can be far more loving, powerful, cooperative and enthusiastic about life than most of us have imagined. These traits, along with intelligence itself, are diminished by emotional distress, but we have the capacity to recover from such distress through the innate healing mechanism of emotional discharge. The more we recover, the better we function. See *Chapter 19, The Overlooked Adaptation.*

We are good for each other. In fact, we are indispensable to each other. Much of our most profound fulfillment is found in intimate connection with other people. Hence, the more we make close connections with others, the better off we are. Closeness aside, our survival depends on cooperation with others, so the more clearly we communicate with them, the better off we are. It is advisable to learn to share intimacy and to communicate clearly.

We have an innate sense of morality. The few of us who don't—psychopaths who lack conscience and empathy—we find so horrifying that they seem almost not human. But we do not all have the same sense of morality. Our moral impulses are filtered through the lenses of different cultures and different temperaments. People respond to moral quandaries with different instinctive moral judgments. Each of us needs to think carefully to determine how to act and what kind of person to be, rather than accept uncritically the morality handed to us in our culture.

We have an innate sense of religion. Even atheists find satisfaction in aligning themselves with a purpose greater than themselves. In a talk at the 2002 TED conference, noted atheist Daniel Dennett says that the secret of happiness is to "Find something more important than you are and dedicate your life to it."[238] There are many causes to which we could dedicate our lives. The trick is to determine which of the many candidates to choose.

We are prone to self-deception. One might argue that since we are good at self-deception, it must be a human characteristic that should be encouraged, but that would be a misreading of the premise of this inquiry. Self-deception is good under certain circumstances for propagation of genes but not for the healthy functioning of the human being. What is good for the genes is not necessarily good for the individual; and this inquiry is about how to live a fulfilling life, not about how to propagate genes. Genetic propagation is a mechanism that explains much of our behavior, as do, in their own way, physical, chemical and biological mechanisms; but now that we know about the genetic basis of self-deception, we have a choice as to what to do about it. Certainly self-deception is harmful, as it interferes with accurate perception of reality, and thereby impairs our ability to think and plan accurately. Fortunately, we know how self-deception works, and that gives us ammunition against it. We can be on the lookout for it and intervene from the vantage point of self-observation and knowledge. Stephen Pinker puts it well:

> Still, thanks to the complexity of our minds, we need
> not be perpetual dupes of our own chicanery. The mind
> has many parts, some designed for virtue, some designed
> for reason, some clever enough to outwit the parts that

are neither. One self may deceive another, but every now and then a third self sees the truth.[239]

Self-deception is an instance of a larger point: *Our rationality is not perfect and is often not in control.* We are both rider—the rational, step-by-step thinker and planner—and elephant—the impulsive, emotionally reactive pattern-recognizer. Without the rapid emotional evaluations of the elephant we would be paralyzed with indecision. Without the foresight of the rider we would (and often do) get ourselves in trouble. Haidt says "The elephant and the rider each have their own intelligence, and when they work together well they enable the unique brilliance of human beings."[240] It certainly behooves us to learn to know ourselves well enough and to acquire enough practical know-how to enable the rider to work with the elephant instead of against it. (This is an example of working with nature rather than against it.)

We can know ourselves. Hence, within limits, *we can change ourselves.* In the movie *The African Queen* Katherine Hepburn says to Humphrey Bogart, "Nature, Mr. Allnut, is what we are put in this world to rise above."[241] We cannot rise above it completely, so we would be better advised to learn to live well within it. But in order to do so, we must indeed rise above it enough to perceive, understand, plan and strategize about not only the world around us but ourselves as well. Rising above nature requires us to utilize our capacity for second-order thinking, the ability to take ourselves as an object of thought and perception. Understanding evolutionary psychology helps. As Robert Wright says, "We're all puppets, and our best hope for even partial liberation is to try to decipher the logic of the puppeteer."[242]

Part IV: Conclusion

Chapter 29, To Be Of Service

We have now had two quite different accounts of human nature, one from the point of view of metaphysics, first-person subjectivity and panpsychist mysticism; and the other from the point of view of objective, scientific knowledge. How shall we reconcile the two?

We do not need the mystical premise to understand that the Goodness Ethic makes sense as a worthy ideal for living our lives. It is clear from the biological and evolutionary data that we humans do not live apart from nature and do not live apart from each other. There is ample evidence that we are deeply interconnected with all of life. We see images of ourselves in our primate cousins and realize that we have evolved as an integral part of a world that nourishes us and sustains us. We live in a universe that is, at bottom, friendly to us. It is our home, it is where we live. Hence, purely from a self-interested point of view, we need to take care of it. Would you refuse to fix a leaky roof or protect your garden from pests on the grounds that you are too special to concern yourself with such things? Of course not. So we should work for the good in all things, not from a sense of duty imposed from without, but from the realization that we are among those things for which we work, and that what benefits the whole system cannot fail to benefit us.

In a sense, however, we *are* special. Uniquely among the beings we know of, we humans have the capacity for second-order thinking, the capacity to pay attention to ourselves; to understand how we behave, act and react; and to change how we do those things so that we can be even more effective at making our plans come to fruition. The other animals, the plants and the minerals just do what they do. There is, no doubt, a deep wisdom in nature, but it is not a self-reflective wisdom. We also do what we do, but we know we are doing it. And that gives us a unique opportunity. If we see that what we are doing is harmful to others (and thereby harmful to us) or using up resources unsustainably (and thereby threatening our future existence) or creating pollution (and thereby undermining our present health), then we can stop doing it, and start doing something else.

And if we see that there is something in us that interferes with our ability to perceive reality clearly and to think and plan effectively, then we can do something about that as well. We can create better habits, intervene when afflictive emotion overcomes us, and discharge away the rigidities that make us stupid. With our powerful intelligence and capacity to plan for the future and implement those plans, we have the opportunity to be stewards of our world. With our capacity for self-reflection, we can be self-correcting stewards, continuously improving our ability to care for our home, our fellow humans and our fellow beings of all species.

This work began by asking "What is the uniquely human function, that which will fulfill us and provide a good life if we exercise it?" From the point of view of down-to-earth, practical, objective inquiry, we find that that function is our capacity for self-reflection, which enables us to improve our ability to make our visions come true. And the most worthy vision, the one that will benefit us the most, is to tend and improve the welfare of all that is.

In this effort, we are not alone.

Each of us is an expression of the One, of The God, the Only Being. The God sees the world through our eyes, hears the world through our ears, feels the world through our skin, and acts in the world through our hands. The more we realize this, the more we make it a reality in our lives by remembering and actually experiencing in ourselves the actions of the Spirit-that-moves-in-all-things, the more we become attuned to what may be called the Spirit of Guidance. The vast intelligence of the All is at our disposal! We are all able to hear that guidance (or see it, or feel it, or intuit it—we each have our own modality) even if that ability has been covered over by the concerns of our daily lives.

But how shall we access that vast intelligence? The wisdom traditions of the world have much to tell us here:

- Do your practices. The wisdom of the All is given freely, as grace, but to receive it we need to make ourselves ready. Whatever your practice may be—meditation, walking in nature, prayer, chanting, yoga postures, stillness or movement, silence or singing, whatever it may be—the practice works only if you do it. Exert the effort, knowing that you as an individual being are serving the whole by opening channels for it to become aware of itself. And in that effort, you become more open to the bliss of communion with the All.

- Don't try to do it alone. The path of the solitary mystic is a hard one and suited only for a few. For most of us, the community of seekers—the *satsang,* the *sangha,* the *jamiya,* the congregation, the fellowship—is a must. There you will find enjoyment, comfort and courage to continue in the face of difficulties.

- Be of service. The Goodness Ethic, to work for the good in all things, is of particular importance because it is not only a natural result of your practice but a means as well. By serving others—human and nonhuman—you overcome the illusion that you are separate from them. Your heart opens with compassion. And the heart, not the intellect, is the conduit for intuition.

- Be grateful. The Sufi mystic says "The attitude is gratitude." To be thankful for the gift of life is to expand and enhance that life. To be thankful for the opportunity to be of service is to expand and enhance such opportunities. To be thankful for your connection with a Whole that is greater than you are is to expand and enhance the feelings of awe and bliss that come with that recognition. To be thankful for the company of others is to attract those who will help you and nourish you with love.

It is all an upward spiral. When you live as if you are part of a web of an organic whole, at the center of which is a vast locus of consciousness, an all-encompassing intelligence, you experience fulfillment. Your feeling of fulfillment is the interior, the feeling state, of a node in the pattern of that whole. That whole incorporates your fulfillment, your satisfaction, in its own experience of itself, yielding a greater feeling of well-being. And you feel the effects of that greater well-being, the bliss and the peace. And feeling that bliss and peace gives you strength and incentive to keep working for the good in all things.

Postscript: Why I Clean Up the Park

I pick up trash when I take a hike through the park near my house. There is often plenty of it, especially in the parts of the park nearest the neighborhood, so the task can keep me busy. I forget how I got into this habit. Probably because I was annoyed by the trash and remembered the story of a man on a long overseas airplane flight who was angry at the dirty bathroom. He sat and fumed and wished someone would do something about it until he realized that most likely nobody would, but he could do it himself. So he did, and he enjoyed the clean bathroom for the rest of the flight. It's like that with me: if nobody else will clean up the trash, then I will. I get a sense of aesthetic pleasure looking at a spot of scenery that is free of human trash, and I like it when I come back the next day and find it still clean.

There are ancillary benefits as well. There is a sense of satisfaction at having accomplished a task. I get a sense of virtue, of being a good citizen. The squatting and bending and reaching are good exercise for me, a person who often sits at a desk in front of a computer. At times there is a bit of a technical challenge; I see a bottle or can that has been thrown back in the brush, hard to get to, and I figure out how I can carefully step and reach through the brambles to get it. It's not in the same league as rock climbing, but when I succeed, I have a happy sense of accomplishment.

All these benefits are self-centered. It's about my getting to see beauty in my surroundings, my getting some exercise, my getting a sense of satisfaction from achieving a challenging task. But there is another dimension as well. I do it in order to reinforce and remind myself of my sense of connection with something greater than myself, with the unity of which each one of us is a part and an expression. I pick up trash so that the All will not have to see ugliness through my eyes.

When I come back the next day or even a few days later and find the place still clean, I wonder if I have created an atmosphere, an aura, of cleanliness that has influenced others to clean up after themselves. That is certainly possible if we are all connected by virtue of being expressions of one Being. Often when I have a great pile of trash, and it's getting too much to handle, I come upon a plastic bag to carry it in. It's as if the universe is helping me.

Frequently I do it out of duty. It's a self-imposed duty, to be sure, but a duty nonetheless. Not that I sat down and decided to impose this duty on myself. It's more like a habit. One decides to act in a certain way or do a certain thing, one does it again and again, and then it becomes habitual. One then feels a sense of duty, or at least a sense of discomfort at the prospect of not doing what one has decided to do.

The way I experience duty is as a burden; it is something imposed on me, which I resent. Often when I first come upon some trash, I dislike feeling that I have to pick it up. I'd rather keep walking, keep feeling the pleasure of that movement, keep getting my aerobic exercise and get to where I am going. I do it anyway, though, even if grudgingly at first. And once I start, I begin to feel a sense of lightness and happiness. Perhaps that is just idiosyncratic to me, a result of my personal history, as if I somehow expect parental approval for doing my chores. Or perhaps it is built in to the human psyche through several hundred thousand years of evolution because we are social animals and to achieve reproductive success in a group setting we have to be attuned to our tribe, the group that sustains us and to which we must contribute if we are to continue to be sustained. We do our duty to gain the approval of the group and to avoid its scorn.

In the end, though, for me, cleaning the park is a spiritual practice, and one does one's practices simply because they are there to be done. One hopes for benefits, and certainly if there were none, one would not continue, but the presence or absence of any particular result at any particular time is not the point.

The point in doing the practice is to become the kind of person to whom benefits generally accrue, the kind of person who experiences the grace, the sense of awe and wonder and gratitude, that comes when one feels deeply one's connection with the Only Being and allows oneself to be a conduit for the actions of that Being.

One of my teachers said this: "The Sufi's choice is to raise her sails to catch the winds of the Divine, which forever blow." Picking up trash, for me, is a way of serving the Divine, and in so doing I am rewarded with beauty.

###

Part V: Appendices

Appendix A, The Good and The Right

This book is about how to maximize the good, but thinking in terms of goodness is not the only way to think about how to live your life. The other way is in terms of rightness. This appendix compares the two paradigms.

There are two ways of thinking about ethics, two clusters of concepts and language, or domains of discourse, that are used to recommend or command specific actions or habits of character. They may be called the Good and the Right. The good has to do with achievement of goals; the right, with laws and rules. The goodness paradigm recognizes that people have desires and aspirations, and it frames values in terms of what enables a being to achieve its ends. The rightness paradigm recognizes that people live in groups that require organization and regulations, and it frames values in terms of duty and conformance to rules. Goodness and rightness "are not complementary portions of the moral field but alternative ways of organizing the whole field to carry out the tasks of morality."[243]

The primary task of ethics is to guide our actions. Many ways of thinking about ethics focus on whether specific actions are good or bad, or right or wrong. These ways of thinking help us decide what we should do in a particular case or class of cases, or evaluate after the fact actions that someone else has done. Another approach, Virtue Ethics, focuses on qualities of character and motives for action. Within Virtue Ethics the distinction between the good and the right is also applicable. Questions about what sort of character traits you should cultivate can be answered on the basis either of what is good or of what is right.

Compassion and insight are typical goodness virtues, and a disposition of conscientious obedience is a typical rightness virtue.

The Good and the Right each have their area of applicability. They often get confused, and their confusion causes no end of trouble. In this appendix I compare and contrast the two in order to promote clarity of thought. In addition, I give reasons for preferring the goodness paradigm over rightness.

The Good

I have already discussed, in *Chapter 3, The Good,* the concept of goodness: that it refers to the consequences or effects of actions, specifically to the benefits or harms that result from what you do or the kind of person you are. The goodness approach to ethics is called teleological, from a Greek word, *telos,* that means "end," "purpose" or "goal." Biologically, what is good for an organism helps that organism survive and thrive. Instrumentally, what is good for a thing enables that thing to serve its purpose.

The Right

I have discussed the concept of rightness in *Chapter 22, Ways to Say "Should".* What is right has to do with conformance to rules or regulations. Conformance to rules is easy to see in nonethical situations. For instance, the right answer to "What is 37 divided by 9?" is "4 and 1/9." We apply a mathematical rule, the rule for how to do long division, and derive the right, or correct, answer. In ethical situations, we apply a moral rule to determine what the right course of action is. If you find a wallet with some money in it and the owner's identification as well, the right thing to do is to return the money to the owner. That is because it is wrong to keep something that does not belong to you, especially if you know who the owner is. The moral rule in this case is "It is wrong to keep something that does not belong to you."

As discussed in that chapter, the rightness approach to ethics is called deontological, from a Greek word, *deon,* that means "duty." You do your duty when you act according to the moral rules. We could also call this a rules-based approach. (By "rules" I mean prescribed guides for conduct, not generalizations that describe physical reality, such as the laws of nature.)

Confusion Between the Good and the Right

All too often people confuse the notions of good and right. The confusion is understandable. Both concepts apply to what we should do, and often the debate is really about persuading someone to act in a certain way. Clarity of language and conceptual rigor seem to be less important than rhetoric. Here is an example:

> In an ideal world, people would be figuring out more ways for proprietary and open source software to work seamlessly with each other ... . All would benefit, and innovation would accelerate appropriately. Unfortunately, it appears the GPLv3 is finding new ways to rip the innovation fabric in half. That is wrong ... .[244]

You do not need to understand what the GPLv3 is (it is the GNU Public License version 3; does that help?) to see that the author is making a point about benefits but then says "That is wrong" as if appealing to some unstated moral rule.

It is this way of using "right" and "wrong"—to express emphatic approval or disapproval—that leads some thinkers to assert that moral discourse is actually meaningless and merely expresses the speaker's preference or the speaker's attempt to influence someone else's behavior.

Why It Matters

If someone says something is good, you can always ask "good for what?" If someone says something is right, you can always ask "according to what rule?" The two domains of discourse really are separate, and it is not useful to mix them. Mixing them is a form of category error, that is, an error "by which a property is ascribed to a thing that could not possibly have that property."[245] That something has good effects does not make it right. That something is in accordance with a moral rule does not make it good.

Making the distinction between Good and Right is important because it promotes clarity of thought. I do not argue that clarity of language is a necessary condition for clarity of thought, but it certainly helps. The clearer your thinking, the more likely you are to succeed in the real world. Accurate thinking based on accurate perception leads to accuracy of action, action that leads to attainment of your goals. Clear thinking enables you to survive and thrive.

Meta-ethics: Good vs. Right

Making the distinction is not just a theoretical issue. Suppose you are living in Holland during World War II and Germany has invaded your country. You are an honest person, and you know that lying is wrong. But you also know that it is good to protect innocent people from harm, so you hide a family of Jews in your house. The Nazis come looking for them and ask if you are harboring any fugitives. You now have two ethical principles in conflict. Shall you protect the Jews or tell the truth? This is a meta-ethical issue: do you do what is good or what is right?

It is hard to decide between framing ethical questions in terms of Good or Right because it is easy to get caught in circular reasoning and beg the question. If we ask which is better, we have already presupposed the Goodness paradigm. If we ask which is right, we have already presupposed the Rightness paradigm. We can assert that people who adopt an ethic based on goodness will be generally healthier and happier than those who focus on rightness, but that assertion already assumes that goodness is superior to rightness. Or we can assert that people who adopt an ethic based on being right are morally superior to those who don't, but doing so already assumes that rightness is superior.

It is not impossible to make a choice, however. I believe it makes more sense to adopt the Goodness paradigm than to adopt the Rightness paradigm. Here's why:

- There is a way to determine which paradigm is better but not a way to determine which is right.

- It is easier to find out what is good than to find out what is right.
- The Goodness paradigm solves the "is-ought" problem.
- It is methodologically easier to resolve conflicts among goods than conflicts among obligations.
- It is easier to justify obeying moral rules on the basis of consequences than to justify paying attention to consequences on the basis of moral rules.
- Excessive focus on being right promotes emotional distress.
- The Goodness paradigm promotes recognition of the connectedness and unity of all things and as such is closer to reality.

There is a way to determine which is better but not a way to determine which is right.

There is a way to determine which one (Goodness or Rightness) works better in the sense of promoting human happiness and welfare: by observation. Observe people who live by a Goodness ethic. Observe people who live by a rule-based ethic. See who seems to be happier and more fulfilled. See which set of people have more beneficial effects on those around them. Try living by the Goodness ethic yourself. Try living by a set of rules. See which one leads you to be happier and more fulfilled. See which one has better effects on those around you. I suspect that you will find that the Goodness ethic works better. Whether or not you do, the point is that there is a method: to observe the effects. The effects are observable publicly, and people can come to agreement about them. If there are disagreements, further observation can help resolve them.

There is not, however, a way to determine which one (Goodness or Rightness) is right. In order to do that, you would have to determine the rules by which to judge that one is right and the other wrong. But there is profound disagreement among philosophers and across cultures about what the rules are. Moral rules are not publicly observable, and there is no easy way to come to agreement about them.

It is easier to find out what is good than to find out what is right.

How do we know what The Good is? How can we find out what is good for us? It's not hard. Observe what makes you healthy and what makes you sick, what makes you happy and what makes you unhappy, what leads to your flourishing (the Greek word is *eudaimonia*, literally "wellness of soul") and what doesn't.

How do we know what the Right is? That is more difficult. So far there is no agreement on which of the many philosophical views is correct.

The Goodness paradigm solves the "is-ought" problem.

In Book III of his *Treatise of Human Nature*, David Hume asserts that normative statements (saying that something ought to be so) cannot be derived from descriptive statements (saying that something is). This assertion has been known ever since as the "is-ought" problem.[246] I suppose it is a problem because we would like to figure out what to do on the basis of what actually exists, but it is a problem only if "ought" is used in the Rightness paradigm. It is easy to derive "ought" from "is" in the Goodness paradigm. The general form is what Kant calls a hypothetical imperative:

- If you want to accomplish x, then you ought to do y.

Here is a particular example:

- If you want to get along with people, then you ought to be honest and friendly.

We can apply this example to a particular case using an argument with two premises and a conclusion, as follows:

- Premise: Those who are honest and friendly get along with people.
- Premise: You want to get along with people.
- Conclusion: You ought to be honest and friendly.

This argument is based on the logical form called *modus ponens:*[xxi]

> A implies B
> A is true
> ---
> therefore B is true

The ethical form replaces the second premise with an assertion about desire or intention instead of about truth and concludes with an imperative, or at least a recommendation:

> A implies B
> One desires B
> ---
> therefore one ought to do A

Instead of asserting that A is true and deriving B, we say that we want B to be true, and hence we should do what we can to make A true.

In the context of the Goodness paradigm, where a good is understood instrumentally as something that enables you to achieve a goal or purpose, it is easy and straightforward to figure out general guidelines for how to live your life from statements of facts. It is notoriously difficult, if not impossible, to do so in the context of the Rightness paradigm. Thus, the Goodness paradigm is superior in this regard.

It is easier to resolve conflicts among goods than conflicts among obligations.

It is all too easy to find conflicts among rules. We can cast the dilemma mentioned earlier entirely in terms of right and wrong instead of Right vs. Good. It is wrong to tell a lie and it is wrong to harm an innocent person. So which rule takes precedence when the Nazis come hunting Jews? We need to modify one of the rules to make it subordinate to the other, or appeal to some higher-level rule. But if we cast the problem in terms of benefits and harm, the choice is obvious: more harm comes from telling the truth, so you should lie and protect the innocent.

[xxi] Logicians, please note: based on, not identical to.

Of course we can find conflicts among goods as well, but it is easier to resolve them by looking at a larger context. It would certainly be to your financial benefit to keep the wallet and the money you found. Without reference to moral rules, it would appear that the best thing to do would be to keep the money. But to do so would harm yourself. It tends to make you less trustworthy; it may well make you feel bad about yourself; and it causes a division between you and the owner, isolating you from that bit of human contact. To give the money back would make the owner happy, make you feel better, and strengthen the bonds of connection between you and other. On balance, returning the money is the better thing to do.

It is easier to justify obeying moral rules on the basis of consequences than to justify paying attention to consequences on the basis of moral rules.

You can always ask why you should obey the moral rules. The answer invariably turns out to be because the consequences of doing so are more favorable than those of not obeying them.

In childhood the rules come from our parents. By obeying them we gain parental approval and avoid punishment. Extending this to the social norms of our community, obeying the rules means being a good citizen. Doing so, we gain the approval and avoid the scorn of those whose opinions matter to us, not to mention avoiding fines and jail sentences. To a more mature mind, the rules might seem to come from the dictates of our conscience, an internal voice that judges our actions as right or wrong, as worthy of approval or disapproval. By obeying, we gain a sense of uprightness, of rectitude, and we avoid feeling guilty. Further reflection leads us to wonder where the voice of conscience comes from and what the justification is for what that voice tells us. We find ourselves with a sense of duty and wonder who or what imposes that duty. Many believe that God defines the moral rules and imposes the duty to obey. God is thus a surrogate parent, and by obeying God's commands we gain divine reward and (we hope) avoid divine punishment. Kant alleges that the dictates of pure reason impose the duty to act so that the basis on which we act could be universalized without contradiction. For a rational being, contradiction is certainly unfavorable. Others postulate an unseen world of values, not unlike Plato's Forms, which the moral sense in some way apprehends. The consequences of doing one's duty in this view are an internal sense of being in harmony with moral reality, of being virtuous and worthy of approval, whether or not anyone actually approves.

In all of these cases, the reason for obeying the rules turns out to be a concern for the consequences of doing so or not doing so. This concern for consequences leads me to believe that the Goodness paradigm, which emphasizes consequences, is more inclusive than the Rightness paradigm, which emphasizes rules.

Coming at it another way, we can ask why one should pursue what is good. If we try to answer the question from within the Rightness paradigm, we find the Utilitarian position, that what is morally right is that which maximizes pleasure and minimizes pain among all concerned. (If we think that the concepts of pleasure and pain are too narrow, we can extend it to say that what is right is what maximizes well-being among all concerned.) But the problem with the Utilitarian position, which is well-known, is that it is in practice impossible to calculate the long-term benefits and harms with sufficient precision. The so-called hedonic calculus is unworkable.

More to the point, there are a great many rules-based positions, and Utilitarianism is only one of them. Many of the deontological positions deny that we should pay attention to consequences in determining what to do. But, as I have shown, the reason for adopting a deontological position in the first place boils down to consequences.

From the Goodness point of view, the answer to why you should pursue what is good is straightforward. If you do, you will feel better and function better than if you don't. If you don't, you will feel and function worse.

(Logically, you could then ask why you should want to feel and function better. Logic fails here, however. The question is, if not logically absurd, at least ridiculous. The fact is, we do want to feel and function better, as does every other living thing, because it is built into our nature, who and what we are.)

The fact that it is easy to justify adherence to moral rules on the basis of consequences, and easy to justify concern with goodness on the basis of consequences, but difficult to justify concern with consequences on the basis of moral rules, leads me to believe that a concern with goodness has logical priority over a concern with moral rules.

Focusing on being right promotes emotional distress, but focusing on goodness promotes emotional health.

I do not know if there have been any controlled studies, but my observation of people tells me that an orientation towards Rightness causes or is at least correlated with emotional distress. Viewed from the outside, the distress manifests as uptightness, defensiveness and a tendency to blame, punish and alienate other people whom the blamer perceives as violating the rules. From the inside, when I feel morally indignant or punishing, I am agitated, angry and compulsive.[xxii] It is not at all a pleasant feeling. When I focus on maximizing benefits, I am alert, inquisitive and thinking about objective reality. It is a much more pleasant way to be.

Those who focus on maximizing benefit, regardless of who is right or wrong, tend to be more open, pleasant, tolerant and happy. Less obsessed by emotional pain, their ability to find workable responses to life situations seems to be greater.

There is, of course, no way to compare one person's emotional state to another's. But you can compare, via memory, your own emotional states at different times. This process requires some degree of self-observation and consequent self-knowledge. If you put in the effort to make the comparison, I think you will find that focusing on how to obtain good outcomes is a much more pleasant way to live than focusing on who is right and who is wrong and feeling resentful toward and blaming those you think are wrong.

[xxii] By "I" I mean I, the author. I suspect this is true of most of us. How do you, the reader, feel?

The Goodness paradigm is closer to reality in that it promotes recognition of the unity and connectedness of all things.

This consideration depends on the assertions that reality is one and that all apparently separate things are connected in that unity.

The Rules-based paradigm implies division and separation. It is all too easy to differentiate between those who obey the rules and those who don't, and to vilify and persecute the latter. Of course the latter have their own set of rules and vilify and persecute the former. The result is strife and discord.

Focusing on goods, you look at the health of the whole and of each part of the whole. You seek to include the parts in the whole. This approach is more conducive to a recognition of Oneness and is thus more aligned with reality.

Lacking a recognition that all things are interconnected, a focus on goods rather than rights or duties may also lead to strife, as numerous wars over territory and resources have demonstrated. But too often the justification for such wars is couched in rules-based morality.[xxiii] It is much harder to break out of the "us vs. them" rules mentality than to consider additional evidence within the mentality that looks for benefits and harms. Better outcomes result from thinking in terms of good and bad than from thinking in terms of right and wrong.

Conclusion

For all these reasons, it makes more sense to frame ethical considerations in terms of good and bad, beneficial and harmful,

---

[xxiii] To give but one example, in the early 21st century the leaders of a powerful nation, most of whose citizens professed to be Christians, whipped up enmity against "Islamic terrorists" to justify invasion of a much weaker country that in fact posed no threat. Many believed the real reason was to gain control of oil resources; but the stated reason was to protect the stronger nation from terrorists, and the subtext was that Christians are right and Muslims are wrong. This entire effort showed ignorance of the greater benefits that could have accrued to everyone—including the misguided leaders—had they recognized that a more lasting security could be had by cooperating and finding common ground.

or effective and ineffective, than in terms of right and wrong, proper and improper, or correct and incorrect. When asking any ethical question—what you should do in a given situation, what kind of person you should strive to be, how to resolve conflict among persons or nations—frame the question in terms of goodness and badness, what is beneficial or harmful, to yourself and those around you.

Advice: Use Goodness Language

To conclude, here is some advice from Christopher Avery, trainer in effective teamwork and author of the book *Teamwork Is An Individual Skill*.

> We request that a group remove the words 'right' and 'wrong' from their shared team vocabulary. We ask them instead to simply substitute the words 'works' and 'doesn't work.'[247]

"Works" and "doesn't work" refer to effects or consequences. Focusing on effects has several advantages:

- It opens us to more possibilities. To say something is "the right thing" to do implies that there is only one right thing. But there may be many good things to do.
- It keeps our attention on the present and open to learning. To say "the right thing" or "the wrong thing" makes implicit reference to a rule, and rules tend not to change. But the real world is always changing, and what works today might not work tomorrow. Relying on moral rules tends to make us overly certain of things; focusing on what works tends to help us keep learning what works and what doesn't, and under what circumstances.
- It promotes healthy relationships. Again from Avery:

> [Using "works" and "doesn't work"] connects us in relationship instead of assigning disconnected states of being. Authoritative use of "right" and "wrong" can numb us into operating as disconnected automatons. Think about it. "That's right" can be falsely affirming

and "that's wrong" can be falsely degrading. I have found myself so sensitive to this that when my young son points and says "That dog's brown," instead of responding "that's right," I affirm him by saying "I agree Thom, that dog appears brown to me too!" I don't know about you, but I prefer the connection that comes with that. It works for me![248]

Appendix B, The Nature of the Good

The idea of maximizing the good for all is close to the utilitarian notion of the greatest good for the greatest number, but the difference is that (a) maximizing the good for all is not justified as being a moral duty but is justified only because on average we (each one of us) will be better off if we try for it; and (b) it does not matter that it is impossible to calculate all possible effects in all possible futures. You just need to do your best in any given situation to make a decision on this basis and then move on. And you need to pay attention to the results of your decisions and become more skillful over time in maximizing goodness.

But what is this goodness? The Good as I define it is not an abstract entity, universally applicable. I am not saying that there is an ultimate purpose to nature as a whole. (Although the mystical approach to life might assert that there is, for the purposes of this discussion it is not a necessary premise.) I am saying that in any situation there are aspects that are good, or beneficial, for the people and other beings involved, and there are aspects that are less good, or even harmful. It is rare to find unmitigated goodness. What's good for the owl is not so good for the mouse. My point, working within the Goodness paradigm, is that it makes sense to try to maximize the amount of goodness while recognizing that (a) we might not entirely succeed, but we will do better than if we don't try; and (b) we will never produce all goodness and no badness.

Goodness is not binary, black or white, on or off, present or absent. It is analog, present in different degrees and to greater or lesser extents. A diet of corn chips, soda and ice cream, for instance, would be good enough to keep a person alive, but not good enough for maximum health. I am not saying that if something is good in a particular time and place it is therefore universally or absolutely good in all times and places. I am not saying that if something has good consequences, it therefore has no bad consequences. I am only saying that there are always consequences and that we can observe and evaluate them and choose good ones.

The good is certainly knowable. One of the benefits of the goodness approach to ethics is that we can find out by observation what benefits a person or organism and what does not. It is not hard to tell if someone is happy and at ease or anxious, angry or in some other way not at ease, just as it is not hard to tell whether a landscape or garden is flourishing and producing abundance or not. In either case with training we become better able to discern nuances and details, but the evidence is not hidden. In order to determine whether something is beneficial or promotes health or sound functioning, you need only observe its effects. The effects may be entirely personal and subjective, observable only by yourself, or public, observable by others.

Here is a small example. One day while hiking in the park, I straightened a bent frond of a saw palmetto near the creek. The frond snapped into place and I felt a sense of satisfaction. The view was more harmonious and the plant looked more whole; but more to the point, the frond could now catch more sunlight than it could before. I submit that this is an unambiguous increase of goodness in the world, both for the plant and for myself. I say this because of three things that are quite observable:

- The view was more harmonious. This is largely subjective. It looked more harmonious to me, but another person might not see it that way. Nevertheless, it was an observed fact (observed by me) that there was more harmony in my experience.
- The plant looked more whole. This also is largely subjective but could more easily be verified by somebody else. The frond used to droop and now it stood upright. Anybody could see that.

- The frond could now catch more sunlight than it could before. This is a publicly observable fact. I could get any number of people to agree that in fact the straightened frond exposes more surface to the sun. Getting more sunlight is beneficial to the plant, enabling it to increase its photosynthesis and get more nourishment and thereby be more able to survive and thrive.

Again, I am not saying what I did was absolutely good, only that it had a better outcome than if I had not done it. Perhaps I stepped on an insect and harmed it while adjusting the frond. Nonetheless, on balance I increased the amount of goodness—I provided benefits that were not there before—in the world.

Goodness as Virtue and Intention

Instead of asking what we should do in particular circumstances or types of circumstances, we can ask what kind of person we should become, what character traits we should cultivate. This question is the domain of Virtue Ethics, and the Goodness Ethic plays an important role here as well.

Virtues are character traits—what we might call habits of character—that elicit the approval of others, and vices are those that elicit disapproval. We need the approval of others, particularly those closest to us or with whom we interact frequently, because we are social beings and cannot function well in isolation.

Here the goodness approach to ethics intersects the rightness approach. Human beings need other human beings; we all need to live in groups. Being a member of a group provides benefits but also imposes duties, with rewards for doing your duty and penalties for disobedience. The fundamental duty is to act for the welfare of the group. From this point of view, living according to the Goodness Ethic is a virtue, and dedicating your life to the Good is a noble, excellent and praiseworthy thing to do. (Of course there is the very real possibility that the group may be shortsighted, just as individuals are, and that what it takes to be its good is actually detrimental to the whole. In practice there are knotty, but not insoluble, problems with hierarchies of goods.)

A virtue (or a vice) is not just a habit, however, because it includes motivation and intention. Strictly speaking, behavior is publicly observable but motivations are not. Nevertheless human beings have a finely tuned ability to intuit the motivations and intentions of others based on hundreds of thousands of years of evolution in small groups. Motivations and intentions are important because they form the basis of trust.

When other people judge you, they look at your behavior, at your actions, but also at what they believe are the moral properties of your character, your motivation. People want to know that your intention is to benefit the community or society by obeying its rules or living up to its ideals. Knowing that your intention is to benefit the community gives more assurance that you will be a good member than mere habit would and certainly more than calculated self-interest would. A good member of the community abides by its customs and conventions, the moral rules that constitute its sense of right and wrong. If you do so from calculated self-interest—as a certain reading of the Goodness Ethic might suggest—then there is always the possibility that your calculations might cause you to defect, to act selfishly or cheat rather than obey the moral rules. If you abide by community morality habitually, then others can have more confidence that you will do so in the future. If you do so because of a motivation or intention to honor and benefit the community that is integral to your character, then others have the highest degree of confidence that you can be trusted to continue to do so.

This being the case, it is of great benefit to cultivate your character, to mold yourself to become the kind of person that others will admire and trust because you can be counted on to contribute to the community.

You might question whether the moral quality of an act depends on its effects or on the intention of the actor. This is not a useful dichotomy, because intentions have effects, in particular on your character. I was once driving in heavy traffic on a four-lane divided road and saw a car coming up from behind me on my right. (This was in a nation in which one drives on the right side of the road; slower vehicles are supposed to keep to the right.) I sped up to prevent the car from overtaking and cutting in front of me. As it turned out, the car exited to the right, so my speeding up had no effect on it. But my intention to compete and get ahead rather than relax and be generous had an effect on me. My inner state was contracted and agitated. If you act on such an ungenerous intention often enough, your character will become contracted and agitated, less pleasant and happy and contented than it could be.

Just as you observe the effects of your actions and choose actions to produce desired effects, you can observe the effects of your intentions and choose to nurture the intentions that produce the effects you want.

In the realm of character, motivation and intention, no less than in individual predicaments, it makes sense to work for the good in all things.

Appendix C, In Defense of Panpsychism

Panpsychism, the idea that everything has an aspect of *psyche* or mind to it, seems nutty to most people. In our everyday experience some things are alive and some aren't, and the difference is obvious even if there are some grey areas. Living things have minds. At least we ourselves do, as we know from direct experience, and it is not too much of a stretch to say that all living things do. But what sense does it make to say that dead things have minds?

First, some context. This is all about the mind-body problem. Mental objects, such as thoughts and feelings, have no extension in space and are directly perceivable only by the person thinking or feeling them. Physical (bodily) objects have extension in space and are perceivable by more than one person. The question is, how are they related?

Here is the argument in its bare logical form as adapted from contemporary philosopher Galen Strawson:[249]

0. Reality is made of only one type of stuff. There is   *assumption*
   only one ultimate category that applies to everything. We call this view Monism.

1. Everything real has a material aspect. That is,   *premise*
   every instance of the one type of stuff of which
   reality is made is observable from an external,
   publicly-available point of view.

2. Our own experience, directly observable only   *premise*
   from the point of view of the one who is having it,
   is indisputably real.

3. Hence, at least some of reality has an experiential aspect as well as a material aspect.   *lemma (1,2)*[xxiv]

4. There is no radical emergence of experience from non-experiential stuff. The experiential aspect of something does not radically emerge from the material aspect. (By "radical" I mean strong, as opposed to weak, emergence. See discussion below.)   *premise*

5. Hence, experience is as fundamental to reality as matter.   *conclusion (3,4)*

5. Experience is fundamental to reality.   *lemma*

6. What is real is ultimately made up of very tiny elements; these are its fundamental constituents.   *premise*

7. Hence, at least some fundamental constituents of reality are intrinsically and irreducibly experiential as well as material in nature. For short, we call this idea "micropsychism."   *conclusion (5,6)*

7. Micropsychism is true.   *lemma*

8. The assertion that all fundamental constituents of reality are experiential as well as material is simpler than and preferable to the assertion that some are and some are not.   *premise*

9. Hence, all fundamental constituents of reality are intrinsically and irreducibly experiential in nature as well as material. For short, we call this "panpsychism."   *conclusion (7,8)*

That is terse, but it shows the logical structure of the argument. As in all logical arguments, the final conclusion is demonstrated to be true only if the logic is sound and all the premises are true. There is a surprisingly large body of recent work on this subject examining each of the premises in detail. I am certainly

---

[xxiv] A *lemma* is a conclusion that is then used as a premise in a further chain of argument.

not going to reproduce it all, but I will go over the premises and give some reasons why I think each of them makes sense.

We start off by assuming *monism*, the view that everything is made of the same kind of stuff. Depending on whom you ask, that might be matter (wholly non-experiential), the view known as materialism; mind (wholly non-material), the view known as idealism; or something in between that takes on aspects of both matter and mind. The alternative is dualism, which says that matter and mind are two entirely distinct kinds of stuff. The problem with dualism, of course, is how to explain the interaction between the two. I take it that monism is not a controversial assumption.

The first premise says that everything has a material, or physical, aspect; so the argument starts off agreeing with the materialists. I am giving an operational definition of "material." What is material is detectable or observable by more than one person. The first premise says that what is real is objectively there, and can be discerned by anyone with suitable training and instruments.

You would think that the second premise, that our own experience is indisputably real, would be equally uncontroversial, but that is not the case. Surprisingly, some people say that experience isn't really real. Most notoriously, Daniel Dennett, a materialist, makes the following assertion, where "phenomenology" means the various items in conscious experience:[250] "There seems to be phenomenology. That is a fact ... . But it does not follow ... that there really is phenomenology."[251]

As Strawson points out, seeming itself is a type of experience, so the argument fails on the face of it.[252] Dennett's claim is not so absurd as it sounds, because Dennett is arguing that what is really real is the brain activity that creates our experience. He says, for instance, that our experience seems smooth and continuous, but the physiology behind it is discontinuous and full of gaps. Hence, our experience is not really continuous at all.[253] But that just begs the question. In order to know anything about brain activity we have to see readings on dials, squiggles on paper, etc., and seeing is a kind of experience. The one thing we cannot doubt, when we are experiencing something, is that experience is going on. We can find out that we are mistaken about the objects of our experience, as when we see a hallucination or an optical illusion, but that we are experiencing is the bedrock of everything.

The conclusion from the first two premises is that experience is an undeniable aspect of whatever the universe is made of. And so is matter, of course. Now the question is, what is the relationship between experience and matter? A common claim is that experience emerges from non-experiential matter when matter reaches a certain degree of complexity. Premise 4 denies this claim.

The basic idea of emergence is that new properties arise in systems as a result of interactions at an elemental level.[254] A case in point is liquidity. A single molecule of water is not liquid, nor are its constituent atoms. But when you put several molecules of water together, you have a liquid (at certain temperatures). Liquidity is an emergent property, specifically a form of "weak" emergence: the emergent quality is directly traceable to characteristics of the system's components. Water molecules do not bind together in a tight lattice but slide past each other; that's just part of their physical make-up.

Some say that consciousness is an emergent property as well, that it arises when constituent material parts—neurons, sense organs and the like—are organized with sufficient complexity. If so, the emergence of consciousness would be a "strong" emergence. The new quality, consciousness, would not be reducible to the system's constituent parts; the whole would be greater than the sum of its parts.

Strawson denies the possibility of such strong emergence. He says "there must be something about the nature of the emerged-from (and nothing else) in virtue of which the emerger emerges as it does and is what it is. You can get liquidity from non-liquid molecules as easily as you can get a cricket team from eleven things that are not cricket teams."[255] We can do so because in those cases "we move wholly within a completely conceptually homogeneous ... set of notions."[256] But there is nothing about the nature of inert, non-experiential matter that would lead to the emergence of conscious experience. The two notions are not homogenous, but radically different. So consciousness does not emerge from non-conscious matter.

That, at least, is the argument in favor of premise 4. If you want to dispute it (and philosophers certainly have done so), you know where to take aim. But if we assume that it is true, then conclusion 5 follows: Experience is as fundamental to reality as matter; it is not something additional that emerges from what is primitive or more fundamental. In Strawson's argument this is a stopping place; the rest is elaboration.

The next premise, 6, is that the ultimate constituents of reality are quite tiny: electrons, protons, quarks, muons and the like. This reflects the current findings of the physical sciences, and there is no reason to doubt it.

Hence (conclusion 7), at least some fundamental constituents of reality are intrinsically and irreducibly experiential in nature as well as material. For short, we call this idea "micropsychism."

Micropsychism should make the idea of panpsychism a bit more palatable. The theory does not assert that inert substances such as rocks and concrete walls are conscious or have any kind of experience. It does assert that the ultimate components of such materials do have a kind of experience, some way of taking into account of their surroundings in a manner that, were it expanded and amplified quite a bit, would be like our waking consciousness of our world.

Premise 8 is an application of Occam's Razor, which advises us to adopt the simplest theory that adequately explains all the facts. Conclusion 7 says we have reason to think that at least some elemental parts of reality are experiential as well as material. We have no positive reason not to think that they all are. So it makes the theory simpler and more elegant to apply it to everything. Hence we end up with full-blown panpsychism (conclusion 9): all fundamental constituents of reality are intrinsically and irreducibly experiential, as well as material, in nature.

There is no way to tell for sure, of course. We cannot perform a scientific experiment to demonstrate that tiny particles or waves or whatever they are have some kind of experience of their surroundings. Physics tells us, with mathematical precision, how they interact, but physics tells us nothing of their internality. It's just that it makes a more coherent and refined theory to assume that every element, rather than only some of them, has some sort of experience. As I like to say, everything has an inside and an outside, the inside being the world as experienced by the entity itself and the outside being the way that the entity is experienced by other entities.

That's the argument in a nutshell. The whole thing hinges on premise 4, the denial of strong emergence. Materialism requires strong emergence to account for human consciousness. Panpsychism requires emergence as well, but only of a weak sort. If the fundamental units of reality are experiential as well as material, then it makes sense in principle that elaborate combinations of them would result in the vivid consciousness that we all enjoy while awake. But what is the nature of that combination? Without an account of that, panpsychism has little more explanatory plausibility than materialism.

If everything has both an inside, as panpsychism suggests, and an outside, as both panpsychism and materialism agree, then the organization of the outside should have some bearing on the richness of the inside. Let's go back to the initial conundrum, the difference between what is living and what is not. Is there something unique about how matter is organized in living beings that would account for the emergence of the complex and vivid form of experience that we know as waking consciousness? The answer is yes; it is what persists through time. The physical matter of non-living things persists through time, and their form changes through the impact of external forces. Living beings are the opposite: their physical matter is constantly changing through time, and only their form persists.

The physical matter of dead things just persists from moment to moment without changing, or changing only through external forces. In any given slice of time, the substance of a dead thing is the same as it is in any other slice of time. The totality of what it is can be encompassed in a single instant.

Living things are strikingly different. The physical matter that composes living things is constantly changing through *metabolism*, the process by which matter is ingested, transformed and excreted. What persists is not the matter itself but the form in which that matter is organized. A single slice of time does not encompass the unity of the living being at all. Only across time can we grasp its functional wholeness. I follow Hans Jonas here.[257] The sense of being a whole conscious entity emerges with metabolism, the ability of a simple organism to maintain its structure through time by exchanging physical matter with its environment. The physical matter changes, but the organizational form doesn't. (Or, it does, but it evolves so there is a continuity.) The structure of the material aspect—a changing material process that has a unity of form over time—gives rise to a unity of experience over time, a macroexperience, which is of a higher order than the microexperiences of the constituent elements.[xxv]

Jonas' insights map nicely to those of other panpsychists, the process philosophers. Charles Hartshorne has made the distinction between "compound" and "composite" individuals, which is roughly the distinction between what is living and what is not.[258] A compound individual is one which (or who), on a macro level, has a "dominating unit," an inclusive locus of experience, a single subject that unifies the experiences of its components into a coherent whole. Non-living things, although made up of actual ultimates that each have a mental or experiential aspect, have no such unification of experience. Hartshorne calls them "composite" rather than "compound." David Ray Griffin calls them "aggregate."[259] In compound (living) individuals the experiences of the components bind together and reinforce each other, giving birth

---

[xxv] A student under Heidegger, Jonas is rooted in both existential phenomenology and in biology, so his language is quite a bit different from Strawson's. He is germane because he takes seriously the possibility that other beings besides the human have subjective experience, which he, along with many existentialists and phenomenologists, calls "interiority." The germ of many aspects of human interiority is found in the simplest of living beings: a sense of freedom, of independence from the givenness of the material, along with a sense of necessity, of dependence on the material for one's existence; a sense of Being, of life, in opposition to the ever-present possibility of Non-being, of death; a sense of value, of the attractiveness of what is nourishing and repulsiveness of what is dangerous; a sense of selfhood, of inner identity that transcends the collective identity of the always-changing components, and a sense of the world that is other than oneself.

to a higher-level experience, a dominant subjectivity among the micropsychic components, which is in some ways superior to and capable of directing them. In composite (dead) things, or aggregations, the experiences of all the component simple individuals remain separate, and no higher-level inclusive experience arises. It is the persistence of form in compound individuals that enables the merging of the mentality of the micropsychic units into an inclusive subjectivity that, in its most developed instantiation, includes all the richness of human mental life, including a sense of freedom and a knowledge of its own mortality.

Appendix D, Truth

How do we know that any of this is true? There are several factors that determine the truthfulness of a theory or an explanation of events:

- The theory is *congruent* with our experience. It fits the facts. No fact is left unexplained by the theory. The theory is falsifiable, and no falsifying fact or event has been found.
- The theory is internally *consistent*. It has no contradictions within itself, and it all hangs together elegantly.
- The theory is *coherent* with everything else we consider true. It confirms, or at least fails to contradict, the rest of our knowledge, where "knowledge" means beliefs we can defend with rigorous reasons.
- The theory is *useful*. It has predictive power. It allows us to gain control of the world and to make accurate choices concerning what is likely to happen. It gives us mastery. When we act on the basis of the theory or explanation, our actions are successful.

I am in the pragmatist camp here. I think the chief quality of a theory that causes us to believe it, that is, to act as if it is true, is its usefulness. Let's look at each of these characteristics in turn.

Congruence

We think of truth as correspondence to reality, but I prefer the term "congruence." Truth is said to be a quality of propositions such that they correspond to the facts. If someone says the car is in the driveway, we can go look at the driveway to see if the car is really there. What's true, on this view, is an accurate reflection or statement of reality. But we don't have direct contact with reality, where "reality" means something completely independent of us. We have direct contact only with our experience, and our contact with reality is filtered through our experience. When what we experience is predictable, and our actions have favorable results, then we can infer that what we are basing our actions on is true. Our theory is congruent with the facts, as we experience them. And when we discover new facts, we can change our theory. Truth is always provisional, not an end state.

Consistency

A consistent theory is one whose elements all hang together; it contains no contradictions. An inconsistent theory has little or no predictive value. If elements of the theory contradict each other, we can't make consistent logical inferences from the theory. We can make inferences, but they are contradictory, and we do not know which inference to base our actions on. An inconsistent theory is not useful.

Related to consistency is simplicity. The recommendation to simplify theory is called Occam's Razor.[xxvi] The simpler a theory is, the more easily disprovable and the more easily understandable it is.

[xxvi] "Occam's razor (also spelled Ockham's razor) is a principle attributed to the 14th-century English logician and Franciscan friar William of Ockham. [It is] a heuristic maxim that advises economy, parsimony, or simplicity in scientific theories. Occam's razor states that the explanation of any phenomenon should make as few assumptions as possible, eliminating those that make no difference in the observable predictions of the explanatory hypothesis or theory. ... Furthermore, when multiple competing theories have equal predictive powers, the principle recommends selecting those that introduce the fewest assumptions and postulate the fewest hypothetical entities." (Wikipedia, "Occam's razor.")

Coherence

A good theory is coherent with other theories. We take as true those assertions, ideas or theories that cohere with all the rest of what we take as true, including our empirical observations as well as our theoretical knowledge. (We should always be ready, however, to revise such judgments on the basis of new information, else we risk falling into dogmatism.) A good example of this attribute of truth is found in the physical sciences. The theories of physical science hold together quite well. Physics, chemistry, geology, biology and astronomy all reinforce each other.

Usefulness

Truth increases our mastery of our lives and environment; it enables us to exert our power, in the sense of our ability to get things done. I include in the term "environment" both the world of physical things and the world of ideas, of theory. What is true is what works to organize our practice and our thought so that we are able both to handle reality effectively and to reason with logical rigor to true conclusions.

The physical sciences exemplify this attribute of truth. The scientific method is a method of evidence-based argument consisting of systematic observation and explanation. Since observation is central, assertions must include reports of the data on which they are based, including enough description of how the data was acquired to enable others to acquire similar data and look for alternative explanations. What authorizes belief is objective confirmation (or contradiction) of expected results by independent observers. The more rigorous the specification of expected results, the more compelling the confirmation (or contradiction). In other words, a theory we take to be true is useful in that it enables us to make predictions that are verified by further observation.

The authority structure of science is anarchic, with scientists deciding for themselves whom and what to believe. The occasional data fakers, professors who tyrannize their graduate students, or national academies that install an orthodoxy pretty quickly get outrun by events. The result is an accumulation of theories (i.e., systematic explanations) that are better established than anything else in human experience (although still incomplete— perhaps with big holes in some areas).

If multiple theories explain the observations, we choose the one that explains more of the observations or explains them with more precision or to a greater level of detail. In other words, we choose the one that is most useful for making further predictions and hence for enabling us to master our lives.

Truth is useful. Does that mean that what is useful is true? That is not a useful question. Let's not ask what truth is; let's ask instead how we can recognize it reliably when it appears.

A good theory points out aspects of our experience to which it would be beneficial to pay attention. A good philosophical expla- nation identifies patterns in our experience. (By "pattern" I mean repeated regularity, a configuration of events or things.)

The relationship between theory and pattern is two-way. Theory describes patterns found in experience, and the patterns found in experience inform theory. We can use other words as well:

Theory   Patterns (regularities)
------->
incorporates
sees, grasps
goes out and gets

<-------
inform
are incorporated into
give input to

Ultimately, truth is good. It works to promote human flour- ishing. Truth promotes goodness, love, harmony and beauty, both in the short term and in the long term. Truth promotes health.

Confidence

Truth gives us confidence. To believe something to be true is to be willing to act on it and, in fact, actually to act on it when the occasion arises. Confidence alone is not a guarantee of truth.

People can have great confidence in something that is false, or at least has bad consequences. People with confidence in what is false have faith, in a disparaging or pejorative sense of the term "faith." But if someone has clear perception and tends to believe true things, then the higher that person's confidence in something, the more likely it is to be true. This likelihood is the basis in reality for the appeal to authority for the truthfulness of propositions.

Non-Falsifiable Theories

Metaphysical theories, theories intended to be universally applicable and to explain all elements of experience and the objects of experience, are not falsifiable. For example, the theory that everything has an inside and an outside—a subjective, privately observable aspect and an objective, publicly observable aspect—cannot be disproved. We cannot prove that some things have no subjective aspect because to do so would require us to observe the inside, the subjectivity, of those things and determine that they had no subjectivity. But by definition we cannot directly observe the subjectivity of anything other than our own subjectivity.

In cases where a theory is not easily or at all falsifiable, for instance a metaphysical explanation of life, we cannot verify its congruence or correspondence with reality. We can, however, make judgments on the basis of the other criteria. We can decide to act as if it is true or not on the basis of its consistency, its coherence and its practicality for achieving our ends.

What Is Knowable and What Is Believable

What we can know from direct experience: That the Transcendental Self is unobservable.

What we believe to be true on the basis of the best science to date: That the quantum-mechanical level of reality is indeterminate.

What may be true and does not contradict what we know:

- That everything has an inside and an outside.
- That the Transcendental Self of each person is the Self of all, The God.

- That the quantum-mechanical level of reality is where The God intervenes in the physical world.

Notes

1 Wikipedia, "Eudaimonia" and "Eudaimonism."

2 Wikipedia, "Arete."

3 Mackey and Sisodia, *Conscious Capitalism*.

4 Wikipedia, "Panpsychism."

5 Dennett, *Consciousness Explained*, p. 367.

6 I have consulted the following sources for this chapter:

- Liebach, "Shape-shifting Fish."
- Underwater Photography Guide, "Huge School of Fish Loved by Photographers."
- Pardeau, Bo, "Schooling Behavior."
- Wikipedia, "Bigeye Scad."

7 Pinker, *How the Mind Works*, p. 322.

8 Wikipedia, "Ant."

9 Thomas, *The Lives of a Cell*, p. 12.

10 Emerson, "Essays, First Series [1841]: The Over-Soul."

11 This chapter summarizes information from a variety of sources:

- Blanton," Does Bell's Inequality rule out local theories of quantum mechanics?"
- Felder, "Spooky Action at a Distance."
- Harrison, "Bell's Theorem."
- Harrison, "The Stern-Gerlack Experiment."
- National Science Teachers Association, "The Stern-Gerlack Experiment."
- Rothman, Doubt and Certainty, pp. 173–180.

- Thinkquest Library, "Bell's Inequality and The EPR Paradox."
- Wikipedia, "Bell's Theorem."
- Wikipedia, "EPR Paradox."
- Wikipedia, "Interpretations of quantum mechanics."
- Wikipedia, "Introduction to quantum mechanics."
- Wikipedia, "Pion."
- Wikipedia, "Quantum entanglement."
- Wikipedia, "Stern-Gerlach experiment."
- 12 A more complete version of this chapter is found at Meacham, "The Quantum Level of Reality." I have consulted the following sources:
- Ask A Scientist. "Size of Hydrogen."
- Bast, Felix, "Ca2+ : An Ion of Biological Cybernetics."
- Encyclopædia Britannica, Standard Edition. "Divisionism."
- Encyclopædia Britannica, Standard Edition. "Nervous system."
- The Physics Factbook, "Number of Neurons in a Human Brain."
- Pratt, David, "Consciousness, Causality, and Quantum Physics."
- Rothman, Doubt and Certainty, pp. 156-160.
- Schwarts, The Mind and The Brain: Neuroplasticity and the Power of Mental Force.
- Stapp, Henry P., Mind, Matter and Quantum Mechanics.
- Stapp, Henry P., Mindful Universe: Quantum Mechanics and the Participating Observer.
- Wikipedia, "Calcium in biology."
- Wikipedia, "Causality."
- Wikipedia, "Chemical synapse."
- Wikipedia, "Consciousness Causes Collapse."
- Wikipedia, "Double-slit Experiment."
- Wikipedia, "Henry Stapp."
- Wikipedia, "Interference."
- Wikipedia, "Interpretations of Quantum Mechanics."
- Wikipedia, "Nerve."

- Wikipedia, "Neuron."
- Wikipedia, "Quanta."
- Wikipedia, "Quantum Decoherence."
- Wikipedia, "Quantum Physics."
- Wikipedia, "Quantum Superposition."
- Wikipedia, "Wave Function Collapse."
- Wikipedia, "Chemical synapse."

[13] Husserl, *Ideas*, p. 156.

[14] Ibid.

[15] Ibid., p. 214.

[16] Ibid., pp. 315, 316

[17] Heidegger, *Being and Time*, p. 27, translator's footnote 1.

[18] Ibid., p. 160, translator's footnote 2.

[19] *Buddhist Writings*, Majjhima-Nikaya, Sutta 63.

[20] Tao Te Ching #1.

[21] Brihadaranyaka Upanishad, IV, iv, 5, in Zaehner, Hindu Scriptures, p. 71. See also Mandukya Upanishad, 2, in Zaehner, Hindu Scriptures, p. 201.

[22] The Bhagavad Gita, tr. Mascaro, p. 99.

[23] Emerson, "Essays, First Series [1841]: "The Over-Soul."

[24] Tao Te Ching #40.

[25] Ram Dass, *Grist for the Mill*, p. 15.

[26] Jewish and Christian Bible. 1 Kings 19: 11–12 (King James Version).

[27] Wikipedia, "Primate."

[28] Wikipedia, "Hominini."

[29] Hare, p. 92.

[30] de Waal, *Peacemaking Among Primates*, p. 51.

[31] de Waal, *Chimpanzee Politics*, p. 164. de Waal backs his conclusions with an impressive amount of observational data. He and his team recorded every instance of each type of interaction—submissive greeting, dominance display, fighting, reconciling, grooming, entreating, copulating and more—among more than 20 apes over five years, and then correlated the data on computers. He graphs the relative percentage of submissive greetings, of mating activity and of group support among the various males and the data clearly show that during the first year of Luit's reign, Yeroen got as much sex as the other two combined.

[32] de Waal, *Chimpanzee Politics*, p. 141.

[33] de Waal, *Primates and Philosophers*, p. 33.

[34] de Waal, *Peacemaking Among Primates*, pp. 38–39.

[35] de Waal, *Primates and Philosophers*, pp. 7–12.

[36] de Waal, *Our Inner Ape*, pp. 139–141.

[37] de Waal, *Primates and Philosophers*, p. 71.

[38] Ryan and Jetha, *Sex At Dawn*, pp. 1–15.

[39] Wrangham, *Catching Fire*, pp. 14, 112–114.

[40] de Waal, *Our Inner Ape*, p. 141.

[41] See, for instance, the section titled "Predictive Power" in Wikipedia, "Evolution as Fact and Theory."

[42] Dobzhansky, "Nothing in Biology Makes Sense Except in the Light of Evolution."

[43] Ibid.

[44] Wikipedia, "Artificial Selection," "Evolution," "Evolution as theory and fact," "Gene," "Introduction to evolution."

[45] Dawkins, *The Selfish Gene*, chapter 11, pp. 189–201.

[46] Pinker, *How the Mind Works*, p. 23.

[47] There are numerous examples of experimental verification. See, for example, Griskevicius et al., "Blatant Benevolence and Conspicuous Consumption: When Romantic Motives Elicit Costly Signals." Trivers, in "The Evolution of Reciprocal Altruism," cites many instances of experimental evidence for hypotheses arising from evolutionary psychological theory. See Pinker, *How the Mind Works*, p. 505, for elegant anthropological verification of hypotheses regarding reciprocal altruism.

[48] The EEA is not a single place but a statistical composite of the properties of the ancestral environment that exerted selective effects on human ancestors. Tooby and Cosmides, "The Past Explains the Present," p. 386.

[49] Dutton, *The Art Instinct*, pp. 14, 19–22.

[50] Orians and Heerwagen, "Evolved Responses to Landscapes," p 556.

[51] Pinker, *How the Mind Works*, p. 21. See also Cosmides and Tooby, "Evolutionary Psychology and the Emotions," p. 98.

[52] Cosmides and Tooby, "Evolutionary Psychology and the Emotions," p. 99.

53 Ibid., p. 96.

54 Ibid., p. 98.

55 Ibid., p. 99.

56 Ibid., p. 92.

57 Pinker, *How the Mind Works*, p. 373.

58 Cosmides and Tooby, "Evolutionary Psychology and the Emotions," throughout.

59 Ibid., p. 93.

60 Ibid.

61 Pinker, *How the Mind Works*, p. 373.

62 Pinker, "So How *Does* the Mind Work?" p. 4.

63 Solomon, *The Passions*, p. xvii.

64 Cosmides and Tooby, "Consider the Source," pp. 53–54.

65 Ibid., p. 54.

66 Tooby and Cosmides, "The Past Explains the Present," p. 420.

67 Ibid., p. 406.

68 Pinker, *How the Mind Works*, p. 62.

69 Cosmides and Tooby, "Consider the Source," pp. 57–58.

70 Ibid., pp. 59–60.

71 Ibid.

72 Ibid., p. 64.

73 Ibid., p. 80.

74 Ibid., p. 74.

75 Ibid., pp. 74 ff.

76 Ibid., pp. 79 ff.

77 Ibid., pp. 82 ff.

78 Ibid., pp. 85 ff.

79 Ibid., pp. 89 ff.

80 Ibid., pp. 93 ff.

81 Haidt, *The Happiness Hypothesis*, pp. 47 ff.

82 de Waal, *Primates and Philosophers*, p. 4.

83 Wikipedia, "Theory of Mind."

84 Hauser, *Moral Minds*, pp. 313–322. Also Steen, "Theory of Mind."

85 Hauser, *Moral Minds*, pp. 337–341.

86 Shakespeare, *A Midsummer Night's Dream*. Plot summary at http://en.wikipedia.org/wiki/A_Midsummer_Night's_Dream as of 30 Nov. 2010.

[87] Information in this section comes from the Re-evaluation Counseling Communities. You can find out about Re-evaluation Counseling by contacting its headquarters at 719 Second Avenue North, Seattle, WA 98109, USA, or visiting its website, http://www.rc.org/.

[88] Re-evaluation Counseling Communities, *Fundamentals of Co-Counseling Manual*, pp. 3–7.

[89] Ibid., p 3.

[90] Re-evaluation Counseling Communities, *RC Theory*.

[91] De Waal, *Primates and Philosophers*, p. 4.

[92] Re-evaluation Counseling Communities, "About Re-evaluation Counseling."

[93] Frankfurt, *The Importance of What We Care About*, pp. 11–25.

[94] Ibid., p. 12.

[95] Ibid., p. 14.

[96] Ibid., p. 16.

[97] Ibid,, pp. 20–21.

[98] Heidegger, *Being and Time*, p. 220.

[99] Henley, *Invictus*.

[100] Pinker, "The Moral Instinct."

[101] Ibid.

[102] Hauser, *Moral Minds*, pp. 112–121. See also Pinker, "The Moral Instinct."

[103] Pinker, "The Moral Instinct."

[104] Pinker, *How The Mind Works*, pp. 336–337.

[105] Pinker, "The Moral Instinct."

[106] Haidt and Joseph, "Intuitive Ethics," p. 56. Note that "consciousness" here means a container. See Meacham, "Consciousness and Experience."

[107] Ibid.

[108] Haidt and Joseph, "The Moral Mind," p. 14.

[109] Haidt and Joseph, "Intuitive Ethics," p 57.

[110] Ibid, p 56.

[111] Haidt, *The Righteous Mind*, pp. 123–127, "Moral Foundations Theory," and pp. 170–176, "The Liberty/Oppression Foundation." See also earlier works that omit Liberty/Oppression: Haidt and Joseph, "The Moral Mind;" Haidt and Joseph, "Intuitive Ethics;"

Haidt and Graham, "When Morality Opposes Justice;" and Haidt and Graham, "Planet of the Durkheimians."

[112] de Waal, *Our Inner Ape*, p. 187.

[113] Ibid., p. 191

[114] Haidt and Joseph, "The Moral Mind," p. 18.

[115] Ibid.

[116] This section is taken from Haidt, *The Righteous Mind*, pp. 170–176.

[117] de Waal, *Primates and Philosophers*, p. 27.

[118] Ibid. p. 25.

[119] Ibid. pp. 33–25.

[120] Ibid. p, 71.

[121] Hauser, *Moral Minds*, p. 395. de Waal, *Primates and Philosophers*, pp. 44–49.

[122] de Waal, *Primates and Philosophers*, p. 43.

[123] Ibid., p. 54.

[124] Ibid.

[125] de Waal, *Our Inner Ape*, pp. 132–135.

[126] Ibid. p. 135.

[127] de Waal, *Primates and Philosophers*, p. 55.

[128] Ibid., p. 6.

[129] Haidt and Joseph, "The Moral Mind," p. 1.

[130] Haidt and Joseph, "The Moral Mind," p. 11.

[131] Ibid., p. 14.

[132] Wong, "Making An Effort To Understand," p. 13.

[133] Adapted from Little, Margaret, "The Moral Right to do Wrong." Little's examination shows the strength of analytic philosophy: By clarifying conceptually what we are talking about, we can avoid confusion and make progress toward insight.

[134] Meacham, "The Good." See also *Appendix B, The Nature of the Good* in this work.

[135] Wong, "Making An Effort To Understand," p. 12.

[136] Joyce, "Moral Anti-Realism."

[137] Sartre, "Existentialism Is a Humanism."

[138] Wikipedia, "Mirror Neuron."

[139] de Waal, *Our Inner Ape*, p. 186.

[140] Pinker, "The Moral Instinct."

[141] Ibid.

142 King, *Evolving God*, p. 13.

143 Wade, *Before the Dawn*, pp. 72–73.

144 Wikipedia, "Group Selection."

145 Fisher, "Still Here," p. 41.

146 Wikipedia, "Meme."

147 Dennett, *Breaking the Spell*, pp. 108–112.

148 Wikipedia, "Evolutionary Psychology of Religion."

149 Dennett, Breaking the Spell, pp. 112–113.

150 Ibid., pp. 125–131.

151 Ibid., pp. 132–135.

152 Ibid., pp. 167–173.

153 Wright, *The Evolution of God*, pp. 468–470.

154 Dennett, *Breaking the Spell*, p. 109, and Wright, *The Evolution of God*, p. 477.

155 Wright, *The Evolution of God*, p. 468.

156 Ibid., p. 464.

157 Dennett, *Breaking the Spell*, pp. 167–173.

158 Ibid., Chapters 6–8, pp. 153–246.

159 Wright, *The Evolution of God*, p. 482.

160 Haidt, *The Righteous Mind*, pp. 190–191.

161 Ibid., pp. 191–192.

162 Ibid., p. 217.

163 Ibid., p. 195.

164 Ibid., p. 214.

165 Ibid., p. 220.

166 Pinker, "The False Allure Of Group Selection."

167 Dennett, *Breaking the Spell*, p. 184.

168 Haidt, *The Righteous Mind*, pp. 221–233.

169 Ibid., p. 223.

170 Ibid., p. 256.

171 Ibid.

172 Ibid., p. 257.

173 Ibid., p. 264.

174 Ibid., p. 267.

175 Ibid., p. 265.

176 Dylan, "Gotta Serve Somebody."

177 This section is drawn from Wright, *The Moral Animal*, pp. 33–92.
178 George Williams, quoted in Wright, *The Moral Animal*, p. 41.
179 Ibid.
180 Wright, *The Moral Animal*, p. 62.
181 Ibid., p. 265.
182 Trivers, "The Evolution of Reciprocal Altruism," p. 35.
183 Wikipedia, "Inclusive Fitness."
184 Dawkins, *The Selfish Gene*, p. 90.
185 Trivers, "The Evolution of Reciprocal Altruism," p. 35.
186 Ibid. p. 37.
187 Pinker, *How the Mind Works*, p. 505.
188 Trivers, "The Evolution of Reciprocal Altruism," p. 36.
189 Ibid. p. 46.
190 Ibid. p. 49.
191 Ibid. p. 50.
192 Pinker, *How the Mind Works*, p. 404.
193 Wright, *The Moral Animal*, p. 264.
194 Trivers, quoted in Wright, *The Moral Animal*, p. 264.
195 Wright, *The Moral Animal*, p. 268.
196 Pinker, *How the Mind Works*, pp. 421–423.
197 Parker-Pope, "How the Food Makers Captured Our Brains."
198 Tierney, "Message in What We Buy, but Nobody's Listening."
199 Taleb, *The Black Swan*, pp. xvii–xviii.
200 Ibid., pp. 87–88.
201 Ibid., p. 88, p. 157.
202 Ibid., p. 88.
203 Kahnemann, *Thinking, Fast and Slow*, pp. 20–21.
204 Ibid., p. 43.
205 Ibid., p. 23.
206 Goleman, *Destructive Emotions*, p. 75.
207 Ibid., p. 78.
208 Ibid., p. 76.
209 Haidt, *The Happiness Hypothesis*, p. 4.
210 Ibid., pp. 5–6.
211 Scholarpedia, "Enteric Nervous System." Rubin, "The Brain-Gut Connection."
212 Haidt, *The Happiness Hypothesis*, pp. 6–8.

213 http://dictionary.reference.com/browse/confabulation as of 3 February 2010.

214 Haidt, *The Happiness Hypothesis*, p. 9.

215 Ibid., p. 12.

216 Ibid.

217 Ibid., p. 13.

218 Ibid., p. 16.

219 Ibid., p. 17.

220 Ibid., p. 22.

221 Versenyi, *Socratic Humanism*, p. 80.

222 Haidt, *The Happiness Hypothesis*, p. 17.

223 Haidt, *The Happiness Hypothesis*, p. 16.

224 Wikipedia, "PDCA."

225 Wikipedia, "Existence Precedes Essence."

226 James, "Habit" in *Principles of Psychology* and "The Laws of Habit" in *Talks to Teachers*.

227 James, "Habit."

228 James, "The Laws of Habit."

229 Goleman, *Destructive Emotions*, p. 145.

230 Ibid. p. 146.

231 Ibid., p. 83.

232 Taylor, *My Stroke of Insight*, p. 146.

233 Goleman, *Destructive Emotions*, p. 83.

234 Ibid., p. 145.

235 Ibid., p. 144.

236 Ibid., pp. 144–145.

237 Ibid., p. 146.

238 Dennett, "Dan Dennett on Dangerous Memes," 5:25.

239 Pinker, *How the Mind Works*, p. 424.

240 Haidt, *The Happiness Hypothesis*, p. 17.

241 The Internet Movie Database, http://www.imdb.com/character/ch0011313/quotes as of 11 February 2010.

242 Wright, *The Moral Animal*, p. 37.

243 Edel, "Right and Good."

244 URL: http://blogs.zdnet.com/carroll/?p=1592, as of 5 September 2006

245 Wikipedia, "Category Mistake."

246 Hume, *A Treatise of Human Nature*, p. 469. Slawson, "Ought vs. Is." Wikipedia, "Is–Ought Problem."

247 Avery, "Use 'Works' And 'Doesn't Work.'"

248 Ibid.

249 Strawson, "Real Naturalism." I am paraphrasing Strawson's terminology. Strawson starts by agreeing with materialists that concrete reality is entirely physical in nature and then argues for a meaning of "physical" that includes both the material and the mental. I prefer to use the term "physical" as most people do, to mean material only.

250 Dennett, *Consciousness Explained*, p. 45.

251 Ibid., p. 366.

252 Strawson, "Realistic Monism," p. 6, footnote 7.

253 Dennett, *Consciousness Explained*, p. 356.

254 Wikipedia, "Emergence."

255 Strawson, "Realistic Monism," p. 15

256 Ibid.

257 Jonas, "Evolution and Freedom," pp. 64-67.

258 Hartshorne, "The Compound Individual," pp. 215-217.

259 Griffin, *Whitehead's Radically Different Postmodern Philosophy*, pp. 58-61.

Bibliography

Aristotle, *Nichomachean Ethics*, I.7 1097b, pp. 22–29. Tr. W.D. Ross. *Introduction to Aristotle,* Ed. Richard McKeon. New York: Random House Modern Library, 1947, p 318. Available online at http://classics.mit.edu//Aristotle/nicomachaen.html.

Ask A Scientist. "Size of Hydrogen." Online publication http://www.newton.dep.anl.gov/askasci/chem00/chem00452.htm as of 1 November 2007.

Avery, C. M., *Teamwork Is an Individual Skill: Getting Your Work Done When Sharing Responsibility.* San Francisco: Berrett-Koehler Publishers, 2001.

___. "Use 'Works' And 'Doesn't Work.'" Partnerwerks Collaboratory, 20 March 2000. Online publication http://archive.maillist.com/teamwisdom/msg00084.html, archived at http://www.bmeacham.com/whatswhat/AveryArchive.htm.

Bast, Felix. "Ca2+ : An Ion of Biological Cybernetics." Online publication http://www.bbc.co.uk/dna/h2g2/brunel/A2417654 as of 10 December 2007.

The Bhagavad Gita. Tr. Juan Mascaro. Baltimore: Penguin Books. 1962.

Blanton, John, et. al. "Does Bell's Inequality rule out local theories of quantum mechanics?" Online publication http://math.ucr.edu/home/baez/physics/Quantum/bells_inequality.html as of 25 August 2011.

Buddhist Writings, Translated and Annotated by Henry Clarke Warren. Vol. XLV, Part 3. The Harvard Classics. New York: P.F. Collier & Son, 1909–14; Bartleby.com, 2001. http://www.bartleby.com/45/3/201.html as of 15 November 2012.

Cosmides, Leda, and John Tooby. "Consider the source: The Evo-
    lution of Adaptations for Decoupling and Metarepresenta-
    tion." *Metarepresentations: A Multidisciplinary Perspective,*
    Ed. Dan Sperber, pp. 53–115. New York: Oxford Press, 2000.
    Available online at
    http://www.psych.ucsb.edu/research/cep/metarep.html as of
    25 May 2009.
___. "Evolutionary Psychology and the Emotions." *Handbook of
    Emotions, 2nd Edition,* Eds. Michael Lewis and Jeannette
    Haviland-Jones, pp. 91–115. New York: Guilford Press, 2000.
    Available online at
    http://www.psych.ucsb.edu/research/cep/publist.htm as of 26
    May 2009.
Dawkins, Richard. *The Selfish Gene, New Edition.* Oxford and
    New York: Oxford University Press, 1989.
de Waal, Frans. *Chimpanzee Politics: Power and Sex Among
    Apes, 25th Anniversary Edition.* Baltimore: Johns Hopkins
    University Press, 2007.
___. *Our Inner Ape.* New York: Riverhead Books, 2005.
___. *Peacemaking Among Primates.* Cambridge, MA: Harvard
    University Press, 1989.
___. *Primates and Philosophers: How Morality Evolved.* Prince-
    ton: Princeton University Press, 2006.
Dennett, Daniel C. "Dan Dennett on Dangerous Memes." Online
    video publication, February 2002,
    http://www.ted.com/index.php/talks/dan_dennett_on_dangero
    us_memes.html as of 16 October 2008.
Dennett, Daniel C. *Breaking the Spell: Religion as a Natural
    Phenomenon.* New York: Penguin Books, 2006.
___. *Consciousness Explained.* Boston: Little, Brown and Compa-
    ny Back Bay Books, 1991.
Dobzhansky, Theodosius. "Nothing in Biology Makes Sense Ex-
    cept in the Light of Evolution." American Biology Teacher
    vol. 35 (March 1973), reprinted in *Evolution versus Creation-
    ism,* Ed. J. Peter Zetterberg. Phoenix: ORYX Press, 1983.
    Available online at http://www.2think.org/dobzhansky.shtml
    as of 14 May 2012.

Dutton, Denis. *The Art Instinct: Beauty, Pleasure and Human Evolution*. New York: Bloomsbury Press, 2009.

Dylan, Bob. "Gotta Serve Somebody" on *Slow Train Coming*. New York: Columbia Records, 1979. Lyrics available online at http://www.bobdylan.com/us/songs/gotta-serve-somebody as of 5 October 2012.

Edel, Abraham. "Right and Good." *Dictionary of the History of Ideas*. Online publication http://etext.lib.virginia.edu/cgi-local/DHI/dhi.cgi?id=dv4-24 as of 17 July 2008. Archived at http://www.bmeacham.com/whatswhat/OP/Edel_RightAndGood.htm.

Emerson, Ralph Waldo. "Essays, First Series [1841]: The Over-Soul." Online publication http://www.vcu.edu/engweb/transcendentalism/authors/emerson/essays/oversoul.html as of 22 August 2011.

Encyclopædia Britannica, Standard Edition. "Divisionism." Chicago: Encyclopædia Britannica, 2007.

___. "Nervous system." Chicago: Encyclopædia Britannica, 2007.

Felder, Gary. "Spooky Action at a Distance: An Explanation of Bell's Theorem." Online publication http://www4.ncsu.edu/unity/lockers/users/f/felder/public/kenny/papers/bell.html as of 25 August 2011.

Fisher, Corey. "Still Here." The Sun Magazine, December 2005. Chapel Hill, NC: The Sun Publishing Company, 2005.

Frankfurt, Harry. *The Importance of What We Care About*. New York: Cambridge University Press, 1998.

Gilbert, Daniel. *Stumbling on Happiness*. New York: Vintage Books, 2005.

Goleman, Daniel. *Destructive Emotions: How Can We Overcome Them? A Scientific Dialogue with the Dalai Lama*. New York: Bantam Books, 2003.

Griffin, David Ray. *Whitehead's Radically Different Postmodern Philosophy*. Albany: State University of New York Press, 2007

Griskevicius, Vladas, et al. "Blatant Benevolence and Conspicuous Consumption: When Romantic Motives Elicit Costly Signals." Journal of Personality and Social Psychology, 2007, Vol. 93, No. 1, pp. 85–102.

Haidt, Jonathan. *The Happiness Hypothesis: Finding Modern Truth in Ancient Wisdom.* New York: Basic Books, 2006.

___. *The Righteous Mind: Why Good People Are Divided by Politics and Religion.* New York: Pantheon Books, 2012.

Haidt, Jonathan, and Craig Joseph. "Intuitive ethics: How Innately Prepared Intuitions Generate Culturally Variable Virtues." Online publication http://faculty.virginia.edu/haidtlab/articles/haidt.joseph.intuitive-ethics.pdf as of 6 October 2008.

___. "The Moral Mind: How Five Sets of Innate Intuitions Guide the Development of Many Culture-Specific Virtues, and Perhaps Even Modules." Online publication http://faculty.virginia.edu/haidtlab/articles/haidt.joseph.2007.the-moral-mind.doc as of 8 October 2008. Subsequently printed in Carruthers, Peter, et al., *The Innate Mind: Foundations and the Future*, Volume 3, pp. 367ff. New York: Oxford Press, 2007.

Haidt, Jonathan, and Jesse Graham. "Planet of the Durkheimians, Where Community, Authority, and Sacredness are Foundations of Morality." Online publication http://faculty.virginia.edu/haidtlab/articles/haidt.graham.planet-of-the-durkheimians.doc as of 6 October 2008. Also available at Social Science Research Network: http://ssrn.com/abstract=980844.

___. "When Morality Opposes Justice: Conservatives Have Moral Intuitions that Liberals may not Recognize." Online publication http://faculty.virginia.edu/haidtlab/articles/haidt.graham.when-morality-opposes-justice.pdf as of 8 October 2008.

Hare, Brian. "What Is the Effect of Affect on Bonobo and Chimpanzee Problem Solving?" *The Neurobiology of the Umwelt: How Living Beings Perceive the World*, Eds. A. Berthoz and Y. Christen. New York: Springer Press, 2009, pp. 89–102. Available online at http://evolutionaryanthropology.duke.edu/research/3chimps/publications as of 3 October 2011.

Harrison, David M. "Bell's Theorem." Online publication
http://www.upscale.utoronto.ca/PVB/Harrison/BellsTheorem/
BellsTheorem.html as of 22 August 2011.
___. "The Stern-Gerlach Experiment, Electron Spin, and Correlation Experiments." On-line publication
http://www.upscale.utoronto.ca/GeneralInterest/Harrison/Ste
rnGerlach/SternGerlach.html as of 29 August 2007.
Hartshorne, Charles. "The Compound Individual." *Philosophical Essays for Alfred North Whitehead*. New York: Longmans, Green and Co., 1936.
Hauser, Marc D. *Moral Minds: The Nature of Right and Wrong*. New York: Harper Perennial, 2006.
Heidegger, Martin. *Being and Time*. Tr. John Macquarrie and Edward Robinson. New York: Harper and Row, HarperSanFrancisco, 1962.
Henley, William Ernest. "Invictus." Available online at
http://www.bartleby.com/103/7.html as of 12 March 2010.
Hindu Scriptures. Tr. R.C. Zaehner. London: J.M. Dent & Sons, 1966.
Hume, David. *A Treatise of Human Nature*, Ed. L. A. Selby-Bigge. Oxford: Clarendon Press, 1896. Book III. Online publication,
http://www.class.uidaho.edu/mickelsen/texts/Hume%20Treati
se/hume%20treatise3.htm as of 5 October 2010.
Husserl, Edmund. *Ideas: General Introduction to Pure Phenomenology*. Tr. W. R. Boyce Gibson. New York: Collier Books, 1967.
James, William. "Habit." Chapter IV of *Principles of Psychology, Vol. 1*. New York: Henry Holt and Company, 1890, 1918. Online publication
http://psychclassics.yorku.ca/James/Principles/prin4.htm as of 8 February 2010.
___. "The Laws of Habit." Chapter 8 of *Talks To Teachers On Psychology; and To Students On Some of Life's Ideals*. New York: Henry Hold and Company, 1914. Online publication
http://www.des.emory.edu/mfp/tt8.html as of 8 February 2010.
Jonas, Hans. "Evolution and Freedom: On the Continuity among Life-Forms." In *Mortality and Morality: A Search of the Good*

after Auschwitz, Ed. Lawrence Vogel. Evanston, IL: North-western University Press, 1996.

Joyce, Richard. "Moral Anti-Realism." The Stanford Encyclopedia of Philosophy (Summer 2009 Edition), Ed. Edward N. Zalta. Available online at http://plato.stanford.edu/archives/sum2009/entries/moral-anti-realism/.

Kahneman, Daniel. *Thinking, Fast and Slow*. New York: Farrar, Straus and Giroux, 2011.

King, Barbara J. *Evolving God: A Provocative View of the Origins of Religion*. New York: Doubleday, 2007.

Leibach, Julie. "Shape-shifting fish in Hawaii offer a compelling lesson: There's safety, and beauty, in unity." Audubon Magazine, Volume 113 Number 4 (July-August 2011), page 68. Available online at http://mag.audubon.org/articles/nature/art-school as of 8 November 2012.

Little, Margaret. "The Moral Right to do Wrong." Lecture presented at the 2012 Royal Ethics Conference, University of Texas at Austin, 25 February 2012.

Mackey, John and Raj Sisodia. *Conscious Capitalism: Liberating the Heroic Spirit of Business*. Boston: Harvard Business Review Press, 2013.

Meacham, Bill. "Consciousness and Experience." Online publication http://www.bmeacham.com/whatswhat/ConsciousnessAndExperience.html as of 8 May 2012.

___. "Do Humans Have Free Will?" Online publication http://www.bmeacham.com/whatswhat/FreeWill.html as of 9 December 2011.

___. "The Good." Online publication http://www.bmeacham.com/blog/?p=554 as of 14 February 2012.

___. "The Quantum Level of Reality." Online publication http://www.bmeacham.com/whatswhat/Quantum.html as of 27 June 2008.

National Science Teachers Association. "The Stern-Gerlach Experiment." On-line publication; URL =

http://www.if.ufrgs.br/~betz/quantum/SGtext.htm as of 29 August 2007.

Orians, Gordon H., and Judith H. Heerwagen. "Evolved Responses to Landscapes." *The Adapted Mind*, Ed. Jerome H. Barkow, Leda Cosmides and John Tooby, pp. 555–579. New York: Oxford University Press, 1992.

Pardeau, Bo. "Schooling Behavior" (Photos of Akule). Online publication http://www.flickr.com/photos/bodiver/sets/7215762679429089 9/ as of 27 July 2011.

Parker-Pope, Tara. "How the Food Makers Captured Our Brains." Online publication http://www.nytimes.com/2009/06/23/health/23well.html as of 23 June 2009.

The Physics Factbook. "Number of Neurons in a Human Brain." Online publication http://www.hypertextbook.com/facts/2002/AniciaNdabahaliye 2.shtml as of 1 October 2007.

Pinker, Steven. "The False Allure Of Group Selection." Online publication http://edge.org/conversation/the-false-allure-of-group-selection as of 19 September 2012.

___. "The Moral Instinct." Online publication http://www.nytimes.com/2008/01/13/magazine/13Psychology-t.html as of 12 January 2008.

___. "So How Does the Mind Work?" Mind and Language, 20(1), 1–24. Available online at http://pinker.wjh.harvard.edu/articles/ as of 23 June 2009.

___. *How the Mind Works*. New York: W. W. Norton & Company, 1997.

Pratt, David. "Consciousness, Causality, and Quantum Physics." Online publication http://ourworld.compuserve.com/homepages/dp5/jse.htm as of 29 August 2007. Originally published in Journal of Scientific Exploration, 11:1, Spring 1997, pp. 69–78.

Ram Dass. *Grist for the Mill*. Santa Cruz, CA: Unity Press, 1977.

The Re-evaluation Counseling Communities. *About Re-evaluation Counseling*. Online publication http://www.rc.org/index.html as of 25 September 2009.

___. *RC Theory*. Online publication
http://www.rc.org/theory/index.html as of 25 September 2009.
___. *Fundamentals of Co-Counseling Manual*. Seattle: Personal
Counselors, Inc., 1970.

Rothman, Tony, and George Sudarshan. *Doubt and Certainty*.
NY: Helix Books (Perseus Book Group), 1998.

Rubin, Jordan S. "The Brain-Gut Connection." Online publication
http://altmedangel.com/gutbrain.htm as of 5 February 2010.

Ryan, Christopher, and Cacilda Jetha. *Sex At Dawn: The Prehis-
toric Origins of Modern Sexuality*. New York: Harper, 2010.

Sartre, Jean-Paul. "Existentialism Is a Humanism." Online publication
http://www.marxists.org/reference/archive/sartre/works/exist/
sartre.htm as of 17 September 2011.

Scholarpedia. "Enteric Nervous System." Online publication
http://www.scholarpedia.org/article/Enteric_nervous_system
as of 5 February 2010.

Schwarts, Jeffery M., M.D., and Sharon Begley. *The Mind and
The Brain: Neuroplasticity and the Power of Mental Force*.
New York: ReganBooks, an imprint of HarperCollins, 2002.

Slawson, Kim. "Ought Versus Is, Government Versus Autono-
my." Online publication
http://www.everything2.net/e2node/Ought%2520versus%2520
Is%252C%2520Government%2520versus%2520Autonomy as
of 18 July 2008.

Solomon, Robert. *The Passions: Emotions and the Meaning of
Life*. Indianapolis: Hackett Publishing Company, 1993.

Stapp, Henry P. *Mind, Matter and Quantum Mechanics, Second
Edition*. Berlin: Springer-Verlag, 2004.
___. *Mindful Universe: Quantum Mechanics and the Participat-
ing Observer*. Berlin: Springer-Verlag, 2007.

Steen, Francis F. "Theory of Mind: A Model of Mental-state At-
tribution." Online publication
http://cogweb.ucla.edu/CogSci/ToMM.html as of 25 August
2009.

Strawson, Galen. "Real Naturalism." Draft paper delivered at a
colloquium for the Department of Philosophy at the University of Texas at Austin, 20 October 2011.

___. "Realistic Monism." *Consciousness and its Place in Nature*,
     Ed. Anthony Freeman. Charlottesville VA: Imprint Academ-
     ic, 2006.
Taleb, Nassim Nicholas. *The Black Swan: The Impact of the
     Highly Improbable*. New York: Random House, 2007.
Tao Te Ching. Tr. Gia-Fu Feng and Jane English. New York:
     Random House (Vintage Books), 1972.
Taylor, Jill Bolte. *My Stroke of Insight*. New York: Viking, 2006.
Thinkquest Library. "Bell's Inequality and The EPR Paradox."
     Online publication
     http://library.thinkquest.org/C008537/cool/bellsinequality/bell
     sinequality.html as of 24 August 2011.
Thomas, Lewis. *The Lives of a Cell*. New York: Penguin Books,
     1978.
Tierney, John. "Message in What We Buy, but Nobody's Listen-
     ing." The New York Times, 18 May 2008. Available online at
     http://www.nytimes.com/2009/05/19/science/19tier.html as of
     1 September 2009.
Tooby, John, and Leda Cosmides. "The Past Explains the Pre-
     sent: Emotional Adaptations and the Structure of Ancestral
     Environments." Ethology and Sociobiology, 11, 375–424. New
     York: Elsevier Science Publishing Co., 1990. Available online
     at http://www.psych.ucsb.edu/research/cep/publist.htm as of
     26 May 2009.
Trivers, Robert L. "The Evolution of Reciprocal Altruism." The
     Quarterly Review of Biology, Vol. 46, No. 1 (March 1971) pp.
     35–57. Available online at
     http://education.ucsb.edu/janeconoley/ed197/documents/triver
     sTheevolutionofreciprocalaltruism.pdf as of 3 November
     2009.
Underwater Photography Guide. "Huge School of Fish Loved by
     Photographers Almost Captured by Fishermen near Kona."
     Online publication
     http://www.uwphotographyguide.com/Akule-school-captured-
     kona as of 25 July 2011.
Versenyi, Laszlo. *Socratic Humanism*. New Haven: Yale Univer-
     sity Press, 1963.
Wade, Nicholas. *Before the Dawn: Recovering the Lost History of
     Our Ancestors*. New York: The Penguin Press, 2006.

Whitehead, Alfred North. *Process and Reality: An Essay in Cosmology*. New York: Harper and Row Harper Torchbooks, 1957.

Wikipedia. "Ant." Online publication http://en.wikipedia.org/wiki/Ant as of 28 July 2011.

___. "Arete." Online publication http://en.wikipedia.org/wiki/Arete as of 30 October 2012.

___. "Artificial selection." Online publication http://en.wikipedia.org/wiki/Artificial_selection as of as of 12 February 2009.

___. "Bell's Theorem." Online publication http://en.wikipedia.org/wiki/Bell's_Theorem as of 19 September 2011.

___. "Bigeye Scad." Online publication http://en.wikipedia.org/wiki/Bigeye_scad as of 27 July 2011.

___. "Calcium in biology." Online publication http://en.wikipedia.org/wiki/Calcium_in_biology as of 10 December 2007.

___. "Category mistake." Online publication http://en.wikipedia.org/wiki/Category_mistake as of 18 July 2008.

___. "Causality." Online publication http://en.wikipedia.org/wiki/Causality as of 29 August 2007.

___. "Chemical synapse." Online publication http://en.wikipedia.org/wiki/Chemical_synapse as of 2 October 2007.

___. "Consciousness Causes Collapse." Online publication http://en.wikipedia.org/wiki/Consciousness_causes_collapse as of 29 August 2007.

___. "Double-slit Experiment." Online publication http://en.wikipedia.org/wiki/Double-slit_experiment as of 29 August 2007.

___. "EPR Paradox." Online publication http://en.wikipedia.org/wiki/EPR_paradox as of 24 August 2011.

___. "Emergence." On-line publication http://en.wikipedia.org/wiki/Emergence as of 1 February 2012.

___. "Eudaimonia." Online publication
http://en.wikipedia.org/wiki/Eudaimonia as of 16 December
2008.

___. "Eudaimonism." Online publication
http://en.wikipedia.org/wiki/Eudaimonism as of 16 December
2008.

___. "Evolution." Online publication
http://en.wikipedia.org/wiki/Evolution as of 14 May 2012.

___. "Evolution as Fact and Theory." Online publication
http://en.wikipedia.org/wiki/Evolution_as_fact_and_theory as
of 14 May 2012.

___. "Evolutionary Psychology of Religion." Online publication
http://en.wikipedia.org/wiki/Evolutionary_psychology_of_relig
ion as of 21 October 2012.

___. "Existence Precedes Essence." Online publication
http://en.wikipedia.org/wiki/Existence_precedes_essence as of
12 March 2010.

___. "Gene." On-line publication,
http://en.wikipedia.org/wiki/Gene as of 4 December 2002.

___. "Group Selection." Online publication
http://en.wikipedia.org/wiki/Group_selection as of 6 December 2009.

___. "Henry Stapp." Online publication
http://en.wikipedia.org/wiki/Henry_Stapp as of 2 October
2007.

___. "Hominini." Online publication
http://en.wikipedia.org/wiki/Hominini as of 28 August 2012.

___. "Inclusive Fitness." Online publication
http://en.wikipedia.org/wiki/Inclusive_fitness as of 12 January 2010.

___. "Interference." Online publication
http://en.wikipedia.org/wiki/Interference as of 29 August
2007.

___. "Interpretations of quantum mechanics." Online publication
http://en.wikipedia.org/wiki/Interpretations_of_quantum_mec
hanics as of 20 September 2011.

___. "Introduction to evolution." Online publication
http://en.wikipedia.org/wiki/Introduction_to_evolution as of
12 May 2012.

___. "Introduction to quantum mechanics." Online publication http://en.wikipedia.org/wiki/Introduction_to_quantum_mecha nics as of 24 August 2011.

___. "Is-Ought Problem." Online publication http://en.wikipedia.org/wiki/Is–ought_problem as of 5 October 2010.

___. "Meme." Online publication http://en.wikipedia.org/wiki/Meme as of 21 October 2012.

___. "Mirror Neuron." Online publication http://en.wikipedia.org/wiki/Mirror_neuron as of 4 November 2009.

___. "Nerve." Online publication http://en.wikipedia.org/wiki/Nerve as of 2 October 2007.

___. "Neuron." Online publication http://en.wikipedia.org/wiki/Neuron as of 2 October 2007.

___. "Occam's Razor." Online publication http://en.wikipedia.org/wiki/Occam's_razor as of 27 July 2008.

___. "Panpsychism." Online publication http://en.wikipedia.org/wiki/Panpsychism as of 23 June 2008.

___. "PDCA." Online publication http://en.wikipedia.org/wiki/PDCA as of 12 March 2010.

___. "Pion." Online publication http://en.wikipedia.org/wiki/Pion as of 24 August 2011.

___. "Primate." Online publication http://en.wikipedia.org/wiki/Primate as of 28 August 2012.

___. "Quanta." Online publication http://en.wikipedia.org/wiki/Quanta as of 29 August 2007.

___. "Quantum Decoherence." Online publication http://en.wikipedia.org/wiki/Quantum_decoherence as of 29 August 2007.

___. "Quantum Entanglement." Online publication http://en.wikipedia.org/wiki/Quantum_entanglement as of 24 August 2011.

___. "Quantum Physics." Online publication http://en.wikipedia.org/wiki/Quantum_physics as of 29 August 2007.

___. "Quantum Superposition." Online publication
http://en.wikipedia.org/wiki/Quantum_superposition as of 29
August 2007.

___. "Stern-Gerlach experiment." On-line publication
http://en.wikipedia.org/wiki/Stern–Gerlach_experiment as of
29 August 2007.

___. "Theory of Mind." Online publication
http://en.wikipedia.org/wiki/Theory_of_mind as of 24 October
2008.

___. "Wave Function Collapse." Online publication
http://en.wikipedia.org/wiki/Wavefunction_collapse as of 29
August 2007.

Wong, David. "Making An Effort To Understand." Philosophy
Now Magazine, Issue 82 (January/February 2011), pp. 10–13.
London: Anya Publications, 2011. Available online at
http://www.philosophynow.org/issues/82/Making_An_Effort_
To_Understand as of 12 April 2012.

Wrangham, Richard. *Catching Fire: How Cooking Made Us Human*. New York: Basic Books, 2009.

Wright, Robert. *The Evolution of God*. New York: Little, Brown
and Company, 2009. Appendix, "How Human Nature Gave
Birth to Religion," is available online at
http://www.evolutionofgod.net/excerpts_appendix/ as of 20
August 2009.

___. *The Moral Animal. Why We Are The Way We Are: The New
Science of Evolutionary Psychology*. New York: Vintage
Books, 1994.

Made in the USA
Charleston, SC
09 March 2013